A GRAMMAR OF THE CORPSE

A Grammar of the Corpse

NECROEPISTEMOLOGY IN THE EARLY MODERN MEDITERRANEAN

Elizabeth Spragins

FORDHAM UNIVERSITY PRESS NEW YORK 2023

This book was a recipient of the American Comparative Literature Association's Helen Tartar First Book Subvention Award. Fordham University Press is grateful for the funding from this prize that helped facilitate publication.

Fordham University Press gratefully acknowledges financial assistance and support provided for the publication of this book by the College of the Holy Cross.

Fordham University Press also publishes its books in a variety of electronic formats. Some content that appears in print may not be available in electronic books.

Visit us online at www.fordhampress.com.

Library of Congress Cataloging-in-Publication Data available online at https://catalog.loc.gov.

Printed in the United States of America

25 24 23 5 4 3 2 1

First edition

Contents

PREFACE vii

Introduction: Necroepistemology 1

1 Presence: Here Are the Dead 25

2 Absence: Disappearing the Royal Dead 45

3 Vitality: Wounded Narrators and the Living Dead 69

4 Assemblage: Recovering Diplomatic Power with Corpses 89

5 Erasure: Corpse Desecration for Narrative Control 110

Epilogue 135

ACKNOWLEDGMENTS 141

NOTES 145

BIBLIOGRAPHY 195

INDEX 215

Preface

The seeds of this project took root early in my graduate career when I first encountered an Aljamiado devotional text, "El alhadis de la calavera que encontró ʿAissa" (Account of Jesus and the Skull), which occupies four folios in one of two Aljamiado codices held by the Colegio Escuelas Pías in Zaragoza.[1] The term "Aljamiado" (derived from the Arabic *ʿajamī*, literally "foreign" or "not Arabic") refers to Romance languages written out phonetically using Arabic script, most frequently Aragonese and Castilian dialects. Crypto-Muslims living under Catholic rule used this writing system in a predominantly religious context during the so-called Morisco century (1500–1614). The manuscript begins, as do many Aljamiado texts, by invoking God with the formulaic *tasmiya*: "Bismillāhi al-raḥmāni al-raḥīmi [In the name of God, the Clement, the Merciful]." It then recounts the "alḥadīs" (Cl. Ar. *ḥadīth*, account or tradition) of how ʿAissa son of Maryam (Jesus, son of Mary) finds a skull in a valley and asks God to make it speak to him. Before approaching the skull, he performs ritual ablutions—*wuḍuʾ*, or *al-guwaḍu*, as it is rendered in the manuscript, the more minimal "partial" ablution in which the devotee washes face, hands, arms, and feet before formal prayer—and then prays. After invoking the name of God and the prophets, he sees himself addressed by the skull "con lengua paladina" (with a clear tongue), whom he interrogates about what has happened to his beauty, flesh, bones, and *arrūḥ* (soul). The skull describes his process of death: the disintegration of his body into the earth, its consumption by worms, and how the angel of death ripped his soul from him, taking it from the house where his brothers prepared his body for burial to be interrogated repeatedly by a series of terrifying angels. The text ends with ʿAissa telling the skull to ask of him whatever it wishes. The skull begs ʿAissa to intervene with God on his behalf to allow him to return to the "caša del mundo" (house of the world) so that he may do good works among the living and follow the right path to his eternal reward. The reader or listener of this tale should know that this request is futile—if God has allowed for the small miracle of the skull's revivification to talk to ʿAissa, any hope of a do-over among the living is out of the question. Surprisingly, ʿAissa's intervention with God makes a difference: the skull is returned to live again in his body and live a more righteous life for twelve years. Even so, the skull's mistakes and regrets should serve as an example for the living to do good works and live piously while they still have the chance.

The text immediately caught my attention with the macabre image of the animated talking skull, an image that no doubt served well its pedagogical and mnemonic purpose for its audience. It skillfully combines engaging images with details that instruct its audience on how to live and die as a good Muslim and what to expect in the grave: anticipating the painful separation of body and soul after death, the different angels that intervene at different points in the dying process, the punishment in the grave, and the ongoing importance of praying for the dead.[2] The descriptions of Morisco eschatology were vividly unforgettable—the Angel of Death with "un azote de fuego" (a fiery whip); Mankar and Nakīr, the black-skinned blue-eyed angels that test the faith of the dead in their graves; the soul being torn through the throat, causing the dead man eternal pain. In particular, the posthumous torments of the soul were brought to light in dramatically corporeal terms: "llegamos a una puerta de las puertas de[l] Infierno y miré y vi honbres que los mordian las culebras y los alacranes y los despedazaban sus carnes (we arrived at one of the gates of Hell and I looked and saw men bit by serpents and scorpions that tore apart their flesh)."[3] The complex and multifaceted lesson this story taught instructs the reader in the complex metaphysics of body and soul, while also serving as a reference for some of the basic tenets of quotidian Islamic practice, including one of the two forms of ritual ablútion, prayer measured through the number of repetitions of *al-rakʿa*, the sequence of utterances and actions performed by the believer as part of the act of worship. This seemingly simple story communicated a complex and nuanced vision of what it meant to be a devout Muslim to an audience of readers or listeners whose very lives were at risk because of their desire to preserve and transmit this information under a repressive regime.

Despite these numerous embodied details, my early work with this text focused on the spectral presence of the skull's *rūḥ* and its eschatological interrogation and punishment in the grave. I defined that haunting following Giorgio Agamben's theorization of an architectural mode of spectrality, which considers how ghosts are bound up with particular geographical spaces.[4] Agamben's specter is the city of Venice itself, once a cadaver, now a phantom that "carries with it a date wherever it goes; it is, in other words, an intimately historical entity." This architectural spectrality can wear one of two faces. The first is utterly aware of its own state of extinction, and has, "with respect to life, the incomparable grace and astuteness of that which is completed, the courtesy and precision of those who no longer have anything ahead of them." The second, "larval" specter, however, is in denial of its own passing and "must pretend to have a future in order to clear a space for some torment from their own past, for their own incapacity to comprehend that they have, indeed, reached completion." The Agambian specter thus retains its historical materiality despite the disintegration of its associated body, its intimate presence in a particular space, and a complex sense of temporality that binds together past, present, and uncertain future resolution.

It is a commonplace in ghost stories that specters emerge from trauma, violence, or injustice. Their lingering presence indexes a life that was brutally cut short, that demands justice and that its work somehow be completed. Crucial to understanding haunting is recognizing that ghosts are, by their very definition, out of time. The clock of their existence has quite literally expired. Their tenaciously persistent presence and feigned future places them inherently out of joint with the time and place that they haunt. That temporal disjuncture is directed toward a traumatic past that the ghost drags not just into the present to be resolved but also tugs toward a future. The "larval" ghost is a potentiality, a being not fully formed, a not-entirely-present past that seeks to close in the future. From within its chrysalis, it "rather obstinately look[s] for people who generated [it] through their bad conscience."[5] This form of spectrality is best understood as a kind of latency, a being, and a state of being that has been bricked behind the walls of history. All of these elements invite narration to reopen the possibility of resolution, just as 'Aissa in the *ḥadīth* renews the possibility of the skull's redemption through formal invitations to recount its story. The spectral latency can be unlocked and made accessible by tapping into the stories contained by the flesh archive of the specter's material remains—the "calavera blanca echada sobre la cara de la tierra" (the white skull flung upon the face of the earth).[6] These are the stories I investigate in this book.

Although I began this project looking for ghosts, as I sought to establish my corpus, I kept stumbling over the bodies. It became clear that if there is a presence that haunts the space of early modern Iberian, Western Mediterranean, and colonial Latin American literature, it is characterized by none of the shadowy insubstantiality of the Gothic ghost story. Instead, as is perhaps already obvious from the image of the talking skull in the story of ʿAissa, the things that appear suddenly in this literature are not shadowy apparitions but are instead unavoidably material. Their history is grounded not just in the architecture of the region's cities but even more concretely in the "guešoš" (bones), "junturaš" (joints), and disintegrating flesh that appear in some of its most canonical texts. In works as varied as the Inca Garcilaso's *Comentarios reales*, Tirso de Molina's *El burlador de Sevilla*, Catalina de Erauso's *La monja alférez*, María de Zayas's *Desengaños amorosos*, Fernão Mendes Pinto's *Peregrinação*, and even *Don Quixote*, corpses interrupt the flow of the text and demand attention. The Inca Garcilaso describes a trove of mummified royal bodies near Cuzco, kept secret in an act of resistance that protects this cache of power and history from the depredations of Spanish troops, while Erauso lingers in agony over her brother's corpse, whom she just killed in the latest of many duels fought in the name of masculine honor.[7] Mendes Pinto journeys widely as part of Portuguese imperial enterprises in Asia, as the death toll charts the itinerary he traces throughout the region. Back on the Iberian Peninsula, Zayas's female narrators tell harrowing tales of women buried alive behind walls or in pieces in wells and caves, incontrovertible evidence that to fall in love with a man is a perilous and often fatal enterprise.[8] Sancho and Don Quixote encounter several corpses—moving creepily along the road at night, commemorated by noblemen and women playing at shepherding, dangling from cork trees on the border with Aragon.

I set out to answer what role these dead bodies play in the various texts, under what circumstances, and for what reasons narrators dwell upon and contemplate material remains. The possible corpus for such a project was enormous, as already suggested through the examples given here. As a universally shared human experience, mortality and its uglier and smellier by-products can be found across time periods, regions, and cultures. Even so, the attention those material remains garner waxes and wanes, depending on the needs and attitudes of their survivors. The body is most vividly put to use at a moment of crisis in belief, "when some central idea or ideology or cultural construct has ceased to elicit a population's belief," and narrators resort to "the sheer material factualness of the human body . . . to lend that cultural construct a 'realness' and 'certainty.'"[9]

To focus the scope of my inquiry, I thus limited my study of the early modern Mediterranean corpse in text to a single event: the Battle of al-Qaṣr al-Kabīr, whose survivors regarded its dead bodies with particular interest and anxiety. As a thought experiment, this approach thus reduced a number of variables that might get out of hand. The military nature of the event means that I am considering primarily male bodies—with one royal exception—whose deaths were caused by a single violent event with well-documented, though under-studied, repercussions. By responding to the demand these corpses made on my attention, I chart a new way of writing narrative that emerged during the early modern period, one that can be tracked on both the Iberian and North African sides of the early modern Western Mediterranean. These bodies stand up and speak most persuasively to the manner and causes of their death, and through their presence become the most convincing evidence for that version of the story. The perhaps artificial limitations I imposed on this book mean, of course, that my findings will also be circumscribed. Nevertheless, other related projects with some of the aforementioned canonical texts, read with some of the theoretical parameters I lay out in the pages of this book, reveal the broader applicability of these ideas. It will, I hope, inspire other readers of the early modern Mediterranean to look again and consider more closely the bodies that make up the ground of this body of literature.

A GRAMMAR OF THE CORPSE

Introduction

Necroepistemology

A king dies, his ailing body wracked by a seizure as, against his doctor's orders, he mounts his horse to lead his troops into battle. His body is quickly hidden away in a litter, tightly controlled by his court, and made to give orders through the mouth of that same doctor. Unaware of their political decapitation, his soldiers fight on and defeat their enemy, animated and directed by the medical ventriloquist who sequesters this privileged information and sustains the illusion of a fully viable body politic. Only when the day is won does the dead king's brother reveal the cadaver of Abū Marwān 'Abd al-Malik (r. 1576–78), assume the throne, and dub himself the Victorious by God's Command, al-Manṣūr bi-amr Allah (r. 1578–1603).[1]

The skin of the dead king's dead nephew, Abū 'Abdallah Muḥammad al-Mutawakkil II's (r. 1574–76), is flayed from his corpse, stuffed with straw, and then paraded about the city of Marrakesh to serve as an example to any who might dare to challenge the new ruler. Al-Mutawakkil's living uncle takes a personal interest in ensuring that this corporeal text of mutilated skin is read by all who encounter it on its circumambulation of the public spaces of the city. The waterlogged and mutilated remains of al-Mutawakkil are buried in ignominy near the place of his death and kept under control by his uncle, the new king.

A mound of undifferentiated Moroccan, Portuguese, Spanish, and mercenary soldiers' corpses lie putrefying in the hot August sun, topped with the fluttering banners of the victorious but dead Moroccan king. A surviving Portuguese soldier, a member of the elite *terço dos aventureiros*, recites an interminable list of the names of his dead compatriots, even though he cannot bring himself to give an eyewitness account of the fate of Sebastian I of Portugal

(r. 1557–78). Sebastian is tentatively identified by several captive and wounded vassals, but his rotting, three-days-dead cadaver has been pillaged of its rich armor and clothing and has bloated his features past recognition. The uncertain identification will haunt his kingdom for centuries to come through a millenarian cult that insists he will return to redeem them.

These are just a few of the images of the dead littering the narrative landscape that portrays the Battle of al-Qaṣr al-Kabīr (August 4, 1578).[2] By effectively managing information about and access to dead bodies, the narrators who recount these stories show how corpses ensured military victory, smoothed transfers of dynastic power, and, most critically, transmitted knowledge through channels the living struggled to legitimize. A mere seven years after the Battle of Lepanto (1571), the Battle of Wādī al-Makhāzin marked another major encounter among Muslim and Christian forces that all sides couched in terms of religious war. In this battle, also known as the Battle of al-Qaṣr al-Kabīr and the Battle of the Three Kings, Sebastian clamored to fight a crusade against a Muslim enemy, while his adversaries ʿAbd al-Malik and al-Manṣūr named themselves defenders of the faith and were lauded by chroniclers of the Saʿdī dynasty for their commitment to jihad. Despite these adversarial characterizations, stories of Wādī al-Makhāzin exemplify the intimate interpenetration of Christian, Muslim, and Jewish elements in the Western Mediterranean. At its most basic level, this was not a battle fought along clearly defined North African/Muslim and Iberian/Christian lines. On the contrary, the battle pitted Moroccan forces bolstered by elite Morisco fusiliers, recently expelled from Spain following the Second War of the Alpujarras (1568–71), against Portuguese soldiers allied with Moroccan forces loyal to al-Mutawakkil, Sebastian's ally. The most common tale of this battle portrays a reckless, inbred, and immature young king hankering for a crusade against Muslims. That story, however, is itself complicated by the simple fact that Sebastian eagerly allied himself with a Muslim army led by a Muslim king. On that day in August 1578, the deaths of all three kings who entered the battlefield—Sebastian, ʿAbd al-Malik, al-Mutawakkil—precipitated two major shifts in the Avis and Saʿdī dynasties of Portugal and Morocco. The Battle of Wādī al-Makhāzin also catalyzed an outpouring of interlocking Mediterranean stories, each of which sought to tell the definitive version of the battle and unseat other competing narratives.

No matter when or where one starts recounting the Battle of al-Qaṣr al-Kabīr, one always stumbles across dead bodies—rotting in the sun on abandoned battlefields, publicly displayed in marketplaces, exhumed and transported for political uses. These bodies function not only as representations of military loss but as a narrative resource within early modern Mediterranean historiography. The eyewitness and the corpse cooperatively produce what I term *necroepistemology*: a system of knowledge grounded in or transmitted through firsthand experiences of the material dead. The presence of the corpse in historical narrative is neither incidental nor offhand. Rather, it fills a central gap in testimonial narrative: it provides tangible evidence of the narrator's reliability while simultaneously provoking a visceral, affective response to the disgusting presence of the dead.

The use of corpses as a source of narrative authority mobilizes the latent power of the dead for generating social and political meaning, legitimacy, authority, and knowledge. This book suggests, however, that in addition to that latent social and political power, the corpse in textual representation also holds semiotic significance. Thus, I analyze the literary and epistemological function these socially and historically significant bodies serve within text and consider how they manifest in and through language. Over the course of this book, I derive a grammar of the dead by asking fundamental questions of textual analysis: Where and when are corpses found? How do they behave as subjects? How are they acted upon as objects? Through these questions, I find that corpses are indexically present and yet disturbingly absent, a tension that informs their fraught relationship to their narrators' bodies and makes them useful but subversive communicative and epistemological tools.

I establish the framework for the concept of *necroepistemology* at the productive intersection of Mediterranean and transatlantic studies and theories of death and the corpse. I survey the Battle of al-Qaṣr al-Kabīr as a Mediterranean event for which the status of the body, living and dead, was renegotiated alongside epistemological standards that shifted through imperial, religious, and bureaucratic innovations in the region. Narratives produced in this complex intellectual environment had to grapple with shifting terms of authority, authenticity, and orthodoxy and a crisis of knowledge about the fate of key casualties of the battle. Restoring narratives of al-Qaṣr al-Kabīr to their Mediterranean context opens alternate methodological possibilities beyond simplistic categories of language, religion, or nation. I articulate a grammar of the dead that emerged in response to this epistemological crisis, considering not just what is said about the dead but also how it is said, and how that generates knowledge in historical text. I center my reading on the semiotics of the corpse, an approach to the corpse that theorizes it both in terms of its symbolic significance (representing human mortality and representable in terms of linguistic signs) and its materiality (as a real thing that requires attention and engagement).

Understanding the corpse as a referential and mediating hybrid object through linguistic pragmatics, narratology, and affect theory reveals the epistemological implications of its representation in text. Across these linguistic, narrative, and affective levels, I show how the corpse's different functions (establishing place, manipulating time, retaining subjectivity, cooperating with other agents, serving as textual objects) operate in diverse literary traditions—Arabic, Spanish, Portuguese—to establish a sense of truth in text.

al-Qaṣr al-Kabīr/Wādī al-Makhāzin

We could begin the story of al-Qaṣr al-Kabīr on August 21, 1415: João I's sons have imagined Portuguese troops spilling the blood of Moors in the center of Ceuta, a dream they try to make reality when the Portuguese fleet arrived in the port.[3] This first incursion onto the African continent set the stage for the next century of Portuguese overseas imperial expansion into and colonial occupation of Africa, Asia, Brazil, and the Indian Ocean. It a process weighed down by a body count whose numbers are represented throughout the literature of this period, carpeting battlefields, filling *naos* (ships), overpowering the noses of their survivors.[4] Portuguese domination of the most proximate of these spheres in North Africa had begun to wane by the middle of the sixteenth century, when João III relinquished some of the kingdom's key Atlantic presidios at Safim and Azamor in 1541. It was this long history of military domination that Sebastian sought to resurrect and sustain through his expeditions into the Maghreb in the 1570s.

Or perhaps we can discern the roots of al-Qaṣr al-Kabīr, known in the Arabic sources as Wādī al-Makhāzin, emerging in the south of Morocco during the first half of the sixteenth century, with the rise of a family that claimed to be able to trace its ancestry back to the prophet Muhammad's daughter Fatima (a status known as *sharīf* and linked to political and religious authority). They grounded their legitimacy in part in their success resisting and confronting the same Portuguese presence on the Atlantic coast that Sebastian would later seek to restore. The first Saʿdī sultan, Muḥammad al-Shaykh al-Saʿdī (r. 1549–57), rose to prominence by taking back control of Agadir from the Portuguese. In 1549, the same year the Portuguese abandoned their forts at Asilah and al-Qaṣr al-Saghīr, Muḥammad al-Shaykh would decisively and violently overthrow the waning Wattasid dynasty and unify Fez and Marrakesh under his power.

The story of the Three Kings might get underway in 1557, a year filled to the brim with royal corpses and dynastic violence. In Morocco, Muḥammad al-Shaykh was assassinated by his own Turkish guard, paid off by the Sublime Porte to contain the upstart ruler and extend the Ottoman political sphere across the whole of North Africa. His eldest son, ʿAbd Allah al-Ghālib (r. 1557–74), acceded to the throne and fortified control by promptly exterminating most of his relatives with claims to power. Three of his brothers—'Abd al-Mu'min, 'Abd al-Malik, and Aḥmad Abū al-'Abbas—managed to escape the slaughter and fled to Tlemcen in Turkish-controlled Algeria. 'Abd al Mu'min soon suffered the same fate as other members of his family when he was assassinated in Tlemcen by men sent by al-Ghālib.[5] 'Abd al-Malik and his younger brother Aḥmad lived for nearly two decades under the protection of the Ottoman Turks and Algerian Pashas. 'Abd al-Malik even fought in the Battle of Lepanto in 1571 and in the Ottoman conquest of Spanish-controlled Tunis in 1574 and is said to have learned Spanish in Oran while in captivity after Lepanto.[6] In the same year on the Iberian Peninsula, João III of Portugal died and left the throne to his three-year-old grandson, Sebastian, whose own father, João Manuel, had died several weeks before his birth. Sebastian's grandfather, the king of Spain and Holy Roman Emperor, Charles V, had abdicated the Spanish throne the previous year in favor of his son, Philip II of Spain (r. 1557–98), and would die the following year in Yuste. On reaching his majority, Sebastian would endeavor to rekindle his grandfather's military prowess by wearing Charles's armor on the battlefield at al-Qaṣr al-Kabīr.

We could begin our tale in 1569, when the fifteen-year-old Sebastian visited his ancestors' tombs at the monastery of Alcobaça. He solemnly swore to their bones that he would recover Portugal's glory by recapturing the kingdom's possessions in North Africa.[7] This macabre occasion was itself embedded in a period of death and dying, since the young king traveled to his ancestors' graves to escape an outbreak of plague in Lisbon, leaving behind thousands of dead and dying subjects in the capital to focus on these more glorious cadavers.[8] This moment in Diogo Barbosa Machado's narrative of Sebastian's doomed reign foreshadows the moment when Sebastian's own corpse (or one that closely resembled it) would join his predecessors and be interred in a royal pantheon in the Hieronymites Monastery in Belem after being plucked from the dead around him. It also reinforces the importance of royal bodies as a recurring topos in the tellings of Sebastian's downfall.

One must certainly begin to track events leading to the deaths of the three kings by 1574, when the Sa'dī dynastic struggle came to a head. 'Abd al-Malik and Aḥmad had managed to stay alive for the remainder of their brother's regime, which ended with al-Ghālib's death in 1574, bringing into conflict two competing modes of royal succession: prevailing Sa'dī practice, in which the throne passed to the eldest male in the family, and the alternative system of primogeniture, in which the throne would pass from father to son.[9] The same year al-Ghālib's son al-Mutawakkil claimed power through primogeniture, 'Abd al-Malik, now the eldest living Sa'dī male, returned to Morocco with his brother and an army funded with Ottoman support to defend his claim to the throne.[10] This civil war between uncles and nephew would last for two years.

The drumbeat toward al-Qaṣr al-Kabīr was throbbing steadily by 1576, the year ʿAbd al-Malik and Aḥmad succeeded in ousting al-Mutawakkil from power. ʿAbd al-Malik's forces engaged al-Mutawakkil's south of Fez, and defeated them handily, in part because al-Mutawakkil's best infantry unit, a group of Morisco fusiliers, deserted to ʿAbd al-Malik's side.[11] Al-Mutawakkil fled Fez for the Spanish fort at Peñón de Vélez, where he first appealed to Philip of Spain to intervene and restore his throne.[12] By the time al-Mutawakkil solicited the aid of the Spanish, however, ʿAbd al-Malik had already forged diplomatic ties with Philip, a relationship that culminated in a treaty in 1577. This agreement points to shifting Mediterranean power balances between Habsburgs and Ottomans and suggests that establishing peace terms with ʿAbd al-Malik was part of Philip's efforts to neutralize a North African threat.[13] When Philip refused to support al-Mutawakkil, the ousted king turned to Philip's nephew, the king of Portugal. The young Portuguese monarch, who in 1574 already had attempted an unsuccessful expedition to North Africa, jumped at the chance to regain a foothold on the Atlantic littoral in Asilah.

Nearly all accounts of al-Qaṣr al-Kabīr from the early modern period through the present day tend to dismiss Sebastian's involvement in this conflict as the result of some combination of Habsburg inbreeding, religious fanaticism, and a proto-quixotic desire to prove his chivalric skills.[14] The inherent contradiction between Sebastian's obsession with crusade against Muslims and his alliance with Muslims was not lost on his Iberian contemporaries.[15] His obsession with defeating Muslims became the central policy guiding the young king's decisions about the administration of his empire from at least the early 1570s.[16] Henry Kamen and Ruth MacKay argue that the young Sebastian identified with his grandfather, Charles V, who was known for his active participation in military campaigns.[17] Dias Farinha instead contends that this expedition was driven by rational motivations, however misguided, including political, social, and economic factors.[18] Sebastian's interest in military action in North Africa also seems to have derived from his frustration with the relinquishing of Portuguese possessions along the Atlantic coast of North Africa.[19] The young king interpreted these territorial capitulations as his predecessor's failure to maintain the Portuguese empire.

The alliance between al-Mutawakkil and Sebastian had to be negotiated in legal terms in the Maghreb, too. Muḥammad al-Ṣaghīr al-Ifrānī, a court historian writing at the end of the Saʿdī dynasty and beginning of the ʿAlawite period, was troubled by the legal implications of al-Mutawakkil's alliance with nonbelievers against other Muslims. According to al-Ifrānī, al-Mutawakkil himself recognized the legally precarious situation of this alliance, and sought a fatwa to justify it and to deny the legitimacy of ʿAbd al-Malik's claim to the throne.[20] The qadis to whom he appealed not only denied him legal grounding for the alliance with Sebastian, but also chastised the overthrown monarch for attempting to delegitimize his uncle, stating that any argument that he could make for the illegitimacy of ʿAbd al-Malik's claim to the throne would also delegitimize his own claim to it.[21] Whether or not this legal exchange actually took place, al-Ifrānī certainly uses it to good effect in his narrative legitimizing al-Manṣūr's monarchy.

Sebastian so fervently embraced the idea of military action in the Maghreb that he issued conscription orders and gathered in Lisbon what parts of the Portuguese naval fleet were not already engaged in Portuguese colonial ventures in Africa and Asia, with harsh penalties for noblemen who failed to participate in the invasion.[22] These orders would prove disastrous for Portugal in the aftermath of the battle, because the death and capture of these conscripted participants stripped Portugal of the leadership of both the current and future generations of nobility, as well as of its heirless king. The taxes he raised mostly affected the poor after the Portuguese nobility vigorously protested the levies, while the remainder of the forces mustered were said to be either the poorly trained dregs of society or foreign mercenaries.[23] It would take Sebastian another year and a half before he managed to assemble the necessary money, men, supplies, and transport. In the meantime, another prominent royal corpse appears on the scene, this time Sebastian's former regent and grandmother, Catherine of Austria. As will be analyzed in chapter 4, her death on February 11, 1578, after an accident and long illness, silenced her important voice, which had spoken out against Sebastian's crusading mania.

After many negotiations both in and outside Portugal, the expedition departed Lisbon on June 8, 1578, in at least five hundred ships filled with some fourteen thousand infantry, two thousand cavalry, one thousand drivers, and several thousand camp followers, servants, and noncombatants. The fleet stopped first in Cádiz, sailed on to Tangiers, and finally reached Asilah, where it arrived on July 13 and disembarked. It waited there for over a week for the promised Spanish support. On July 29, impatient for action, Sebastian ignored ʿAbd al-Malik's letters pleading for (or, depending on who tells the story, demanding) peace (surrender) as well as his uncle's stipulation for Spanish support, and began to lead his troops overland toward al-Qaṣr al-Kabīr, supplied with about ten days' worth of rations.

By August 3, the Portuguese were encamped near the junction of the Makhāzin River and Loukkos River, just north of the town of al-Qaṣr al-Kabīr. This river is the third largest in Morocco and connects the northern interior of Morocco with the Atlantic at Larache. The town, which sits to the southeast of the Larache estuary, itself dates to Roman times and remains the hub of one of Morocco's most productive agricultural regions. The valley in which the battle was fought has been described by one modern observer as "one of the least inviting towns in Morocco" for its swampy topography, with "pestilential air, and swarms of greedy mosquitoes."[24] The region's propensity for flooding may have been a key factor in the battle, as the strategic destruction of the lone bridge spanning the river cut off a main line of retreat, leading to al-Mutawakkil's and possibly Sebastian's drowning in the waters of the Makhāzin.

On the morning of August 4, Sebastian ordered the Portuguese cavalry to attack Saʿdī forces in response to cannon and arquebusier fire. He fatally disregarded the advice of some of his advisers to wait to engage the enemy. Several contemporary accounts on both sides argue that the Portuguese were ignorant of ʿAbd al-Malik's illness, and that the Moroccans' success in concealing their leader's death directly contributed to their victory. Other accounts condemn Sebastian's decision making further by suggesting that he did, in fact, know that ʿAbd al-Malik was seriously sick, and chose to continue with his original plan, regardless of the advantage that could have been gained from patiently waiting for the Moroccan sultan's malady to run its course. Whether or not Sebastian knew what was happening to his adversary, we do know that it was a closely guarded secret in ʿAbd al-Malik's camp, as will be explored in greater depth in chapter 2. The outcome of the battle hinged upon who knew about this body, when, and how they kept others from finding out.

In little more than four hours, the inexperienced Portuguese army was neutralized, with all but a few hundred of its troops killed or captured. The battle was so devastating that of the approximately twenty thousand Portuguese men (of more than sixty thousand participants on all sides) who took the field on the morning of August 4, nearly half were killed. Al-Manṣūr's forces captured most of the rest.[25] Joseph Valencia, ʿAbd al-Malik's doctor, writes in a letter to his brother that in the aftermath of the battle, the dead and captive Portuguese were so numerous that even humble Maghrebi soldiers took Portuguese captives for servants.[26] Moroccan sources agree with the Portuguese accounts that the crux of the battle was ʿAbd al-Malik's death in the middle of the battle from a mysterious illness. Unlike the Portuguese, the Moroccan chroniclers do not speculate that he was poisoned but refer only to an unnamed illness in general terms.[27] The deposed al-Mutawakkil drowned when he tried to escape by fording the al-Makhāzin River. According to several Portuguese sources, after several close calls, Sebastian was finally killed when he plunged once more into the breach along with his intimate friend, adviser, and leader of the noble *terço dos aventureiros*, Christóvão de Távora. In contrast, Moroccan sources say that the king drowned in the river while trying to flee for safety with his ally, al-Mutawakkil. While ʿAbd al-Malik's body was buried in state, his nephew's body, once recovered downstream, was flayed and stuffed with straw to be displayed throughout the realm.

Plunderers, meanwhile, stripped Sebastian's corpse of its rich armor and arms, rendering it indistinguishable from the other bodies among which it lay. A chamberlain to the Portuguese king, Sebastian de Resende, identified a corpse as Sebastian's remains in exchange for his freedom. This corpse, whether it was in fact the Portuguese king's, was brought to a tent, where it was laid out next to the corpses of the two other kings and scrutinized by a group of Portuguese captives, who confirmed its identity. This confirmation was tentative, as by the time the Portuguese noblemen were asked to recognize the body, most distinguishing marks had been stripped away by looters or had decomposed beyond any hope of certainty. The body was finally interred at al-Qaṣr al-Kabīr in a coffin full of lime after a third and unsuccessful attempt to confirm its identity by two more compatriots.[28]

News of the Portuguese defeat reached the Iberian Peninsula piecemeal, beginning on August 10 at the courts of Lisbon and Madrid. Philip was first apprised of the news at the Escorial on August 12 but was unsure of the fate of his nephew until August 18, when rumors of the death were confirmed. As the weeks and months after the battle wore on, speculation bloomed about whether Sebastian had truly been killed or if he had managed to survive the battle.[29] This story, predicated on the claim that his body had never been recovered, evolved into the messianic Sebastianist legend.[30] In the two years preceding his assumption of the Portuguese throne, Philip promulgated a version of the events which would bolster his own claim to the throne both in Portugal and throughout Europe.[31] Even so, officials in Portugal and Spain sought with difficulty to control the story and, along with restrictions on textual iterations of the story, made a point of publicly mourning the death of the king. Sebastian, disinterred twice, enjoyed no fewer than three funerals in the four years following his demise, for at least two of which his body was absent, "among other reasons to make it clear that he was dead, very dead."[32]

In Portugal and Spain, the Battle of al-Qaṣr al-Kabīr led to chaos: the emergence of pretenders to the throne, and even a messianic cult. In Morocco, however, Wādī al-Makhāzin resulted in a quarter century of relative political stability, economic prosperity (in part thanks to the ransom collected from prisoners taken at the battle), and even imperial expansion to the south.[33] In both cases, it was the fate of certain, important bodies that, at least in the eyes of the event's narrators, contributed to these vividly contrasting results. While the uncertain fate and disconnected custody of Sebastian's corpse left room for speculation about his possible survival and challenges to his successors' legitimacy, al-Manṣūr and his supporters left no such doubt in the minds of his subjects as to the circumstances and final resting places of his predecessors' remains, as will be discussed in chapter 5. The very toponyms each side used to refer to this conflict point to these centrally important bodies. For Moroccans, Wādī al-Makhāzin, the river in which 'Abd al-Malik's and al-Manṣūr's adversaries drowned and secured the victory, became the place to give the event its widely used name of *ghazwat wādī al-makhāzin* (Battle of the River of al-Makhāzin). It is also the last place to which most Moroccan chroniclers bother to track the corpse of the defeated Portuguese king. Meanwhile, for those telling the story from the Portuguese perspective, the battle is most commonly known by the speculated first of Sebastian's several burial places—the town of al-Qaṣr al-Kabīr.

Transoceanic Story

A *Grammar of the Corpse* responds to responds to the fundamental provocation of Mediterranean studies to work beyond the linguistic limitations of modern national boundaries to study the region.[34] Rather than track Arabic sources as subservient, contributing to, or achieving their ultimate expression in a Eurocentric story, I incorporate the ties between early modern Iberia and North Africa into larger narratives about the region, its people, and its cultural productions.[35] By considering this moment in terms of a single, shared literary strategy instead of cultural influence, hybridity or conflict, I bypass narratives that focus on, manifest, or reinscribe binaries between European and non-European, Muslim and Christian, East and West.

More than six decades have passed since Américo Castro first coined the term *convivencia* to describe the interfaith relationships that defined medieval Iberia.[36] Since Castro first proposed his vision of Muslims, Jews, and Christians living alongside one another in symbiotic accord, the idea has come under fire from all directions: Hispanists who portray the Reconquest as the fulfillment of an eternal Spain's manifest destiny as a Catholic power; historians who seek to recreate a more fine-grained understanding of the social, political, demographic, and ecological dynamics that governed its lived reality; or literary scholars who reject the simplistic notions of influence that obtain from Castro's account.[37] Viewed reductively from the framework of the early *convivencia* debates, Catholic persecution of Muslims and Jews during the early modern period either naturally emerged from the contentious preexisting conditions of the Reconquest, or represented a shocking rupture from the idyllic golden age of medieval coexistence among the three major monotheistic religions—Christianity, Islam, and Judaism. In either case, however, the earliest formulations of *convivencia* were saturated with nationalist narratives of "conflict, competition, and victory," that, without careful interrogation, limited its methodological utility by inscribing it within suspect teleologies of Castilian exceptionalism.[38]

The stories we tell now about the medieval and early modern Iberian Peninsula have long since moved beyond ones of enmity or blissful coexistence governed by strict confessional divisions.[39] In the decades since Castro's first intervention, scholars have nuanced the discussion, drawing our attention to the complex environment of the medieval and early modern Iberian Peninsula: the economic foundations of multiconfessional coexistence, reframing *convivencia* as instead a marriage of convenience, the immeasurable impact Muslim Iberia had on medieval and early modern European cultural productions and development, the central and systematic role of violence in regulating the coexistence of majority and minority groups, the transmission of literary genres, tropes, and figures across religious and cultural lines.[40] Such work recognizes the region as a complex society that for at least seven hundred years was populated by individuals of different ethnic, religious, and cultural backgrounds who interacted, cooperated, and clashed with one another for many reasons including but not limited to religious ideologies.[41]

Arbitrary conventions of periodization are only reinforced by the geographies of the Strait of Gibraltar and the Atlantic Ocean, aqueous divides that seem to partition Catholic Iberia from Muslim North Africa, metropolitan center from peripheral colonial possessions overseas.[42] These geographical divisions carry significant methodological implications for early modern Iberian, Mediterranean, transatlantic, and, more recently, transoceanic or global studies.[43] According to this partitioning of the Western Mediterranean, the second half of the sixteenth century marked a particularly divisive epoch.[44] Both the Ottoman and Habsburg empires grappled with the repercussions of the expulsion and forced conversions of Spain's and Portugal's Jewish and Muslim populations, and the Ottoman consolidation of its control of the Balkans, the Levant, and the Maghreb. Throughout the sixteenth century, a series of battles between these Mediterranean powers at Malta, Cyprus, Lepanto, and elsewhere would help shape a logic of binaries.[45] In the decades leading up to Spain's expulsion of the Moriscos, for example, Spain would be "imagined as a pure, contained space from which even Christian Moors ultimately had to be excluded."[46] While these confessional distinctions are significant, to read interactions among these groups as determined only by these macrocategories is to ignore the local, individual, cultural, and historical context of particular events, as well as the richer structure they created in aggregate.

Despite efforts to expand our understanding of the cultural, linguistic, religious, political, ethnic, and social complexities of the medieval and early modern Iberian Peninsula and Mediterranean basin, we nonetheless continue to reify chronological and geographic categories that perpetuate many of the same ethnic, religious, linguistic, and geographical divisions that humanists and social scientists alike have sought to transcend. The year 1492 still stands in synecdoche for divisions between medieval and early modern, Mudéjar and Morisco, Jew and *converso*, Reconquista and imperial conquistadores, Mediterranean and Atlantic.[47] Although some scholars have sounded the call for responding to the true complexities that inflect that date, we continue to use that year to define the disciplinary perimeters that separate medievalists and early modernists, Iberianists and colonial Latin Americanists, Arabists and *moriscólogos*, scholars of Sefarad and the Sephardic diaspora.[48] By continuing to respect these divisions, we limit the toolkit that can be brought to bear on cultural productions from Habsburg Iberia, Marinid and Saʿdī Morocco, the Ottoman Mediterranean, the Sephardic diaspora, the Spanish Netherlands, Naples, and Milan, and the global Iberian monarchy.

Beyond the confines of the Mediterranean basin, every American schoolchild recognizes 1492 as the inception of transatlantic European imperialism and the irruption of a new world order that would reshape the globe.[49] Local negotiations at different nodes throughout the world resonated throughout imperial networks, transforming and linking the Iberian globe in economic, political, and cultural terms that carried profound epistemological and historiographical implications.[50] The distances between the seats of power and colonial possessions across expanding Portuguese and Spanish empires created epistemological voids.[51] Early modern historiographic conventions across the globe thus evolved directly from the unifying axis of imperial systems, whose economic, legal, epistemological, and bureaucratic structures invested new authority into the human body as a source of knowledge and truth.[52] These evolving conventions not only inflected the stories being written about global imperial enterprises but also modulated the means by which information was communicated, validated, and deployed within Mediterranean spaces.

After 1580, the union of the Iberian crowns of Portugal and Spain amalgamated a connected, composite history of global imperialism under a single unified crown.[53] Before and after annexation, those consolidated histories explode 1492 as the culmination of Spanish peninsular consolidation and transatlantic crossing and incorporate moments of Portuguese and Moroccan history as inextricable parts of the early modern Mediterranean story. The rupture of 1492 is bridged by the ongoing contact, negotiation, and coexistence maintained through Portuguese and Spanish presidios in Ceuta (1415), Asilah (1471), Oran (1509), and other North African cities, not to mention the constant circulation and exchange of bodies and goods throughout the region.

The picture of medieval and early modern Iberia that emerges from this scholarship is emblematic of the Mediterranean: a complex "zone of conflict and competition" that was fractured by shifting religious, political, social, and cultural priorities, but still characterized by a "commonality of culture."[54] Scholars across archaeology, classics, medieval and early modern history, Islamic studies, and Ottoman studies working in a Mediterranean studies paradigm have dominated discussions of the region, recognizing the rich ground for studying coexistence, empire, diaspora, conquest, and captivity.[55] By acknowledging Iberia and the Western Mediterranean as a fraught site of cultural intermingling, these scholars are attentive to the dynamics of personal and economic interests and obligations during medieval times that continued to motivate actors in this space.[56] Nevertheless, they are in some ways less limited in their research than are those of us working in medieval and early modern Mediterranean literary studies. We continue to be constrained by the priorities of post–nineteenth century nationalism that constitute our monolingual home departments, in which such multicultural histories are most often mobilized as exotic prehistories to the consolidation of the nation rather than compelling fields of study in their own right.[57] Ultimately, however, recognizing the Mediterranean as an interconnected, multilingual, and multiethnic space, a "linguistic polysystem," reveals a more complex picture than such protonationalism allows. In that system, cultural, social, political, and economic networks enmeshed rather than segregated the lives of Muslim, Christian, and Jewish actors, in spite of their differences in belief, before and after 1492.[58]

Even as scholars of the early modern Iberian Peninsula have begun to account for the linguistic and cultural multiplicity of Iberian literature, the focus of these studies frequently, though not always, follows a vector from Semitic languages in service to Romance languages.[59] Early modern Iberianists continue to attend primarily to how dominant powers perceived, portrayed, and oppressed minority groups, despite our use of terms like "Iberia" and "early modern" to describe our field of study to signal that we have stepped away from the teleological nationalism of the earlier "Spanish Golden Age."[60] Such approaches reflect the fact that early modern Iberian literary scholars have still not responded coherently to the vision of the Mediterranean as an deeply interconnected, coherent geographical and cultural space.[61] Inversely, many scholars in Arabic and Near Eastern studies continue to resist the incursions of comparatist scholars whose training in Arabic language and literature diverges from traditional philology training in an empiricist mode.[62]

Such approaches hew more closely to the realities of the sixteenth century Western Mediterranean by responding to "the ways in which those living in and moving through the Iberian Peninsula—past and present—produced and responded to the richness of linguistic, cultural, and historical threads that extend far beyond the peninsula's geographical borders."[63] The Battle of al-Qaṣr al-Kabīr destabilizes the easy division of north and south, Christian and Muslim, over the Straits of Gibraltar and epitomizes the interpenetration of diverse actors in the Western Mediterranean. At its most basic level, this was not a battle fought between purely North African, Muslim forces and Iberian, Christian forces—a distinction that in all cases would have left much to be desired in terms of ethnic "purity."[64] The leaders of these forces were invested in protecting and furthering the interests of their realms, not only within the confines of the Muslim/Arabophone or Catholic/Latinate worlds, but cognizant of the interconfessional religious and political currents that swept the early modern Mediterranean and Western Europe as far north as England. Such awareness was not exclusive to Moroccan leaders but also factored into Iberian statecraft. The sources thus suggest that this conflict was viewed not as a clearly delineated fight between two distinct religious civilizations, but rather between two contingent iterations of factions that emerged from the mutually imbricated populations that resided in these spaces at the end of the sixteenth century.

What emerges from this framework is thus a study that, while it recognizes the complex religious, cultural, and political dynamics that ebbed and flowed through the Middle Sea, steps out of the linguistic and confessional strictures that bind us to the same limiting categories that have defined our field for the past sixty years. Centering the figure of the dead human body as a narrative resource, and considering the complex modes of expression that its narrators use to cope with the problems of its appearance across multiple language traditions offers new insight into the shared cultural context of the early modern Western Mediterranean, while also engaging with an ongoing conversation among scholars of early modern about embodiment and the material body.[65] This book focuses the theoretical insights of these scholars onto the importance of the dead human body, partial and whole, extending research on the power of the dead body to the early modern Mediterranean.[66] A *Grammar of the Corpse* challenges the Eurocentric and media-specific assumptions that undergird these projects, instead offering a precise portrayal of the epistemological work done by the dead in the writing of transnational history.

The Corpse as Index

The basic building block for the grammar of the corpse is the index. In classical semiotics, an index is a sign that exists in physical, existential, or causal proximity to its object: smoke reveals proximal fire, a footprint in sand points to the foot that created it, an elevated heart rate can announce an underlying physiological problem, and, most classically, a photograph records the light that reflected off the object that was photographed.[67] The index points or refers back to that antecedent, retaining a potentiality that the reader must activate to decode its meaning or recognize to apprehend the referent: the sophisticated woodsman can follow the traces of smoke to their origin, the forensic specialist can divine information about the body whose foot marked the sand, the medical professional can interpret vital signs in the diagnostic process. Indexes are concerned with position and context, whether spatial, temporal, or social.[68] For lexical indexes, this means that their interpretation hinges on understanding the situations or frameworks surrounding or producing speech or text.[69] That framework is, however, subject to change: deictics are so tied to the present situation of utterance that they do not consistently refer to the same stable, fixed objects.[70] They also manifest linguistically in elements such as demonstrative adjectives and pronouns, verb tenses, or even anaphora (language most meaningful when considered in the context of preceding or subsequent expressions). Unlike more classic examples of indexes—the weathervane, smoke, a fingerprint—the corpse is not inscribed with a single moment in time but archives the remains of multiple moments, a referentiality that only proliferates as the corpse disintegrates.

Representations of the corpse deploy these semiotic strategies alone or in combination, displaying it as a physical index of a past life, its meaning mutable and context dependent, and signaled or coupled with lexical deictic markers. As Heather Dubrow convincingly argues, such references rarely appear in isolation, but rather cooperate in clusters or groups within textual representation. I argue that these clusters work together to generate a foundation of reliable knowledge in historical narrative.[71] I investigate the patterns of such indexical clusters as and in language, analyzing how indexical corpses as linguistic, rhetorical, and material phenomena converge to support narrative in its major components: space, time, people, interactions, and objects. I understand the more granular details of language (i.e., deictic reference, verb inflection, subject animacy) to be indicative and constitutive of narrotological or affective effects and read such details accordingly, seeking to explain how these indexical building blocks create a credible, narrative whole. As a grammar of the corpse, then, this book identifies and explains its basic forms and structures (in space, in time, as subject, in collaboration, as object), and then analyzes how those fundamentals ladder up into more complex manifestations in narrative (as ideological support, as propagandistic tool, as a medium for bridging the gap between the written page and the eyes of the reader).

Some theorists of the corpse are deeply concerned with the indexicality of the dead as a guarantee of mimetic reality. In particular, photographic and cinematic representations of the body "as a purveyor of facts and evidence" date to the earliest developments of these visual technologies, and evidential truth claims continue to feature in visual representations of the body and corpse, but, I argue, are not limited to these media.[72] While photography and cinema theorists have productively formulated a semiotics of death and the dead, some have mistaken the medium for its semiotic and rhetorical modality by contending that the indexicality of death is a purely modern phenomenon.[73] These theorists overlook the dead as a key indexical phenomenon within representation and the grammar that governs its portrayal by fetishizing the photograph as index of death rather than the corpse *itself* as an index of death. That said, I mobilize cinema theory's understanding of the index because, unlike cultural historical, anthropological, or sociological investigations of the dead, I begin from the same starting point as these scholars: the corpse in representation. We are left, then, with what Margaret Schwartz refers to as a "rhetoric about death in the medium of the flesh."[74] Schwartz shows that any representation of the dead already traffics in indexicality and referentiality, regardless of the medium in which it is portrayed.[75] If indexing the dead is a matter of rhetoric, then what is the grammar of that rhetoric? How do those modes of reference get deployed in text? How does its manifestation in text differ from its visual presentation? Even though the image or description of a corpse figures as an archetypal symbol of human mortality, it is more than just a metaphor or mimetic likeness. By focusing on the corpse as the central object of analysis, the critic can better understand the nature of mediation and referentiality itself in the corpse as a "material substrate of communication."[76]

The irreducible units of analysis for a representation of the corpse are, perhaps unsurprisingly, the semantic elements that compose it in text. My methodology will be familiar to literary scholars, built as it is on a foundation of close readings of the language used to describe corpses in my chosen archive. My analysis of these constituent semantic parts of the corpse's representation reveals how on a word-by-word basis the dead body appears as subject, as object, in space, and in time. I build my understanding of a corpse starting from the basic building blocks of communication—subjects, verbs, objects, prepositions, and so on—and following how those elements correspond with and constitute the range of communicative functions a corpse assumes within a text. Scaled up to the syntactical level, such grammatical features reveal and express space, time, subjects, objects, and the interactions among these different elements. In this grammar of the corpse, a detailed analysis of grammatical structures within these texts (verb inflection and tense, deictic reference, or active and passive participles) discloses the conceptual patterns that dictate the functions served by the corpse's representation. Emphasizing the pragmatics of the corpse, how it configures the textual space and time through deixis and other rhetorical and linguistic strategies, exposes the literary ways these linguistic strategies play out.[77] How these details are expressed structurally also sheds light on the visceral responses narrators have to the presence or absence of corpses and the ways in which they position themselves vis-à-vis these bodies.

I build out from these more granular functions of the corpse in text by considering the broader effect these details have in narrative, bringing the tools of narratology to bear on the semantic material the initial linguistic analyses identify. Narratology focuses on the commonalities in storytelling across communicative media, seeking to identify and understand the ways in which stories are produced, transmitted, exchanged, and interpreted.[78] Narrative, and indeed textual, analysis can be reduced to six basic questions: *Who? What? Where? When? Why? How?* These initial questions, of course, propagate other more specific and nuanced lines and areas of inquiry, but, from the outset, they allow us to identify key actors and actants within the story, the objects that populate the worlds in which those actors and actants move and upon which they act, their situatedness in those worlds in time and space.[79] The convergence of these questions onto the corpse enable me to attend to the different functions the corpse serves narratologically within the text as a feature and producer of its world.

Finally, narrative representations of corpses affect other figures within and beyond the text. Affect theory focuses on the resonances between and among human and nonhuman bodies, of the rich sensibilities that arise in the in-between spaces. This becomes a central resource that grounds my understanding of how intradiegetic interactions between corpse and other entities come to bear upon the extradiegetic reader.[80] These resonances in the spaces among bodies and between bodies and texts point us beyond the semiotic significance of these textual representations of dead human bodies and ask us to attend to the ways in which they exceed and expand the limits of representation. If theorists of the dead highlight the corpse as a trace, as inherently referential, affect theory provides a framework for considering how that trace manifests in and between bodies.[81] By locating the corpse's ability to affect others in narrative spaces and the experienced world, rather than on a reader's internal response, affect theory facilitates observation of those effects and affects on the written page.

This methodology allows me to trace the effect of the corpse on text from the granular, semantic level up through the impact it could have on the reader of that text. A *Grammar of the Corpse* thus recognizes the dead human body as an expression that must be interpreted according to the terms of its inscription into text and its interaction with the social world. Since a dead body is an inherently referential object, all interpretation of the corpse, whether in representation or material reality, must engage in hermeneutics—a process that responds to it as index while considering its position within and as a constitutive part of narrative. The resonances the stories that are grounded in and emerge from the dead human body constitute the world that both living and dead inhabit and in which they interact. A grammar of the dead must respond to the rhetoric of those resonances and expose the structure undergirding the material substrate of their communication.

A Grammar of the Corpse

Al-Qaṣr al-Kabīr was recognized by its contemporaries and particularly by those who narrated it as having lasting social and political consequences on both sides of the Strait of Gibraltar, much like the Battle of Lepanto had six years earlier. In the final quarter of the sixteenth and first quarter of the seventeenth centuries, numerous accounts of the battle spread throughout the Iberian Peninsula, Morocco, and into Europe and the Ottoman Empire.[82] What began as a flurry of textual creation to determine what precisely happened at the battle, over the course of the seventeenth, eighteenth, and nineteenth centuries became rich territory for the likes of literary and dramaturgical luminaries both on the Iberian Peninsula and beyond, including Lope de Vega, Calderón de la Barca, Philip Massinger, and George Peele.[83] Few of these texts, chronicles or otherwise, have received attention from a literary perspective. Instead, the texts have almost exclusively served as sources for a limited number of historical studies of early modern Portugal or Morocco, drawing only marginal attention from Hispanists.[84]

Rather than give a comprehensive survey of this extensive archive, I focus on reinterrogating the most widely read and cited accounts of this important battle, drawing on a range of published and archival primary sources written and circulated in Portugal, Spain, Morocco, England, and Ottoman Algiers.[85] The texts analyzed are thus taken from a variety of literary and administrative genres, published and archival sources, including epistolary accounts written during or immediately after the event, formal accounts written by eyewitnesses several decades later, and dynastic chronicles: Juan de Silva's epistolary correspondence from December 1577 through January 1579 with

Philip II of Spain in his capacity as Spanish ambassador to Portugal; a letter from the Moroccan sultan's personal physician, a man of Sephardic descent named Joseph Valencia, to his brother; the polemic work *Jornada de África* (Expedition to Africa, 1607) by Jerónimo de Mendonça, a veteran of the battle; an account included in a work by another veteran, Miguel Leitão de Andrade, the *Miscellânea do sitio de N[ossa] S[enhor]a da Luz do Pedrogão Grande, aparecim[en]to de sua s[an]ta imagem . . .* (Miscellany of the Site of Our Lady of the Light of Pedrogão Grande, Apparition of Her Holy Image, 1629); an anonymous chronicle of the Saʿdī dynasty, the *Tārīkh al-dawla al-saʿdiyya* (Chronicle of the Saʿdī Dynasty, early seventeenth century), and al-Ifrānī's *Nuzhat al-ḥādī bi akhbār mulūk al-qarn al-ḥādī* (The Leader's Strolls on Reports of First-Century Royals, after 1670).[86] Despite my interest in the historiographical tradition of this event and the utility of these sources for historical research, my principal concern is to attend to the images, turns of phrase, grammatical structures, and erasures that the authors employ as they claim their own authority as narrators—in other words, to treat them as literature. My contribution brings scholarly attention to unstudied and understudied sources, printed and manuscript, and brings to bear on them my unique skill set as a reader: literary, multilingual, with an interest in what these texts can teach us about literature and the body, the body in literature, and a literature of the body. I am optimistic that mine will not be the final word on these or other texts treating al-Qaṣr al-Kabīr, and so expect that my necessarily partial vision of this corpus will gradually be fleshed out in other work.

The narratives of the battle that these sources present range from the very heart of the unfolding events—whether told by soldiers (Mendonça and Leitão), actors in an official position of power (Silva), or participants on the side-lines of the event (Valencia)—to more distant reflections on the macroscopic results of the battle—as seen in the anonymous chronicle of the Saʿdīs. It would be tempting to read each of these texts according to the religious or linguistic background and tradition of their authors. A Mediterranean approach challenges us, however, to move beyond that limited methodology and seek other, more meaningful connections between and among the textual productions of this region. My readings of this archive are thus organized not along chronological, linguistic, or intertextual lines, but instead are motivated by the narrative strategies the narrators deploy to cope with their own realistic representations of corpses. The selections I study were chosen with an eye toward these narrators' most extensive and vivid engagements with human remains and are distributed through the chapters according to the principle strategy with which the narrator handles those remains, each of which derives from the corpse's indexicality. Focusing on how the indexical corpse refers to the situations of narrative utterance and parsing how those utterances manifest the reality of discourse allows us to understand how the corpse establishes that particular situation.[87]

Where? At the heart of the corpse's power to generate a sense of narrative certainty is its material presence. Knowledge of human corpses comes to be associated with hermeneutic aptitude and epistemological authority.[88] If dissecting and exposing the insides of the anatomized corpse establishes the surgeon as the expert reader of the corpse as text, textually representing corpses situates the narrator, too, as a present and privileged arbitrator between interiority and exteriority of text, body, and narrative frame.[89] Chapter 1, "Presence," investigates how Mendonça's account represents his access to the remains of his dead companions to defend Portuguese valor and honor in the face of foreign accusations of cowardice and incompetence. This narrator describes the deaths of dozens of Portuguese noblemen in vivid detail, depicting the lethal impact of the events almost in real time as they die "here" before the reader's eyes. These allusive corpses cluster with other verbal markers that collectively orient the reader to the immediate field of interpretation surrounding the body. By insisting upon the presence of these dead bodies within his narrative, Mendonça creates a common ground within the text, a shared plane of reference, upon which he and his reader can meet and experience the events he narrates. The reader thus becomes another witness of this set of events and will feel compelled to testify to what they have witnessed "here," participating in promulgating a revised version of the story more favorable to the Portuguese. This new frame of reference allows narrator, reader, and corpses to coexist in the narrative space of the text, in effect coopting the presence of the reader in text as witness to the events narrated.

When? Having established where corpses can be found in narrative, in Chapter 2, "Absence," I move on to ask *when* they are found. Paradoxically, even as the corpse is undeniably present *here* in space, the physical body points to the absence that identifies it as corpse rather than as living human being.[90] As an index, a corpse's absence is thus most keenly felt in terms of time: although a materially present entity lingers and fragments into significant pieces, temporally, this entity is no longer with us. Even as the corpse tends to consolidate shared textual spaces into mutually intelligible fields of interpretation, so does it converge multiple time frames: living, dying, and dead pasts, living and dead presents, disintegrating and uncertain futures. The collision of these heterogeneous time frames in the *here* and *now* of the indexical display of the corpse can be untimely—what André Bazin theorized as an obscenity. I read two accounts of royal death that grapple with such an obscenity: Sebastian's disappearance in Mendonça's *Jornada de África* and the Moroccan king ʿAbd al-Malik in his final moments in a letter written by his doctor, Joseph Valencia. These accounts consider the problem of royal death, which decouples the temporal systems of royal body natural and the body politic, as a potentially destructive example of such untimeliness. Reproducible access in textual representation to this moment of instability poses an ethical dilemma for the witness of royal death: how can the narrator bear witness to the king's death when knowledge of that death will only emphasize its disruptive asynchrony? The narrators cover up the obscene royal death by resorting to distinct narrative strategies that manipulate time: Mendonça, by avoiding the portrayal of the obscenity of his dead king's corpse; Valencia, by controlling the indexical link to his king's hidden body. Ultimately, their strategies respond to the question, *When is the corpse?* with misdirection. They deny or obfuscate the reality of the corpse's present situation, and emphatically claim that it cannot be *now*. The temporal leaks through which these absences keep the past alive highlight the slipperiness of corpses as epistemological antecedents.

Who? Chapter 3, "Vitality," moves on to ask *who* corpses are as subjects. If a corpse is a sign that points to *a subject who was*, as index, it retains the traces of the subject to which it refers.[91] Its lingering potentiality attracts the attention of narrators who themselves lack agency. In their interactions with corpses, these narrators recognize and inflect corpses as human, animate subjects, even as they inflect themselves as impotent objects. It becomes clear over the chapter that an important facet of the model of testimony that emerges at al-Qaṣr al-Kabīr is eyewitnesses' propensity to associate their own bodies with corpses. Wounded survivors of the battle like Miguel Leitão de Andrade recognize corpses as actants composed of vibrant matter. He presents his own scarred body in conjunction with the corpse of a Dominican friar, the Virgin of Pedrogão Grande, and the material text itself in the hands of its reader, a cooperative body that stabilizes future disseminations of his story. Though his passivity means that, like Mendonça, he is unable to give irrefutable testimony to having witnessed his king's corpse pass through the Moroccan camp in the battle's aftermath, that uncertainty hinges not on avoidance, but rather on the same incapacity that dictated his initial relationship with the Dominican's body. It also condemns him to the prolonged captivity that calls his narratorial authority into question.

With whom? As shown in chapter 3, the corpse is a social entity that disrupts easy distinctions between persons and things, subjects and objects, agency and passivity. Burial is therefore just one possible collaboration among the living and the dead, a subject that chapter 4, "Collaboration," explores in greater depth. Assemblages made up of living, dead, animate, and inanimate entities collaborate to allow all of their members to be carried along a trajectory toward a shared, mutually beneficial goal—motivating action, restoring political stability, burying the corpse, moving living and dead bodies through space. Silva, injured and aware of his own reduced powers to disseminate information, grasps the lingering subjectivity Sebastian's cadaver retains, its manifest traces of viability, and, consequently, its status as a repository of epistemological power. He succeeds in bringing himself within the gravitational pull of its orbit long enough to be carried along the trajectory of its translation from North Africa to a Portuguese mausoleum. This powerless living narrator forges a symbiotic alliance with the more animate and mobile royal corpse, joining its trajectory home. Silva's efforts to associate with or substitute his own injured body with the dead one highlights the deep and abiding power of the corpse in early modern economies of knowledge.

What? Whereas the first four chapters of the book focus on examples of "reactive" necroepistemology—how narrators cope with disaster by scrambling to establish knowledge of its corpses—chapter 5, "Erasure," opens out to consider "creative" necroepistemology—how new knowledge can be produced through corpses from a position of power. While Leitão and Silva embrace the subjectivity that lingers in the material remains of the corpse, other narrators bear witness to its violent reduction to a mere object. In particular, corpse desecration deliberately erases and suppresses the vital subjectivity and humanity of dead bodies, and its documentation within text can inscribe that brutal objectification into the language that describes that process.[92] Such processes feature prominently in *Tārīkh al-dawla al-saʿdiyya*, one of the major chronicles of the Saʿdīs. I focus on the textual erasure that results from necroviolence in a case that describes al-Manṣūr's public flaying of his nephew al-Mutawakkil. This violent episode emerges as one strategy to foreclose potentially disruptive alternate versions of the story, like those that irrupted into the gaping void left by Sebastian's disappearing body.

The narratives about al-Qaṣr al-Kabīr reveal a major crisis of information for all involved in the event, both the winners and losers. What happened? Who died, when, and who was at fault? What proof do we have? How do we marshal that proof to convince others of what we know? At the very center of that epistemological crisis were three questions concerning the kings that each narrator sought to answer: how and when they died, who knew they were dead, and what happened to their corpses. Paradoxically, the turmoil that erupted in the wake of this triple decapitation of royal leadership disrupted the usual lines of communication through which information about such events was usually transmitted.[93] Even as new leadership gradually wrested the Western Mediterranean out of chaos, there remained a nagging sense that the knowable rested on shaky footing. As the narrators grappled with al-Qaṣr al-Kabīr and its aftermath, they began to converge on a common solution: knowledge of the corpses of the battle became the token by which the truthful narrator could be known. The webs of communication, commerce, and knowledge linking the shores of the Western Mediterranean were gradually rewoven and resettled, anchored in place by the scarred, mutilated, and decomposing bodies from al-Qaṣr al-Kabīr.

1
Presence
Here Are the Dead

La muerte no es otra cosa que un apartamiento del cuerpo y del alma.
Death is nothing but the parting of body and soul.
—ALEXO VENEGAS, *AGONÍA DEL TRÁNSITO DE LA MUERTE*

In his narrative account of the Portuguese defeat at al-Qaṣr al-Kabīr, *Jornada da África* (1607), Jerónimo de Mendonça repeatedly describes the bloated and rotting bodies of those who died there: soldiers, nobles, and kings, European and North African, named and unnamed. As part of a narrative strategy to substantiate his own testimony of the battle against the versions given in earlier accounts of the Portuguese failure in North Africa, he invokes the number and immediate presence of these war dead. His access to specific knowledge of their identity and the circumstances of their deaths and inadequate burials allows him to assert the trustworthiness of his own narration as an eyewitness account. Mendonça uses these decomposed corpses to bridge the diegetic world of the text and extradiegetic space of his reader. This strategy emphasizes the emerging value of witnessing as a source of knowledge even as it draws upon the corpses' indexical power to open a sense of presence that narrator and reader can share.

Mendonça was a member of the *terço dos aventureiros*, a regiment that consisted of noblemen who fought at the center of the Portuguese line at al-Qaṣr al-Kabīr and a majority of whom were killed or taken captive after the battle. According to Diogo Barbosa Machado, Mendonça himself belonged to an illustrious family from Porto, though little is known about him beyond what he relates in the *Jornada de África*.[1] He dedicated the book to Francisco de Sá e Menezes, Conde de Matosinhos, who served as *capitão-mòr* of Porto, as well as *camarero mòr* of Sebastian's father Prince João, but who had been dead for nearly a decade by the publication of Mendonça's book.[2] After al-Qaṣr al-Kabīr, Mendonça spent a number of years in captivity before returning to Portugal and publishing his firsthand account of the Portuguese disaster with Pedro Craesbeeck's printing house.[3]

In his account, the dead frequently appear in close proximity to living figures within the diegetic space of the narrative—much like when hanging corpses in cork trees interpellate Sancho by touching him and drawing his attention to them, rather than wait to be discovered.[4] In structural terms, most of his version of this event relates the deaths of his compatriots—beyond the space dedicated in the first tome to the battle itself, the last of the three *livros* is a kind of hagiography of those who died in captivity after the battle that relates the vitae of seven such men.[5] In the narrative itself, corpses are shown to be within reach: the viscera of the dead share the same textual space as the unsettled narrative and social order. The interactions between these dead bodies and living bodies focus the reader's attention on the location and terms of that space and establish grounds for interaction among subjects and objects within it: between living characters and corpses, the narrator and his audience, the material text and its reader. These present dead bodies point to the deaths of the subjects that once animated them. If a single dead body mediates between life and death, a large group of bodies constitutes an even richer referential potential whose capacity to mediate between life and death, here and there, now and then, commands our attention.[6] The semiotics of their presence serve an important authoritative function for Mendonça as he tries to wrest control of the story of al-Qaṣr al-Kabīr away from unauthorized voices. This control is anchored in the ground of the corpse—the first key feature of my theorization of *necroepistemology*.

These strategies of embodied narrative share the sense that a body's presence grounds and validates the story being told. The dead and wounded bodies stand as tangible proof that the reader or the audience can examine carefully to establish the validity of what has been said. Put in other terms, at a moment of crisis in belief in a cultural construct, narrators resort to what Elaine Scarry describes as "the sheer material factualness of the human body."[7] During the early modern period, eyewitness testimony gained prestige as a source of truth alternate to accepted textual authorities, a phenomenon that is especially well documented in the colonial Latin American canon and early modern medical literature. Nevertheless, narrators' consistent reliance on the corpse to shore up eyewitness accounts betrays a degree of lingering uncertainty about the stand-alone credibility of testimony and eyewitnesses.[8] They highlight their somatic corporeal experiences of the dead as a solution to this epistemological problem. Narrators claim, *I know this to be true because I was present and saw it happen*, while also incorporating dead bodies as witnesses that attest to the credibility of this statement—*I know this to be true because I was present and saw it happen, and you, reader, may believe what I say, because I can describe and reembody for you a corpse that I had access to at that time.*[9] Such a narrative asks the reader to join the eyewitness in testifying to shared human mortality, and in that way to become a mediated witness to the events described. The corpse comes to fill the gap between the eyewitness's dubious reliability and the necessary level of epistemic certainty to communicate effectively. The use of corpses to resolve a crisis of belief is not an obvious solution, but it draws on what literary critics, historians, philosophers, and social scientists have pointed to as the latent power of the dead for generating social and political meaning and knowledge.[10] The question I seek to answer throughout this book is: *How* and *why* does it work as a literary trope?

As discussed in the introduction, Schwartz convincingly theorizes corpses as communicative objects whose representational power derives from their referential relationships to absent subjects even as their emotional clout is supported by the visceral reaction provoked by their material form. Understanding the corpse as both fleshy and evocative, figure and figurative, is critical for parsing its meaning. This approach helps us to conceptualize corpses as a powerful tool for generating narrative space in the midst of an unsettled, unstable world. Mendonça, as we will see, mobilizes in the *Jornada de África* the corpse's material and metaphorical significance through deixis to generate a sense of spatiality that makes his account more accessible and more credible to his reader.[11] The act of writing within the scriptural economy of the sprawling Iberian empires took on an embodied meaning through which it participated in shaping and responding to the problems of empire and colonialism.[12]

Access and Knowledge

In the sixth of seven chapters of Book I of the *Jornada de África*, Mendonça describes the Battle of al-Qaṣr al-Kabīr itself and the body count incurred during that battle, again defending Portuguese reputations with bodies, at this point still living.[13] He begins by recounting that the soldiers' final act before the start of battle is to pray the *Ave Maria* and to kneel before the crucifix held up by a Father Alexander. At this moment, the enemy fires the first shot. Mendonça uses his knowledge of this moment to undermine Girólamo de Conestaggio's text, showing that it was written "não sabendo que esta humilhação foi feita á imagem de Christo [not knowing that this obeisance was made to the image of Christ]."[14] More shots are fired, registering the first fatalities of the battle. Mendonça insists that these first victims were not in fact already lying afraid on the ground, as Conestaggio had claimed, but that they had calmly and bravely stared down the assault.[15] Mendonça also challenges Conestaggio and Rivadeneyra on the cause of that prostration the Portuguese had prostrated themselves out of fear: "nem sei certo, como dizem estes dous auctores, que todos os portuguezes se estirassem em terra, como se estivessem já amortalhados, cousa que parece não podia acontecer, ainda que lh'o mandassem com pena de morte [I am not at all sure, as these two authors state, that all the Portuguese stretched themselves out on the ground, as if they were already enshrouded. It seems unlikely that this would have happened, even had it been commanded of them on pain of death]."[16]

Mendonça corroborates his version of this story in two ways. By affecting modesty—"I do not know for sure"—he bolsters his own credibility as a narrator and obliquely critiques his opponent's hubris in claiming to know for certain what happened. He also appeals through the logic of apodixis to his readers, implying that it is a generally accepted principle that even under pain of death the Portuguese would never behave so ignobly. Whether or not the Portuguese began the Battle of al-Qaṣr al-Kabīr lying down in fear before their enemies, as Conestaggio claimed, or praying, invoking this image at the start of the story of the battle prepares the metaphorical ground for the rest of the chapter, in which supine Portuguese corpses accumulate in piles on the battlefield. As the battle's casualties mount, Mendonça appeals apodictically to the reader to judge whether it was possible for the Portuguese to win the battle given how badly outnumbered they were: "Mas emfim, que podiam fer dous mil homens de cavallo, por mais valorosos que fossem, contra quarenta mil que Franqui confessa, fóra aventureiros e Alarves, que vem a ser ainda maior numero do que elle diz que os portuguezes acrescentam? [And yet, in the end, what could two thousand men on horseback, no matter how brave they were, do against the forty thousand who Franchi confesses, whether *aventureiros* or Arabs, came to be an even greater number than that which he says the Portuguese amassed?]."[17] With this rhetorical question, Mendonça prompts his reader to agree with his position: that the Portuguese were put into the impossible position of defending themselves from an enemy that vastly outnumbered them, and that to do so was to comport themselves with valor.

From the first moments of his account of the battle, then, Mendonça links truth, witnessing, and the bodies of his dead companions. He positions himself not as a repository of secondhand information, but as a participant whose locus at the heart of the action gives him access to information about some of the highest-ranking Portuguese noblemen who were captured or killed. Part of Mendonça's strategy for refuting Conestaggio's narrative of Portuguese cowardice is to demonstrate his compatriots' corporeal sacrifice on a granular, body-by-body basis. One might argue that by gathering together long-dead bodies and deictically mapping them in a common textual space, Mendonça responds to a human impulse to care for the dead, the sense that "there is something deeply wrong about not caring for the dead body in some fashion, but also that the uncared-for body, no matter the cultural norms, is unbearable."[18] Semiotically, however, any efforts to care for the dead are subservient to the role their material remains play in creating a common ground that spans the gap between the diegetic world of the text and the world in which the reader consumes the text, and, perhaps, facilitates their mourning and textual burial.

By showing his reader that these men die bravely "here," Mendonça activates that reader as another witness of this set of events. The reader will thus be able to testify to what they themselves have witnessed: a revised version of the story that will be less damaging to Portuguese reputations than other, earlier accounts. While their deaths would seem to silence both the voices of these men as well as their stories, the effect of this effort is to amass a flesh archive whose potential may be tapped in the future.[19] Mendonça displays his access to the annals contained within their bodies in all their gory particularities by rendering them in corporeal form. The index of the dead points to the multiple available narratives of al-Qaṣr al-Kabīr whose recounting would corroborate Mendonça's tale of Portuguese bravery. Their embodied presence brings tantalizingly close the possibility of recovering their stories and maybe honor, if not the material bodies themselves, from beyond the veil of obscurity.

The *Jornada de África*, widely accepted as accurate by Mendonça's Portuguese contemporaries, refutes two earlier accounts of the battle.[20] The first of these, Conestaggio's *Dell'unione*, censures the Portuguese for participating in the expedition and derides their cowardice in their defeat.[21] Conestaggio's denigration of the Portuguese explains why there is no known contemporary Portuguese translation of the text—it was so controversial that Philip actually ordered that it be kept it out of circulation in his realms beginning in 1589.[22] Despite these prohibitions, Mendonça managed to track down and read its third edition and obtained capital support to push back on it from Jorge Artur, a Lisbon-based book merchant who, over the first decades of the seventeenth century, collaborated steadily with the prominent printer Craesbeeck on printing a number of religious texts.[23] Though Conestaggio is his principal adversary, Mendonça also contests the version Fray Antonio de San Román de Rivadeneyra offers in *Jornada y muerte del rey D. Sebastián de Portugal* (Valladolid, 1603), which drew heavily on Conestaggio's account of the events at al-Qaṣr al-Kabīr. While Fray Antonio relies on *Dell'unione* as a source text, he is less scathing than Conestaggio and suggests that the Genoese author took too much pleasure in denigrating Portuguese soldiers' courage.[24] From Mendonça's perspective, however, Fray Antonio does not go far enough in defending the Portuguese. The veteran criticizes both Conestaggio and Fray Antonio for unjustly condemning the Portuguese in their defeat and casts their aspersion back on them by identifying their accounts as the worst disaster of the whole affair: "julgando com razão ser mór mal a mentira que a mesma desventura [the greater ill was the lie, rather than the misfortune itself]."[25] From the very first, then, Mendonça declares his dispute with Conestaggio and Fray Antonio as a matter of epistemological certainty and historiography, and the bodies he details in his story emerge amid social upheaval and epistemological crisis.

Mendonça's insistence on the value of his firsthand experience over writerly authority is typical of sixteenth- and early seventeenth-century Iberian historiography and eyewitness accounts, all of which grappled with the spatial problems of empire.[26] Because of the distances between the seat of power and its colonial possessions, Portuguese and Spanish imperial expansion into new territories catalyzed the need for witnesses to report back to the capitol what was happening on the ground.[27] In this global context, the stakes of trustworthy information forced witnesses of and participants in colonial processes to develop strategies that supported their claims to credibility, specifically ones that emphasized their corporeal access to that information or their embodied presence at events they narrated.[28] The human body thus took on a significant role in producing knowledge in the colonial context as paradigms governing the transmission and reception of information shifted with the scale of colonial possessions and their associated bureaucratic regimes.[29]

Surprisingly, however, the authority of early modern American narrative did not always derive from the demonstrable credibility of information they transmit, but rather followed an *ad hominem* logic in which the author's ethos guaranteed the account.[30] The evidentiary logic of fictional and historical writing alike tracked with judicial or legal conventions.[31] Unlike present-day eyewitnesses, who are commonly understood to attest to factual evidence in a case, early modern witnesses more frequently spoke to the credibility of the accused themselves in ethical rather than ontological terms.[32] In historiographical settings, narrating subjects thus needed to situate themselves with respect to other witnesses who would verify their status as witnesses through a process called *compurgation* and situate them within a reputable community.[33] In colonial soldiers' narratives, for example, compurgation arises from the fraternity of a military community, which Miguel Martínez argues is forged in solidarity through shared experiences of war.[34] The narrated matter that such military voices undertake is limited explicitly to what they can attest to as a result of their physical presence at the time of the event.[35]

While oceanic voyages of discovery and conquest by figures like Bernal Díaz del Castillo, Vasco da Gama, and Columbus violently extended early modern European spheres of knowledge outward, and mobilized those explorers' bodies as proof of the stories they told, anatomical discovery extended that same impulse toward the human body's interior.[36] Early modern anatomists' interest in bodies, especially in the decades after Andrea Vesalius's *De humani corporis fabrica* (1543) was published, however, goes beyond just their utility in establishing scientific truth and heralds a moment at which the fundamental epistemological assumptions that undergirded knowledge production were being reordered and reconstructed, what Sawday has described as the Renaissance's "culture of dissection."[37] Like the writing colonial subject, early modern anatomists and physicians emphasized a shift in their position toward an intimately indexical relationship with the body upon which they acted. Analogous to the authoritative distance imperial historians assumed over their material, Galenic anatomists assumed a position of disinterested authority over the criminal body confirming the past authority of received texts, while a separate, debased *demonstrator* wields the knife that dissects the body in question.[38] In contrast, Vesalius and his successors assumed a more proximal position to the corpse, combining the roles of *demonstrator* and *ostentor*, pointing out key sources of knowledge while confronting the dead body in an equal setting in which the corpse actually consents to and participates in the spectacle of its own destruction.[39] The growing proximity between demonstrator and corpse correlates with the anatomist's ability to overturn established authority—his knowledge becomes more reliable the more intimately he engages with the body, and the more directly he can direct his audience's attention through indexical gesture that connects his own body with the corporeal evidence at his fingertips.[40]

In these different contexts—colonial, historiographical, anatomical—the human body emerged as a source of information that, with the necessary hermeneutical skills, had the potential to generate and serve as referent for a kind of apparently stable truth.[41] That truth tracks tightly with a narrator's embodied proximity to raw sources of information and the indexical relationship he can demonstrate to his audience. It is in this mode of knowledge production that Mendonça ultimately calls into question Conestaggio and Fray Antonio's standing as narrating writers, rather than specific items of misinformation for which they might be responsible.

Here

Upon relating that his countrymen were killed, the narrator pivots for the remainder of the chapter to a lingering and detailed description of the destruction wrought on the Portuguese troops at this battle. He abruptly changes his locus of enunciation from a geographically and temporally distant location to a space that is represented as immediately present through deictic pronouns, as though the shell-shocked narrative voice were being forced to relive the harrowing experiences of the day:

> *Aqui* foram mortos com valor estranho dous irmãos d'aquelles cinco que juntos entraram na batalha: D. Henrique de Menezes, e D. Simão de Menezes, o qual foi visto com uma bandeira dos inimigos na mão, sobre un montão de mortos, incitando aos vivos (já quasi sem vida) a semelhante exemplo; *e assim foi morto* D. João da Silveira, filho do conde da Sortelha, herdeiro da sua casa e do valor de seus ascendentes; D. Manoel de Menezes, bispo de Coimbra, que com a lança em logar de baculo, no sancto augmento dá fé catholica, mostrou por obra que inda nas armas fez vantagem ás lettras.[42]

> *Here* were killed with remarkable valor two brothers of those five who together entered the battle: D. Henrique de Menezes and D. Simão de Menezes, who was seen with an enemy flag in his hand, on top of a mountain of corpses, inciting the living (already nearly dead) to his example; *and so died* D. João da Silveira, son of the count of Sortelha, heir to his house and to the valor of his ancestors; D. Manoel de Menezes, bishop of Coimbra, who with a lance in place of a crosier, in the saintly support of the Catholic faith, showed through his work that arms still surpass letters.

This passage is typical of the many examples in the *Jornada* in which Mendonça names the dead. He draws attention to the family relationships of the deceased and emphasizes the valor they showed during the engagement. And yet, this is not quite the portrait of bravery that he has sought to convey up until now. Mendonça has defined courage against Conestaggio's account of Portuguese incompetence, passivity, and timidity.[43] Against this characterization, Mendonça consistently seeks to portray the Portuguese soldiers as active agents taking decisive action where they can, a theme explored in greater depth by Leitão and Silva, as we will see in chapters 3 and 4. Despite this pattern, however, this passage leaves the reader with a sense of the cost of the battle in human lives as the named dead pile up in an ignominious heap.

The mountain of Portuguese dead "here," topped with the enemy's flag, inverts the imperial image Sebastian had hoped would be the outcome of this conflict. Rather than plant their own flag in the ground, the Portuguese soldiers themselves have been made into the standard bearers for the enemy they meant to defeat. The banner on this mass of dead bodies points to the excruciating but unavoidable evidence of their loss. The punctuated similarity of these deaths, as well as their immediate presence, is beat out rhythmically:

> Da mesma maneira acabou. . . . *Tambem* foi morto. . . . *Aqui* foi morto . . . , e assim pelejando foi buscar a morte . . . *tambem* acabou. . . . *Assim* acabaram *tambem*. . . . *Aqui* morreu tambem . . . onde acabou valerosamente. . . . *Tambem* acabaram . . . e foi morto. . . . *Aqui* acabou *tambem* . . . *tambem* foi morto com grande valor. . . . *Aqui* acabaram *tambem* . . . e foram mortos. . . . De tão illustre sangue *como havemos dicto* andava *n'este* tempo o campo cheio de vivos e mortos, juntamente variando a morte com lamentaveis successos, e sustentando-se a desprezada vida á força de valor e de ventura.[44]

> In the same way died. . . . So too was killed. . . . *Here* was killed . . . and thus fighting he went to seek out death . . . so too ended the life of. . . . Thus, too, died. . . . *Here* died as well . . . where his life ended valiantly. . . . So too ended the lives of . . . and was killed. . . . *Here too* ended the life of . . . also with great valor was killed. . . . *Here too* ended the lives of . . . and were killed. . . . Of such illustrious blood *as we have said* ran *at this time* the battlefield full of living and dead, together interspersing death with lamentable events, and thus did disdained life sustain itself by force of valor and fortune.

This emphasis on the immediacy of these bodies, indexed visually with banners and textually with the repeated deictic "aqui," here, informs the central argument of this chapter. A first reading of these passages shows that the repetition of "aqui" has the effect of turning the reader's mental eye from one corpse to the next, scanning over those who died, lingering over those given names. Readers are asked to accompany Mendonça in witnessing the dead and thereby become themselves witnesses to the moment of their death, displayed in what Vivian Sobchack calls the "ferocious reality" of death.[45] The emphasis on their immediate presence "aqui" introduces this fleshy catalogue of human mortality into his textual archive. An analysis of the complex deictic system this passage creates sheds light on precisely how the agonizing reality of their presence is enacted on the page.

Where Is the Corpse?

Mendonça foregrounds the corpses of those who fought at al-Qasr al-Kabir as "here," imparts information about their deaths in full detail, and identifies each by name, a practice Thomas Laqueur terms *necronominalism*.[46] By insisting on the immediate presence of the corpses within the text, the narrator establishes a common ground, a shared plane of reference, on which he and his reader can meet.[47] The referential bodies occur in deictic clusters with other rhetorical strategies that elicit the cooperation of the reader in remembering and maintaining a shared textual space.[48] Crucially, Mendonça exhibits his command of this newly created narrative space when he turns the reader's attention away from our present time and place and insists on the shared diegetic space of the text through his use of indexes and deictic reference.

Indexes and deictics are sometimes referred to as *shifters* because how they signify can vary depending on the situation, and they can be decoded only with reference to their particular situational context.[49] As shifters, deictics are particularly susceptible to perspectival changes and specific material circumstances. Our ability to interpret these signs is thus fundamentally contingent upon our understanding of when and where they appear, or our cooperation with the speaker to cocreate a space in which they make sense. Losing circumstantial or contextualizing information may make the object of an index hermeneutically impenetrable or reduce it to an empty modifier, open to being appropriated or reinvested with a new, alternate referent, a problem that will be explored further in chapter 2.

Of particular relevance to this chapter is a subclass of deictic references: spatial deictics, which are particularly powerful in generating and orienting our attention to the contours of such shared fields of interpretation. Spatial deictics locate entities, configure spaces, or describe movements in those spaces and are usually discussed in relation to a particular point of reference. To interpret them, the reader or listener needs to establish an origo, which is most often identified as the pivot point from which the speaker enunciates.[50] Such spatial information can be communicated through proximal (*here, this, este*), medial (in Romance languages, *ese* and its equivalents), and distal (*there, that, aquel* and its equivalents) indexes, which ultimately orient the interactants' attention within that arena.[51] Spatial deictics create particular context for their speakers' enunciations and reciprocally are themselves given particular meaning by that context.[52] They also illuminate the disposition of speaker and audience to one another in that they gain meaning not just from the speaker's context, but also from the social and physical positions of speakers *and* listeners.[53] For example, the spatial adverb "there" in the sentence, *There goes Jack*, clearly indicates the disposition of the speaker vis-à-vis Jack, but it also gives us information about the position of the hearer of the sentence. When such an utterance is quoted in a different context—*He said to me, "There goes Jack"*—the indexical ground of reference transposes with it, projecting the origo of the original statement into the narrative space. William Hanks argues that the relationality of deixis makes it "perhaps the clearest indicator of the interactive transformations involved in producing context."[54] Thus, deictics comprise language that is perhaps uniquely suited to conveying the complexity and dynamism of objects and spaces that are themselves in constant flux. When transplanted to new contexts through citation or other reframing techniques, deictics can be particularly striking in their capacity to retain the ground of earlier pivot points even as they take on new meanings in this new territory.

As proposed in the introduction, corpses *are themselves* indexical and iconic signs to be interpreted. As matter, corpses are inherently communicative objects because, Schwartz argues, they "are material things that bear a referential relationship to an absent subject. They are a kind of medium that connects the living to the memory of the deceased."[55] Although in her project Schwartz focuses on corpse as icon, she also recognizes how its indexical features contribute to its power in representation. The corpse is an object that uncompromisingly reminds its viewer of what lies beyond the known world and gestures toward its now deceased subjectivity. The corpse's indexical relationship with what is "not here" mediates between "here" and "not here." That is, any representation of the dead already traffics in indexicality and referentiality, regardless of the medium. When the referential "here" of the grave site is carried over to the page, the spatial ordering it enacts is "now transfigured into *textual* space, an emergent way of relating to the dead."[56] With this temporarily established common ground for narrating and reading, the narrator generates a newly corporeally anchored field and thus maps a new referential cartography that is mutually intelligible to narrator and reader.

In the previous passage from the *Jornada*, there is a characteristic clustering of a set of deictic features within a confined textual space. Rather than a lone deictic, instead we see a deictic chain, or a group of indexes that aggregate within a unit of text, that also coincides with several instances of anaphora. The cooperation among indexes and anaphora converges a set of moments of metaphysical and textual rupture into a single, unified space.[57] Here, that confluence of referentiality happens on several levels. First, the imagery of the passage follows a converging vector along the gravitational pull of those bodies. The narrator initially has described a pile of bodies—themselves indexes, if we follow Schwartz's logic—marked by the index of the banner held aloft in

D. Simão de Menezes's hand. The narrator asserts that this visual index marks the point to which other bodies are drawn to die "here." The men whose deaths are narrated in the subsequent pages thus draw together to form the growing mass of bodies that has collected in this place. Even the use of their names, what I explore later as "necronominalism," labels now detached from the bodies to which they were once affixed, acts as an index to the disappeared subjectivity. The visual index of the flag thus helps amass the hardwired referentiality of the piled-up material bodies of the dead.

The aggregation of language mirrors that of the banner-marked bodies. The indexes themselves converge on the page: the prosody of the textual gesture "aqui, . . . aqui, . . . aqui, . . ." verbally links these discrete events in a web of common experience through the regularity of the textual rhythm. The rhythmically strong deictic elements, marked sharply with the plosive consonants of "aqui" and "acabaram," alternate with the rhythmically weaker elements of names and detail. This cadence establishes and then fulfills readerly expectations over the pages that recount the deaths of these men—upon reading that something happens "aqui," the reader is trained to immediately expect another account of how another brave soldier died. The prosody of Mendonça's mourning is thus beat out percussively on the repeated consonant "k." The linguistic convergence of a cluster of deictics link those moments of sharply marked rupture. Further, the deictic adverbs cooperate with words like "tambem" and "assim," whose anaphoric referentiality continuously requires the reader to keep track of their antecedents.[58] The author and reader thus cooperatively weave together the discursive fabric of the text "here."

When used in conjunction with another type of index—a corpse—deictics produce a new territory between "here" and "not here" that is mutually intelligible and navigable for narrator and reader. Narratologists have elucidated how deixis participates in constituting narrative by defining and establishing the relationship between story and discourse, intradiegetic and extradiegetic space, participants and observers.[59] Deixis efficiently creates a reader's sense of the contours of narrative space, orienting them toward the limits of "the relationship between story and discourse and between an external world and the mind of an observer."[60] Narrative achieves this effect by requiring the reader constantly to reconstitute the indexical ground of reference in which deixis refers not to objects in the reader's world, but instead to a new pivot anchored in the narrative field.[61] Most compellingly, Susan Stewart argues that "deixis fuses form, expression, and theme as one even in place and time . . . it is its own location."[62] The use of deictics in narrative thus effectively causes the reader to translate their plane of reference from the place in which they are reading into the created narrative spatiality and temporality.

Unified thus by the rhythmic regularity of these deictic adverbs and the anaphoric cooperation that words like "tambem" and "assim" elicit from the reader, we begin to see the consolidation of a shared textual space in which the intra- and extradiegetic zones within and beyond the text merge. The deictic gesture marking the conflated "here" of battleground and narrative space also converges the intradiegetic narrated space and extradiegetic space of the reader. Since "deixis involves a triangle of the one who points, the one who is addressed, and the person or object or locale being thus distinguished," the repeated use of the deictic adverb "here" insists upon at least a two, if not three, dimensional space in which that triangle lies.[63] These words, which gesture to the narrator's created space that he and his reader share, scan the reader's attention across the page, regularly reminding them of the continuity of that created space. It is this last effect that I will explore in depth for the rest of this chapter.

Necronominalism

If we return to the textual example from Mendonça's *Jornada de África*, I highlighted three key features that bring us back to the three threads I want to tie together in this chapter: narrative authority, corpses, and deictic reference. As I argued earlier, the driving purpose behind Mendonça's text is to disprove Conestaggio's negative narrative of Portuguese participation at the battle. Mendonça sets out to establish himself as a more trustworthy and authoritative narrator than his rival. He does so in a manner characteristic of other participants in the Iberian imperial process like Díaz del Castillo or Hernán Cortés, who also relied on their positions as eyewitnesses of and participants in events in the Americas to legitimize their claims to narrative authority. Mendonça explicitly identifies himself as "quem viu e passou toda esta jornada" [one who saw and experienced all this expedition]," a position he opposes directly to Conestaggio's position as "escriptor," as a writer.[64] Put in deictic terms, Mendonça claims that his authority derives from the simple fact that he went "there"—the place of the action of the battle—while Conestaggio stayed "here" in Lisbon—the place of writing, publication, and reading.

Except that Mendonça doesn't exactly claim that he went "there," while Conestaggio stayed "here." As we saw in in the first two quotes, Mendonça inverts the expected semantic fields of "here" and "there."[65] This is a clear example of a creative or performative sign.[66] In circumventing our initial understanding of our bodily position not only with respect to the "speaker," but also with respect to other items within the same domain, Mendonça brings our attention to bear most forcefully on the moments that disrupt our expectations and, like other authors of Iberian imperial enterprises, insists upon the localism of the battlefield as preeminent over the center of empire. "Here" in the *Jornada de África* comes to refer not to what we would expect to be the place of writing, publication, and reading—seventeenth-century Lisbon—but instead to the ground piled high with the still-bleeding bodies of Mendonça's compatriots, the "montão de mortos" at al-Qaṣr al-Kabīr. This provocative use of deixis refashions the parameters of this textual world to meet the extraordinary demands of empire." If "in its universalist ambition, empire is essentially placeless," then, by anchoring the spot of death and dying "here," Mendonça stakes out the battleground as the place in which the translated elements of empire can be analyzed and made sense of.[67]

What does Mendonça accomplish by rendering these textually preserved bodies of the Portuguese army unavoidably present? As I suggested earlier, one might read the gesture as a textual funereal service, a way of laying to rest bodies that, by necessity, were left untended on a battlefield. More concretely, however, Mendonça upends any notion of comfortably distant objectivity in the metropole by strategically inverting proximal and distal deictics. He thus translates the site from which one can successfully narrate and understand empire from an expected center toward an ignominious and distant periphery. He collapses and conflates the site of imperial action and witnessing with the site of centralized knowledge collection and judgment, creating a common ground littered with the bodies and limbs for the reader to consider. Mendonça has already exerted significant efforts to ground his authoritative status as an eyewitness to the events of this battle, and to connect his status as one who saw and experienced the events of the day to a notion of truth. By indicating that he and his reader share a common setting in which they are confronted with the embodied aftermath of al-Qaṣr al-Kabīr, he invites his reader to join him in reliving these events of the past within the present setting. This gesture made all the more poignant by the subsequent translation of the center of Portuguese power from Lisbon to the Escorial in Spain in 1580—the placelessness of Portuguese empire has been utterly confirmed with its loss of control even over its own capital. Thus, the boundaries of center and periphery collapse, and the devastation and loss at al-Qaṣr al-Kabīr is indistinguishable from the humiliation of the Iberian Union in Lisbon.

In this way, Mendonça denies his reader the safety of distance and abstraction, the comfort of the convention that, in the words of Scarry, "assists the disappearance of the very event that is the most radically embodying event in which human beings ever collectively participate."[68] On the contrary, Mendonça not only lists the names and injuries of those who died twenty-nine years before the publication of his book but also vividly, if briefly, describes their blood soaking the battlefield which he establishes as distressingly physically present before the reader's eyes: "Da mesma maneira acabou Ayres da Silva, [. . .], que banhando a terra com seu sangue, mostraram a innocencia de seu animo, na maldade por [Conestaggio] injustamente opposta. Tambem foi morto D. Vasco Coutinho, e D. Luiz Coutinho, conde de Redondo, que emfim ousou banhar-se de tal sangue esta terra [In the same way Ayres da Silva died . . . who, bathing the earth with their blood, showed their soul's innocence, which Conestaggio in his spite opposed. D. Vasco Coutinho was killed, too, and D. Luiz Coutinho, count of Redondo, in which blood the earth dared to bathe itself]."[69] These are not neutral, abstracted bodies subsumed into a metaphorical body of an army whose arms or flanks were "severed" or even "neutralized," but corpses who have recently bled out into the dust of "esta terra [this earth]." The deictic *esta* (this) indexes a setting that is shared between narrator and readers. Mendonça is not alone in reliving the bloody deaths of his own companions; rather, he creates a space to share with his reader. This place *here* is defined by the relationship of his own embodied eyes as they witness the spilled blood to the anthropomorphized earth that bathes in the noble blood of his companions, and to the implied readerly interlocutor that accompanies him in his memory.

By emphasizing the immediate presence "aqui" of "hic jacet," or the presence in the established "terra" of these bodies, Mendonça theorizes a common space on the page to which he and the reader can return, perhaps to care for the corpses of these fallen companions in a way neither he nor any other Portuguese survivors were able to do at the time of their comrades' deaths, perhaps to witness the truth. It bears repeating that the "here" of the grave site is carried over to the page a spatial ordering "now transfigured into *textual* space, an emergent way of relating to the dead."[70] These bodies are invoked in a way that uncompromisingly reconfigures their viewer within the spatiotemporal frame of the narrative—the deictic "here" points to a shared and proximal referential space that is neither entirely that of the narrated stuff of the text (*there*, or *not here*) nor that of the space of reading (perhaps, *right here*).

The corpses' indexical relationship with what is *not here* mediates the conceptual transition between the *here* and *not here*. Where the corpse collapses proximal and medial spatiotemporal ground, they also bring an unknown, distal territory into the common ground of textual communication.[71] In the absence of shared common ground, these corpses converge to form a makeshift site of mutual comprehension. The corpses appear to be irrevocably *here*, and thus generate both space and time that can be shared with the reader.[72] If the narrator designates *here* as the place of undeniable truth, the end of a life, then based on this designated positionality the reader must begin to orient and map out the contours of their common grounds for understanding with the narrator. Narratologically, those bodies construct a temporarily stable raft of certainty to which narrator and reader can both cling to encounter a shared sense of truth or authenticity. The corpse thus becomes the new pivot point from which the narrator can attempt to encode markers of credibility for radically new information, and from which the reader can assess those spots in the narrator's ethical topography. As a symbol of the liminal between what is known and unknown, the corpse materializes a localized strategy for reorienting narrator's and reader's epistemological topography.

The chapter closes with a lengthy list of the Portuguese knights slaughtered in the fray and a brief contemplation of the fates of the bodies of the dead and mortally wounded:

> *Aqui* acabou tambem Francisco da Aldana . . . Thomé da Silva, Joanne Mendes de Oliveira, Christovão de Alcaçova, D. Pedro da Cunha, D. Nuno Manoel, Christovão de Brito, André Gonçalves, alcaide-mōr de Cintra, e Alonso Peres Pantoja . . . D. Sancho de Noronha, D. João e D. Luiz de Castro. . . . Tambem houve alguns fidalgos que morreram logo depois da batalha . . . D. Fadrique Manoel, cujo corpo resgatou sua mãe D. Joanna de Athaide, e Nuno Furtado de Mendonça, aos quaes *n'este* logar podêmos tambem dar a sepultura, pois *n'elle* com tanto valor tomaram posse da gloriosa morte que tiveram.[73]

> Here, too, died Francisco da Aldana . . . Thomé da Silva, Joanne Mendes de Oliveira, Christovão de Alcaçova, D. Pedro da Cunha, D. Nuno Manoel, Christovão de Brito, André Gonçalves, alcaide-mōr of Cintra, and Alonso Peres Pantoja . . . D. Sancho de Noronha, D. João e D. Luiz de Castro. . . . There were also some noblemen that died after the battle . . . D. Fadrique Manoel, whose body was rescued by his mother D. Joanna de Athaide, and Nuno Furtado de Mendonça, whom *we* can also bury in *this* place, for it is *here* that they took possession of the glorious death they had.

Naming these dead introduces another level of indexicality into this deictic cluster.[74] The names gesture toward the absent being as *that* which was, whether as stone inscriptions, ink on parchment, oral recitations, or lists of the significant dead.[75] Laqueur argues that the indexical relationship between the named dead and the corpse is haunted by the gap between text and rotting body: "the names on this . . . list forever float close by to, but never quite on, bodies themselves. They are inscribed securely on a memorial wall as the unmoving shadows of men, as stand-ins for the dead whose bodies are nowhere yet everywhere close by."[76] Invoking the dead thus requires pragmatic cooperation among the living in recalling and revivifying what is no longer. Death discursively returns matter that was human, animate, proper, singular, and definite to the non-salient: natural processes of decay make the dead body inhuman, inanimate, common, plural, and indefinite.[77] Necronominalism resists that process of relegation of dehumanized, common objects to anonymous insignificance in the background. Naming the dead insists upon the corpse's abiding humanity that, even as it loses the material qualities that distinguish it from the earth in which it is interred, retains its referential salience in the figural foreground, what I will explore as *prominence* in chapter 3.

In effect, the corpse acts as an empty signifier for a witness that the narrator can fill with meaning. Like the corpse itself, these names retain their existential connection to the absent subject. The names of D. Fadrique Manoel and Nuno Furtado de Mendonça, whether their bodies are laid to rest in Portugal or Morocco, mediate between the world of the living and whatever place to which these men have gone. Mendonça insists upon readerly cooperation in his act of textual burial with a first-person plural conjugation—"*we can* also bury"—and deixis—"in *this* place," "in it"—once more collapsing the space of witnessing, writing, and reading. D. Fadrique Manoel is the only person killed in the entire chapter whose body we know makes it back to his family. All the others, as far as the reader knows, are interred or left untended on the blood-soaked battlefield itself. Contrary to the glory of a burial in the place of one's distinguished death that Mendonça previously extolled, his use here of "resgatou" to characterize the return of D. Fadrique Manoel's corpse to Portuguese soil betrays more equivocation about how much "glory" can be found in being abandoned "in this place" forever. The former patriarchs and heirs of Portugal's greatest families have been reduced to rotting corpses in a place from which their families can never recover their physical remains.

As previously mentioned, the success of Mendonça's strategy fundamentally depends upon his reader's uptake and cooperation. To what extent does the reader allow Mendonça to manipulate their sense of time and place in order to relive the horror of the Portuguese defeat at al-Qaṣr al-Kabīr? Mendonça mobilizes proximal deictics in conjunction with these corpses, forces his reader out of a passive model of reading, and demands a response from his audience, co-creating the deictic field in which lie these untended dead bodies. He relies upon the "the sheer material factualness of the human body" not only to support the undeniable sense of truthfulness of the facts he presents to his reader, but also for their more visceral power in demanding attention and some kind of response.

Figure 1. João Baptista, woodcut of the Battle of al-Qaṣr al-Kabīr, in Miguel Leitão de Andrade, *Miscellânea do sitio de N. Sa. da Luz do Pedogão Grande* (Lisbon: Matheus Pinhero, 1629).

Some of the most striking images from another seventeenth century Portuguese account of al-Qaṣr al-Kabīr—the seventh dialogue of Miguel Leitão de Andrade's *Miscellânea*—were printed as double-folded woodcuts bound within the pages of this account (figures 1 and 2).[78] The woodcut showing the battle's aftermath, in particular, is eye-catching for its casual display of corpses and severed limbs littered on the battlefield. To see the images of the battle and its aftermath, the reader must pull out the double-folded woodcuts that are bound amidst the text of the account of the battle. The physical action of unfolding these pages can be read, in one sense, as the reanimation of the events at the hand of the reader, who as a result joins the ranks of witnesses to this version of the battle. Much as the reader's haptic engagement with the material text serves to anchor its credibility and subsequent propagation, so too does Leitão's textual rendering of his own wounded body emerge as a stable piece of evidence that his reader can examine to verify his narrative authority.[79] While no images accompany Mendonça's account of the battle, he endeavors to accomplish a similar goal through his extensive use of deictics. By making these bodies present before the eyes and within imagination of the reader, he actively involves the reader and asks them to join him in promulgating *his* explanation of the events. The temporal and geographical collapse

Figure 2. João Baptista, woodcut of the aftermath of the Battle of al-Qaṣr al-Kabīr, in Leitão de Andrade, *Miscellânea do sitio de N. Sa. da Luz do Pedogão Grande* (Lisbon: Matheus Pinhero, 1629).

produced by deixis makes the reader himself witness to the events as mediated by Mendonça and marshals this new witness to his narrative agenda.

The mass of dead Portuguese soldiers left on the battlefield at al-Qaṣr al-Kabīr constitute evidence of the utter failure of Sebastian's North African venture. The imperial failure comes, in the *Jornada*, at a distinct, ethical cost. The inability to make territorial gains in the Maghrebi desert carries implications for Portuguese geopolitical power, but, for Mendonça, more critically impedes first-hand access to their bodies as a source of truthful narrative. This, ultimately, seems to be Mendonça's answer to Conestaggio's searing critique of the Portuguese failure at al-Qaṣr al-Kabīr: *you weren't there; you can't know what happened*. Mendonça mobilizes corpses within his narrative to help him construct his narrative ethos, to uphold his status as a reliable witness and speaker. In doing so, he joins the ranks of other early modern narrators of empire in arguing that eyewitness accounts of the imperial enterprise are more trustworthy than those of narrators with more education or social status who have never participated on the ground. For Mendonça, this testimonial project is associated with his efforts to redeem the Portuguese losers from the dishonor of their catastrophic defeat in Morocco and subsequent defamation by non-Portuguese writers. This account goes beyond merely establishing narrative authority, however. Mendonça is not satisfied simply with being recognized as the most authoritative narrator on the subject. He is eliciting a kind of conversion in his reader by textually mobilizing the dead of the battle as martyrs to this cause. It is insufficient that the reader finds him logically compelling, or credible as a narrator. Mendonça insists that they, too, must join him in experiencing the Portuguese defeat, so that they may join him in attesting to this version of the story. Nevertheless, in Mendonça's case, the success of his historiographical agenda is complicated by the truth that his account seeks to represent. The utter destruction of Portuguese imperial place because of al-Qaṣr al-Kabīr requires this author to endeavor to construct and supply a new locale in which he and his reader can find common ground.

2
Absence
Disappearing the Royal Dead

> Lo primero es cubrir el rostro del Defuncto y las partes, que la honestidad calla, y la castidad olvida, y encargo se trate el Cadaver, con mucha decencia y veneración, que a los Defunctos se le debe con mayor justificacion.
>
> The first thing one must do is to cover the face of the Deceased and the parts that honesty silences, and chastity forgets, and I charge you to treat the Cadaver with much decency and veneration, which is owed to the Deceased with the greatest justification.
>
> —JUAN EULOGIO PÉREZ FADRIQUE, *MODO PRACTICO DE EMBALSAMAR CUERPOS DEFUNCTOS*

For an event sometimes known as the Battle of the Three Kings, one might expect that the involved kings would have figured consistently as protagonists of narratives that recount the events. Ironically, however, the kings shaped the action in the combat zone more through their absence than with their presence. Despite his aspirations to follow in the footsteps of his grandfather, the Holy Roman Emperor, as a great military leader, Sebastian's leadership skills on the battlefield are erratic at best—hardly a surprise, given his volatile behavior leading up to al-Qasr al-Kabir. Even Mendonça's apologetic account of his king's actions show an impulsive character more concerned with securing personal glory than strategic victory. He disappears at precisely the wrong moments, depriving the chain of military command of critical instructions at key moments and preventing them from taking action that might have changed the course of the battle. By disappearing from the scene of battle even while he is alive, Sebastian stymies his followers so that they are immobilized by their opponents instead of wielding weapons against them. While he lives, his absence presages the chaos that will ensue after his death. Put in terms of medieval and early modern theories of monarchy, the material absence of Sebastian as royal head of this body politic, along with the rest of his body, incapacitates its most active limbs, in this case, the leaders and soldiers of his army. His death brings no closure, and instead it opens up a fissure at the heart of the state he should have been leading.

Sebastian's is not the only royal body that tends to go missing in these narratives. An ailing ʿAbd al-Malik dies and his corpse disappears from the scene because of the prescient intervention by his attendants. ʿAbd al-Malik's doctor, Joseph Valencia, accurately reads the signs of the king's imminent demise from illness and then fends off disaster when he convincingly makes the royal corpse seem alive for the remainder of the battle. For all but a few witnesses, including ʿAbd al-Malik's brother and heir, Aḥmad al-Manṣūr, Valencia effectively extends the king's public life for several hours beyond his physical death by verbally transmitting orders from the corpse to his subordinates—distorting that time frame long enough for other key events to take place on the battlefield that secure Portuguese defeat.[1] Mendonça, for one, laments that the Portuguese vanguard retreats just a moment too soon from where ʿAbd al-Malik lay dead and loses the opportunity to publicize the Moroccans' decapitation in metonymy: "o que se não acontecêra, fôra muito facil cousa cortar a cabeça a Muley Moluco, e posta como determinavam ém um alto pique [if it had not happened, it would have been easy to decapitate ʿAbd al-Malik, and place the head on a tall pike]."[2] This absent body entirely alters the denouement of the story.

For these narrators, the moment of royal death cannot or should not be represented in the *now* of narrative time. Sebastian's and ʿAbd al-Malik's lifeless bodies refer to the unspeakable obscenity of the moment of their deaths. Representing that moment destabilizes social and political structures by centering the reader's attention on a rupture in the social order that is repetitively accessible through text. The indexical representation of death and the dead produces common ground upon which narrator and reader can meet. Here, however, those corpses cannot or should not be represented as mimetically present *now*; André Bazin's study "Death Every Afternoon" allows us to theorize the indexical representation of royal death as taboo or obscene.[3] Bazin contends that the representation of real death is an obscenity because that representation violates its nature by making a temporally singular, sacred moment available for repeat viewing. Documentary representation allows viewers to "desecrate and show at will the only one of our possessions that is temporally inalienable."[4] Bazin's definition of obscenity—something he is defining normatively as ethically, if not technically, unrepresentable—derives from a very modern attitude toward death as a private moment to be publicly denied or shrouded. Other kinds of representations of death, however, also have warranted circumspection for both ethical and political reasons. Moving beyond Bazin's modern understanding of the singularity of the moment of death, his preoccupation with the temporality of death and the dead is a point of entry for answering the question, *When is the corpse?* Bazin's unease with looking too hard at the newly dead body underscores its untimeliness. The sudden death of a king is an example of an inopportune death whose documentation is necessary but brings attention to bear on the most socially and politically unstable point of monarchy: the vulnerability of the king's body natural.[5] The consequences of an unpropitious royal death can render its representation obscene—it is a singularly destabilizing moment whose availability as a spectacle of consumption violates its very singularity. Two of the battle's narrators produce textual solutions, as we will see, to cope with the obscenity of royal death: evasion and ventriloquism. Through these strategies, narrators manipulate heterogeneous time frames to bring them into moments of synchrony and asynchrony, achieving a delicate balance between continuing to narrate and doing so ethically.

Narrators who witness royal death must assume different postures that justify documenting it and making this disruptive and destabilizing moment available for future consumption and reproduction. Each strategy has temporal connotations and consequences: to use Elizabeth Freeman's term, they drag time.[6] Temporal drag constitutes the *now* as "complex and vascular"—the present is mixed up with and haunted by the past and future.[7] Two gazes drag time to conceal a corpse's obscene absence when witnesses are directly involved in the events to which they attest: (1) The *endangered* gaze, defined by the witness's physical, embodied proximity to sources of danger, is characterized by lacunae that result from the traumatic rupture of two or more heterogeneous time frames. Those gaps conceal royal death and allow the living past to leak into the dead present because when the endangered witness looks away from obscene death, they and their audience can continue to pretend that the dead are not dead. (2) The *interventional* gaze is even more implicated in the events it documents than the endangered gaze. Ethically absolved by the witness's efforts to avert the moment of death they report, the witness is free to narrate their experience of the moment of death in all its sensorial detail. That corporeal involvement and effort to forestall death speaks to a command of a future time frame they hope to keep from happening.[8] In this way, the interventional witness drags the future into the present, a temporal leak that gives them the chance to anticipate the untimely death.

The first of these strategies appears most vividly in a text already familiar to us—Mendonça's *Jornada de África*. In this comprehensive chronicle of the battle, Mendonça presents himself as an endangered witness: as we have seen in chapter 1, the position from which he recounts these events is indexically inflected by his experience at the heart of the battle's action. Nevertheless, he assiduously avoids portraying his dead king's corpse. By insisting on his ignorance about the most important moment of the event he recounts—Sebastian's death—Mendonça reinforces his position as an endangered witness at the height of the action because that position fragments and obscures the horrors in which the witness participates. Meanwhile, a second witness of royal death, Joseph Valencia, recounts his experience of the battle in a letter to an unnamed brother that circulated publicly to Italy and England. He retains the indexical link to another hidden king's body—'Abd al-Malik's—to inscribe his testimonial position in an interventionist mode. That link depends on Valencia's success at ventriloquizing royal death as life, a performance that in effect conceals the untimeliness of 'Abd al-Malik's death by making his corpse temporarily absent but imminently present. As endangered and interventional witnesses, Mendonça and Valencia separately grapple with the representational problems that the absence inherent to the dead royal body poses to its witnesses, and each respond with textual solutions that create temporal drag, which covers up the obscenity of these deaths.

Obscene Royal Death

Although earlier he emphatically insists upon graphically detailing the specific, gruesome deaths of his companions, at this most important point of the narrative, Mendonça refuses to reproduce the moment of royal death and will not present a clear and detailed account of what happened to his king. This elision is not accidental; on the contrary, Mendonça explains his circumspection about the event:

> Até este passo houve algumas pessoas dignas de fé, que ousaram revelar o acontecido, porém se viram mais, não se sabe; o que se viu sempre claramente, é que nunca alguem disse que vira matar a el-rei, e não é muito, realmente, pois nenhum homen que ficasse vivo é razão que tal confesse.[9]

> Until this step, if there were some trustworthy people who dared to reveal the event, even if they saw more, it is not known; what was always seen clearly is that there was never anyone who said that they saw the king killed, which is not saying much, really, as there is not a reasonable man alive that confesses to that.

This omission is dictated by a concern that representing Sebastian's royal death would constitute a semiotic obscenity. That representations of Sebastian's death are thought to be obscene is exposed in the very diction of this passage—witnesses do not dare to reveal what they saw. All those who may have seen Sebastian die—the possible identity of these witnesses is itself delicately hedged—refuse to pull back the veil and expose this moment to the prurient interest of the public. Portraying this event would inappropriately invite the reader's interest in something that inherently warrants repulsion and offers no redeeming social value, and thus abrogates fundamental social norms of respect. After the king's death, therefore, Mendonça maintains Sebastian's absence on the level of representation and avoids making direct references to either the moment of his death or to the material presence of his body. By strategically controlling what bodies he includes in his account, therefore, Mendonça refuses to give them access to an indexical space that they can share with this body and thereby chooses not to satisfy his reader's repulsive desire to relive this moment of abject political instability.

We have seen that the corpse is unremittingly indexically present—it is both *here* and *there*, linking and mediating between those spaces. The corpse is not just present, however, but also absent. Although the corpse is powerfully *here* in space—it insistently draws attention to itself by awakening the senses of sight, smell, and touch—it is just as powerfully *not here* in time. The animating force that previously made this entity fully human has since departed: "a corpse always references a human departure, a specific subject who has left it behind."[10] As an index, as a trace or mark of a presence that is now absent from the narrative space, the corpse is an inherently temporal sign: "Whether it persists, as in the then-ness of a preserved fingerprint, or not, as in the now-ness of a sundial's shadow, the 'thing' inscribes its sign at a specific moment in time. Thus, the index has a privileged relation to time, to the moment and duration of its inscription; it also has a physical relationship to the original of which it is the sign."[11] Unlike the single moment a fingerprint points to, however, when the persisting indexical "thing" is a corpse, references to a lifetime of specific moments are inscribed in this single corporeal entity that is the metonymic trace of a missing life.[12] The process by which a corpse fragments and disintegrates only multiplies its composite referential scope across multiple time frames.[13] Its temporal antecedents—both before and after the moment of death—exist in narrative continuity with one another even as they coincide in and on the body. Those temporally marked remains point back to the absence that defines the corpse. By existing *now*, the corpse points to what was *then*, and already begins to transition to what it will be (and will not be) *soon*.[14]

If *now* is death and *then* was life, then the distance between those two moments can be gauged by legible physical signs: if rigor mortis has set in, how badly the body has decayed, how disgusting it smells, and so on. At times, however, documenting and reproducing such legible signs is obscene: inappropriate for the moment or audience, untimely, or out of sync with what is expected. As briefly outlined earlier, Bazin argues that the representation of death is obscene, especially when that representation provides a temporally mimetic experience.[15] Although not synonymous, change and time are so deeply mutually imbricated that when one is stopped, so ceases the other.[16] Since death "is the culmination of a particular process of duration and change," and cinema as a medium is invested in embalming the passage of time, capturing death mimetically preserves it as an inherently temporal experience.[17] The progress of the film has meaning because the observable and observed passage of time synchronizes with the observable and observed changes in the dying body. Once this process is captured in this medium, it can be accessed and replayed. This iterability is what makes Bazin conclude that the desire to see death represented in real time profanes this singular moment by making it reproducible, and that "this violation is called obscenity."[18]

In 1666, Juan Eulogio Pérez Fadrique defined the practice of embalming as an intervention into the temporal progress of the corpse's decomposition: "*Embalsamar, es conservar un cuerpo en perpetuidad*. No contento con esta difinicion digo. *Embalsamar es practica, y curacion perserbativa de el cuerpo Defuncto cõ Aromas, para en lo posible, hacerlo eterno* [*Embalming is the practice of preserving a body in perpetuity*. Not content with this definition, I say, *Embalming is the practice and preservative cure of the Dead body with aromatic substances, so that insofar as is possible, to make it eternal*]."[19] The temporal problem of representing death is not limited to film, photography, nor even visual media—if embalming is the practice of conserving a body in perpetuity to make it eternal, so too is the act of documenting it visually and in text. The apparently contingent and discordant elements of a narrative, when successfully joined together, create the sense of a teleology along which the constitutive elements of a narrative work.[20] Indeed, a text's situated, reproducible, particular temporality through a sequence of events is one of the properties that make narrative distinguishable from other modes of textual representation.[21] Forward momentum from narrative beginning to narrative end can be understood as plot, where "plotting" is "that which . . . makes us read forward, seeking in the unfolding of the narrative a line of intention and portent of design that hold the promise of progress toward meaning."[22] A narrative's temporal specificity contributes to its legibility—it contextualizes it within a particular place, as indicated by temporal and spatial deixis: *here* and *now* rather than *there* and *then*.[23] The reader immerses themself into this temporal system, internalizes the tempo of the narrative world into their own, and reenacts that alternate time frame with each reading.[24] When the moment of death becomes available and repeatedly reproducible in text, its representation is subject to the same ethical questions that attend cinema.[25]

Rendering a royal corpse available and temporally repeatable in text becomes taboo or obscene because this mimetic representation brings stress in the form of repeatable attention on the weakest point of monarchy: during the interregnum between the death of one king and the coronation of his successor when the body natural's intrinsic failings and weaknesses come to the fore. As Bertelli contends: "If the king was the very personification of the laws, it followed that after his death the bond that kept the community of subjects united and in order might also fail. This loss created a sense of a 'gap': a crisis."[26] When the king's corporeal body dies, the decapitated state "might render the body corporate incomplete or incapable of action."[27] Power transitions smoothly through an interregnum only when the king's temporal mortal body natural successfully syncopates with the timeless body politic, cuing the shift to the body natural that is next in line.[28] While historians of late medieval and early modern Iberian monarchies argue that Ernst Kantorowicz's Tudor model does not map perfectly onto the Iberian context, their critique focuses on its theological underpinnings.[29] The metaphorical embodiment of the state as delineated by Kantorowicz corresponds to corporeal theories of monarchy that circulated in Trastámara Castile, which identified the king as the head, the nobles as limbs equipped for its defense, and the rest of the body as the kingdom led by and subject to the head.[30] Similar organological metaphors were used to characterize Sebastian's reign in Portugal and to identify how he exemplified the worst aspects of a body natural that failed to fulfill his vow to protect and serve the body politic.[31] The tenuous transition of power after Sebastian's death, which decapitated Portugal's body politic, crystallized all of the weaknesses and problems Sebastian's body natural brought to his monarchy.

This central problem of monarchy can be characterized as a moment of acute asynchrony—"different time frames or temporal systems colliding in a single moment of now"—between the heterogeneous time frames of the body politic and that of the body natural.[32] While the body politic marches along in apparently linear progress, the king's death brings the body natural's timeline to a halt. After death, the vacated, static royal body natural no longer evolves in the same temporal system as the rest of the body politic. The asynchrony of body politic and body natural leaves a hole in the social and political fabric that must be patched or filled before the expanding trauma caused by this temporal standstill unravels the social fabric. The problem becomes even more acute if the king's death is followed by a mismanaged interregnum: custody of the royal corpse was not maintained between the moment of his death until the transition of power; the ruler's vassals have failed to adequately protect the body; there is no clearly defined heir or line of succession. The consequences of such a moment render its portrayal obscene: a mimetic representation of this moment of death enables the reader to replay the textually embalmed, politically taxing moment of royal death, a process that is politically, socially, and epistemologically destabilizing because each iteration reopens and renews the stress of the transition period. Representing an untimely death in all of its temporal specificity makes the precarious interregnum, in effect, too available. As a result, the royal death becomes ethically untellable for a loyal subject.

Witnesses of the untimely royal corpse are motivated to be evasive, to justify their presence and failure to intervene, to elude or evade representing the body in all its gory detail, or, in certain cases, to present their account in terms of the actions they took to intervene. The gaze in documentary representations of death is inscribed with the embodied perspective of the observer and encodes the ethical behavior of that witness in the representation itself. Under some circumstances of insurmountable physical or technical distance from the moment of death, the helpless witness's extreme discomfort, injury, or incapacity to intervene is encoded within their testimony.[33] Some testimonials may try to dodge the ethical issue of representing the royal death entirely. Such an omission opens a temporal lacuna at the heart of this account—the obscene absence of royal subjectivity is replicated in the text. In still other cases, the peril an endangered witness faces or their unpreparedness to report on this key moment excuses their failure to keep it from happening and the incomplete information they may offer on the matter. The nature of mimetic representation also means that it is etched with temporal information. The obstructed, stuttering timeline of the traumatic event proceeds as multiple heterogeneous timelines diverge, leaving lacunae that may give cover to the ethically compromised witness. Such gaps allow the living past to leak or drag into the dead present, because where the endangered witness looks away from the obscene moment of death, they and their audience can continue to hope or feign that the dead are not truly dead.

The interventional witness's efforts, on the other hand, may respond to the disruption caused by the abrupt asynchrony of the heterogeneous temporal systems of bodies politic and natural by bringing the body natural back in sync with the body politic.[34] One more creative kind of interventional witnessing can be found in Valencia's ventriloquism of his royal master's dead body—he makes words from his own mouth seem to come from that more authoritative body. Reanimating the royal corpse artificially turns back time to a moment when this powerful body was alive, assertive, and autonomously vocal. The urgency of the interventionist's involvement exonerates the obscenity that documenting this death might represent. Ventriloquism recognizes and approaches the body as an archive of material to be accessed.[35] When the dead are reenacted as if living, what the flesh was once animated to do in the past is restored in the present, while it also simultaneously retains its temporally inflected and constantly decaying, changing residues. The danger presented by such an intervention also poses a temporal question—if sustained too long, in effect, the ventriloquism of a royal corpse constitutes a coup by the external voice animating it. The successfully intervening, ventriloquizing witness, then, must have impeccable timing, whereby they make the corpse seem to keep speaking just long enough for the processes of the interregnum to identify and get back in sync with the time frame of the new royal body natural. The success of this intervention can be measured by the extent to which the corpse passes as living and the living continue to recognize the reanimated corpse as one of themselves, rather than as abject, irreconcilable other. Both strategies—omission and ventriloquism—drag the time of royal death, contaminating the present moment of the dead with living past and uncertain future.[36]

Endangered Evasion

Mendonça's position as an endangered eyewitness—as one who experienced every agonizing moment of the *jornada* of and in Africa—is spatially inflected, as we have seen, but also constructs multiple temporal frames that justify what he does and does not narrate. Strikingly for a narrator whose testimonial pose is built on extensive and exclusive access to accurate information, Mendonça claims to have no knowledge about the fate of Sebastian's body, unlike other witnesses of al-Qasr al-Kabir. Despite recognizing the royal body's power, and the need for information about Sebastian's death for a smooth transition of authority, Mendonça will not recount the circumstances of Sebastian's death. Indeed, he takes pains to omit any knowledge he or other witnesses might have of this royal death, a stance that relies on the obstructed view and harried pace of his proximity to violence and death to avoid condemning himself as a faithless vassal who watched his king die. Mendonça's obstructed representation of Sebastian's death obeys a Bazinian taboo against obscenely representing the dead king under these circumstances. The absent corpse disappears into the asynchrony of the heterogeneous time frames that respectively encompass royal mortality and eyewitness testimony. Nevertheless, sidestepping the problems of representing this death introduces temporal leak into Mendonça's account, a feature that renders Sebastian's body as simultaneously past and present: *then*, *now*, and, most dangerously, projected into the future.

If in the twenty-first century digital photographic and filmic technology are the technological innovations that give mimetic, documentary access to the dead, in the early modern period, the analogous documentary technology was eyewitness testimony. The global early modern imperial process brought the need for reliable information to a spatially and temporally contingent head.[37] During the medieval period, more prestigious historiography took the form of *historia*, a category that "implied authorship by someone who possessed the tools and learning needed in order to make inquiry into a subject, then place it within a context," and was written by professional, court-affiliated historians.[38] As discussed in chapter 1, a medieval historian's ethos, then, was in part based upon his social status, a rank that he had attained through a certain level of education and that reinforced his ability to marshal established textual authorities to corroborate his narrative, or, to use Andrea Frisch's terminology, upon his familiarity with *faits notoires*.[39] Even if the actual epistemological status of eyewitness testimony remained in doubt, the potential for establishing fact began to privilege accounts by participants in the imperial process over the textual erudition of court historians who had not traveled to imperial holdings beyond the Iberian Peninsula.[40] This sense of credibility held true despite evidence of interested testimony by participants in the imperial process.[41] Even as the eyewitness in the juridical context gradually transitioned from a marginal, compurgatory role toward a more central voice that transmitted the impression of credible knowledge, so historiographical standards for authority and credibility followed.

The main axis of the epistemological and historiographical position Mendonça stakes out in *Jornada de África* is grounded in his status as an eyewitness of the events of August 4, 1578, as discussed briefly in chapter 1. In his prologue, Mendonça positions himself as witness in contrast with those he classifies as professional writers: "E não o farei como *escriptor* por certo, que não ha razão para que tal se cuide de mim; mas sómente *como quem viu e passou toda esta jornada,* darei meu testemunho [And I won't do it as a *writer,* certainly, for there is no reason to pay attention to me on that count; but only *as one who saw and experienced all this expedition* will I give my testimony]."[42] In this expressly testimonial mode, then, Mendonça questions Conestaggio and Rivadeneyra's standing as narrating writers, rather than interrogate specific items of misinformation for which they were responsible. According to Mendonça, Conestaggio becomes suspect by writing and relying on secondhand information because this process of attaining knowledge keeps him from discerning falsehoods in his sources or tempts him to extrapolate mistaken information from incomplete knowledge. Mendonça, in contrast, claims to testify as one who saw and experienced the *jornada*—a word that refers both to the period of time that passed and to the expedition itself—a mode of knowledge creation, he contends, that will be prone to fewer fallacies. Here, witnessing the expedition entails experiencing the changes wrought by the passage of this moment of time. Mendonça encodes temporality into his testimony by equating the passage of time with the event itself.

We should consider skeptically Mendonça's protestation that he is not a writer and recognize this statement of false modesty for the writerly mode in which it is made.[43] Mendonça is savvy in delineating the scope of his gaze as a witness, sidestepping events that might compromise his ethical stance as an observer. As an affected rather than authentic disclaimer of the limited capacity of the author, this modesty topos "becomes a device that actually prepares the audience or reader for just the kind of rhetorical skill which it literally denies."[44] Mendonça's protestations depart slightly from the usual formula of the *captatio benevolentiae*—namely: I am not a writer, but still I write—in the second clause of the formula: I am not a writer, but I am a witness who experienced these events as they happened. Mendonça doubles down on the point he believes to be the source of his narrative authority by preemptively acknowledging his own narratorial limitations: as an eyewitness, as one who saw, experienced, and participated in al-Qaṣr al-Kabīr. As he describes how the casualties of the battle mounted, Mendonça appeals to the reader to judge whether it was possible for the Portuguese to win the battle given how outnumbered they were: "Mas emfim, que podiam fer dous mil homens de cavallo, por mais valorosos que fossem, contra quarenta mil que Franqui confessa, fóra aventureiros e Alarves, que vem a ser ainda maior numero do que elle diz que os portuguezes acrescentam? [And yet, in the end, what could two thousand men on horseback, no matter how brave they were, do against the forty thousand who Franchi confesses, whether *aventureiros* or Arabs, came to be an even greater number than that which he says the Portuguese amassed?]."[45] With this rhetorical question, Mendonça prompts his reader to agree with his position: that the Portuguese were put into the impossible position of defending themselves from an enemy that vastly outnumbered them, and that to do so was to comport themselves with valor.

These facts of his account characterize Mendonça as an endangered witness; his perspective is defined by his proximity to the events that he documents.[46] As already discussed at length in the preceding chapter, this position is inflected with signs that "indexically and reflexively point to the mortal danger" he faced, and his physical and embodied presence on the scene. Nevertheless, Mendonça recognizes that his testimony must indicate that this act of witnessing "in no way substitutes for a possible intervention in the event, that is, it must indicate that watching the event of death is not more important than preventing it." Mendonça's textual activity as credible eyewitness is ethically sustainable only if he can construe his activity in the represented scene as an appropriate response to the events he witnessed. Mendonça constructs his embodied experience of this event not just as a helpless onlooker but also as the intimately involved endangered witness: he inscribes the risks to his own life and those of the other key witnesses that were incurred while attesting to these events. As Vivian Sobchack explains: "Endangered vision is frequently obstructed, marking its need for protection, inscribing its fragile yet concerned relation to the horrors of mortality it grasps." This perspective justifies the incomplete information he gives about the death of his king. Mendonça's selectively obstructed perspective, which provides ethical as well as embodied cover, enables him to shield his own vision and that of his reader from that most obscene event: the death of his king.

The position from which Mendonça and his companions witness these events is inflected by the mortal danger they face, an unstable framing that emphasizes that these witnesses are vulnerable human operators acting on the scene, not objective, distant observers.[47] Sebastian's vassals' obligations during the battle are clear—it is their responsibility to endanger themselves to keep him safe. The king's failures as a leader make that dangerous job even more difficult, further imperiling the noblemen who were already prepared to die for him. As the battle winds down, the king and his guard engage with a group of Saʿdī soldiers who demand that the Portuguese surrender. Rather than recognize the consequences his actions might have for his men, the king responds by attacking:

> El-rei n'este tempo, bem certificado de tanta desventura, depois de lhe matarem outro cavallo, fazendo as maravillas que *todo o mundo viu*, andava acompanhado de alguns fidalgos, que pretendiam salval-o, a troco de suas vidas. . . . [El-rei] se lançou a elles furiosamente, acompanhado dos que o seguiam, pelejando todos com desesperada ousadia por sua salvação, *onde dizem que* cahiu depois de morto o cavallo.[48]

> The king at this time, well apprised of so much misfortune, after they killed another horse from under him, performed miracles that *everyone saw*, and rode accompanied by some noblemen, who intended to save him in exchange for their own lives. . . . [The King] flung himself at them furiously, accompanied by those who followed him, all fighting with desperate daring for their own salvation, *where they say that* the king after the horse fell dead.

While the king stays alive, Mendonça does not lack for witnesses who can document the royal body's movements. Sebastian fights in the thick of the action with such valor that multiple horses are killed from under him—marvels that all the world are willing and able to attest to. Since those witnesses are also risking their own lives, their involvement mitigates the ethical compromise that might arise from failing to prevent the king from putting his vulnerable body in peril. Even so, their failure to fulfill their commitment to save him at the cost of their own lives leaves the same witnesses, including Mendonça, unwilling to document, attest to, or represent the king's death. The king's death abruptly causes asynchrony between his actions and the sequence of events those around him witness. The disruptive momentum that carries the rest of the body politic along toward eventual defeat is too disruptive to allow those witnesses to make that moment textually reproducible.

The moment of rupture between what Mendonça claims to have witnessed and those events he leaves out of the frame of the narrative is clear. Mendonça fails to document the actual event of the king's death, an erasure that stands in stark contrast to the king's visibility earlier in the paragraph, which emphasizes the number of witnesses who could testify to his bravery. Whereas Mendonça relies on eyewitnesses and his own experiences to report on the king's actions in the battle, as soon as he turns to relate the crux of his entire narration, the death of the Portuguese king, he can only support his story with hearsay: "onde *dizem* que cahiu [where *they say* he fell]."[49] The time frame in which someone could have witnessed the king die is effectively suspended as a perpetual present, a *now* that is endlessly repeatable so long as this text is available. The asynchrony of the two key time frames—the one in which Sebastian dies, the other in which the potential witnesses move—isolates the events of death and witnessing that occur respectively in them. Rather than collide in a single *now*, their radical divergence generates the space of absence in which Sebastian's death can be hidden away from sight. Nevertheless, the momentum of quickly diverging time frames that carry the royal death into obscurity opens a void within the text that attracts all of the attention it sought to avoid. Mendonça so hastily looks away from Sebastian's death that the time frames of *now* and *then* orbits around the point of omission.

To return to the passage with which we began our discussion of the obscenity of an indexically represented royal death, we again see the disruptive temporal asynchrony that results from Sebastian's death and Mendonça's averted gaze:

> Até este passo houve algumas pessoas dignas de fé, que ousaram revelar o acontecido, porém se viram mais, não se sabe; o que se viu sempre claramente, é que nunca alguem disse que vira matar a el-rei,

> e não é muito, realmente, pois nenhum homen que ficasse vivo é razão que tal confesse.[50]
>
> Until this step, if there were some trustworthy people who dared to reveal the event, even if they saw more, it is not known; what was always seen clearly is that there was never anyone who said that they saw the king killed, which is not saying much, really, as there is not a reasonable man alive who confesses to that.

Sebastian's death is a recognizable weak point in Mendonça's redemptive story. He emphasizes that he and his sources up to this point have been reliable but defends their caution in revealing the circumstances surrounding the event, and even argues that no reasonable survivor, himself included, could be expected to confess to having witnessed such a thing. Mendonça emphasizes that Sebastian's vassals' own time frame syncopates with that of their king—their trustworthiness as eyewitnesses is closely bound up in their ability to recount the events of this *jornada*. The limbs of this body remain coordinated in time with the head they are endangering themselves to protect. Their decapitation at Sebastian's sudden death ruptures that synchronicity, sending limbs and head spinning into radically different time frames. As in the account he gives of his companions' deaths, the deictic "este" collapses the frame between the *here* of the reading frame and the *there* of the battle's events to now. The ambiguous proximal deictic could first be read to refer to the *here* of textual production—up until this page of the text, the reader can verify the facts as reported. "*This* step," however, could also point to the chronology within the temporal system of the battle itself, which in turn would imply the enduring temporal presence of the moments of mortality represented in this text: *here* is *now*, always available to the reader who chooses to subsume their time frame into the logic of the text.

While other narrators of the battle claim to know how Sebastian died and endeavor to leverage that information to prove the significance of their accounts, Mendonça's central agenda is to promote the bravery of the Portuguese men who fought at al-Qaṣr al-Kabīr. Sebastian's death before the eyes of his own men stands as a counterargument to Mendonça's thesis, a fact that he reluctantly acknowledges at this point. By veiling the obscenity of his king's death behind the expected obstructions of an endangered gaze, Mendonça attempts to strike a balance between vindicating the bravery of Sebastian's vassals and exculpating their failures by hiding the most important piece of evidence for their failure. Mendonça recognizes that his perspective as endangered witness is insufficient to justify the violation that representing Sebastian's royal death would constitute. The absence of that corpse in the text ironically becomes the temporal center around which all heterogeneous time frames of the narrative are oriented.

Interventional Ventriloquism

The disappearance of Sebastian's body is mirrored by the absent body of his rival, ʿAbd al-Malik. The witness with most direct access to that body responds to ʿAbd al-Malik's death not by demurely turning away like Mendonça, but instead by embracing that knowledge and manipulating it for the benefit of his king's body politic. Despite their interest in this moment of the battle, the sources do not agree upon the basic facts: what caused the Moroccan king's death, how and when he died, who knew about his death, what was the status of the quick-thinking ventriloquist who mediated between corpse and troops. Joseph Valencia, a Jewish doctor of Sephardic origin, claims that he witnessed the moment of death with multiple senses (eyes, ears, touch) and maintained contact with that corpse well after the moment of ʿAbd al-Malik's death, a dramatically different strategy from Mendonça's self-censorship. Valencia is a remarkable narrator because of the scope, reliability, and depth of the information about royal death to which he claims exclusive access. He responds to the problem of royal death by assuming an interventional gaze: he contends that he witnessed the corpse, possessed the expertise to correctly interpret the embodied information before him, attempted to prevent the king's eventually inevitable death, mediated between living and dead, and knew how to protect and transmit that information appropriately. Valencia intervenes after the moment of death by ventriloquizing ʿAbd al-Malik's corpse and temporarily resynchronizing the heterogeneous temporal systems of the king's inanimate body and the fast-paced events of the battle. Valencia's efforts to reanimate the royal corpse suspend it in time as a flesh archive that lends itself to recovery, interpretation, and transmission—a vocal reenactment that drags this simulacrum of life into the present and future.[51]

Valencia's letter was translated into English soon after he wrote it, and has thus been preserved in Spanish and in English among a collection of state papers from the Barbary States in the National Archives in London.[52] The few scholars who have worked with this letter refer to the edition published by Henri de Castries in his series that collected unedited material from European archives in Portugal, Spain, France, the Low Countries, and England as *Les sources inédites de l'histoire du Maroc*. Castries presents the letter simply under the heading "Lettre d'un médecin juif a son frère," and suggests that it was probably written after August 16, 1578. It was most likely sent from Fez, a city about which the doctor demonstrates intimate knowledge, and a major intellectual center with a population of some forty or fifty thousand Jews from the thirteenth through the sixteenth centuries.[53] This city and its *mellah* (Jewish quarter) would receive many of the Portuguese soldiers captured at Wādī al-Makhāzin and house them until they could be ransomed. Though the letter was directed to the physician's brother, it found a larger audience in the Elizabethan court following its translation into English. It may have disseminated even more broadly in Western Europe and the Mediterranean, as Arthur John Butler suggests that the source of the sixteenth-century English translation may have been an Italian translation of the letter, not the original Castilian.[54] This contemporary English translation reveals the hunger for information about Wādī al-Makhāzin beyond the bounds of the Iberian Peninsula.[55] The manuscript at the National Archive in London does not communicate any information about where the addressee received this letter, but its dissemination into at least two European kingdoms indicates that the doctor's brother may not have been residing in North Africa, but rather in one of the diasporic Jewish communities in Italy or elsewhere on the northern edge of the Mediterranean basin. The details of the king's illness and his treatment depicted in the missive also suggests that the brother could have been a doctor as well and was a receptive audience not just to the latest political news, but also the specifics of the medical case. In all, the letter is a unique vantage point from which to view the events of Wādī al-Makhāzin and makes a compelling case study for understanding the role of royal bodies for establishing narrative authority.

Mercedes García-Arenal identifies the author of this letter as the same Joseph Valencia described by Gonçalo Coutinho, the governor of the Portuguese presidio at Mazagão, in the *Discurso da Iornada de D. Gonçalo Coutinho a villa de Mazagam, e seu governo nella* (*Discourse of the Expedition of D. Gonçalo Coutinho to the town of Mazagam, and his government there*).[56] Coutinho recounts that Mulay Zidān, heir to the southern fragment of al-Manṣūr's realm residing in Marrakesh, sent his personal physician to care for the Portuguese governor when he was ill. Coutinho describes the doctor as "genteely Hispanized" and learned in Avicenna and Galen.[57] Coutinho's description of Valencia perhaps explains why a Maghrebi Jew would write to his brother in Spanish rather than Arabic or Hebrew. The large Sephardic community of Fez is known to have communicated in Arabic and Castilian, so much so that Portuguese captives held in Fez after August 4, 1578, expressed relief at being able to communicate with members of the Jewish community in the *mellah* in Castilian.[58] This community in Fez only began to disperse to Marrakesh following al-Manṣūr's accession to the throne, so the letter's origin there also makes sense for a well-educated Jew. His status in the royal household and loyalty to the ruling family also tracks with broader trends in the Jewish diaspora. Jews working in royal houses and administrations were particularly vulnerable to transfers of power between different parties and generations because of the personal nature of the relationships undergirding their status.[59] Valencia's ability to establish his utility to his royal protectors dictated the ongoing stability of his standing in the Moroccan court. That Valencia survived a quarter of a century into the tumultuous years following al-Manṣūr's sudden death from the plague in 1603 indicates that he was very politically savvy indeed.

Valencia concurs with the simplest and most linear version of the story of ʿAbd al-Malik's death: the king died from an illness that had affected him since days before his forces engaged Sebastian's, not from poisoning or a wound in battle. The doctor narrates that the sultan became seriously ill while his army was encamped outside of Marrakesh, waiting for information about the plans and movements of the Christian forces in Asilah, and suffered from fits of vomiting and fever. ʿAbd al-Malik died near the beginning of the battle, a fact that Valencia participated in hiding from the dead king's forces until a clear transition of power to al-Manṣūr could be ensured. Several of the sources, including Valencia's account, tell how the doctor succeeded in hiding ʿAbd al-Malik's death from his troops by effectively ventriloquizing the royal corpse—he mediated between body in the tent and ʿAbd al-Malik's commanders in the field, transmitting what were purported to be royal orders. The delay in revealing this leader's death is widely credited with ʿAbd al-Malik's forces' victory.

The details he conveys about the king's diet and symptoms suggest that Valencia expects his audience to be familiar with the principles of humoral medicine, which would have attempted to maintain the patient's health through his dietary regimen.[60] Even though Valencia suggests that the illness had progressed so far that the ʿAbd al-Malik could no longer communicate clearly, those closest to the ruler seem to have managed to keep this news from spreading among his followers:

> Al tercero dia, le acudio un hipo mui grande y un temblor en las manos, en especial en la parte derecha, torpedad en la lengua, que me pronostico luego la desventura que avia de ser. Encontreme con Mulei Hamet, e dile quenta del caso, y dixele la verdad de lo que sucedio; fueme mandado por el que lo tuviese en secreto; y dende aquella ora enpeso a entender en los negocios del reino.[61]

> On the third day, he was struck by a great hiccup and a trembling of the hands, especially on the right side, as well as weakness in the tongue. To me, this foretold the misfortune that had to be. I met with Muley Ahmed, and I gave him an account of the case, and told him the truth about what was happening; I was ordered to keep it a secret, and from that hour he began to give orders in the business of the realm.

From the first appearance of this malady, Valencia demonstrates his skill as an expert witness: he read bodies and discern the future that awaits them from the signs he reads on them. Valencia claims that he, as the expert physician, was the only one of ʿAbd al-Malik's intimates to correctly discern and predict the sultan's imminent demise, despite the obvious physical signs of serious illness, as well as the impact of those conditions on the sultan's capacity to communicate with those around him. Valencia's is a story that follows a teleology toward the king's death from signs and symptoms read and interpreted in the archive of the his dying body.

Valencia's initial story of the king's illness positions the doctor as uniquely situated to intervene in the events that he narrates. His warnings during ʿAbd al-Malik's illness anticipate how, after the king dies, his remains will be reenacted performing precisely the same actions, still mediated by Valencia. ʿAbd al-Malik is tongue-tied and interrupted by the effects of his illness, his voice inopportunely silenced, a situation that creates auditory absence at the heart of this monarchy. Valencia recognizes this silence as presaging a future, prolonged silence from this body, and identifies the communicative difficulties that will arise as a result. The doctor's diagnosis thus anticipates the king's death—"la desventura que avia de ser" (the misfortune that had to be)—and al-Mansur's rise to power—"dende aquella ora enpeso a entender en los negocios del reino" (from that hour he began to engage in the business of the realm)—and also foreshadows Valencia's own position as the principal ventriloquist who steps in to resolve the dead king's linguistic torpor. He recognizes that the sick king's body has already begun to fall out of sync with the ordinary linear momentum driving the story forward and is at risk of precipitating out of time altogether.[62] Like Mendonça, rather than allow the disorder that a royal death's asynchrony would open at this moment, Valencia steps in as a fully embodied participant.

Valencia's account invites the reader to experience this event through his sensory experience as witness. He relates a moment the day before the battle in which, against his recommendations, ʿAbd al-Malik mounts his horse to survey his cavalry, and the weakness of his health becomes immediately apparent: "Y, estando a cavallo, *senti* que se havia desmayado; *llegeme* a el, pedindole de merced que se echase en su litera, y de ella podia dar orden [He being mounted on his horse, I *perceived* that he had fainted; *I came to him* and pled with him to retire to his litter, for God's sake, and from there he could give orders]."[63] The diction here is sensorially expansive. Mendonça characterizes his testimony in principally visual terms ("quem viu e passou toda esta jornada" (one who saw and experienced this entire day/expedition); "testamunhas de vista" (testimonies of eyewitnessing)). His status as *eye*witness maintains a sense of perspectival distance from his encounter with death—the witness must be sufficiently removed from the scene to be able to report on its visual impact. In contrast, Valencia here uses a more general verb "senti," I perceived.[64] The ambiguity of which sensory faculty the doctor uses to obtain information that the king had fallen from his horse constitutes him as a fully embodied presence on the scene. His use of the word "senti," I perceived, I sensed that, encodes a more encompassing notion of the experience of a witness. He does not restrict himself to taking in only visual stimuli, but points to a much broader spectrum of sensation, one that in this case could also include hearing and touch. The Spanish "senti" leaves open to interpretation which of Valencia's senses provided the information about ʿAbd al-Malik's swoon, the effect of which is an account inscribed by the bodily presence and involvement of its witness in spatial and sensorial terms.

The same expansive sensory range characterizes the moment of ʿAbd al-Malik's death. The doctor asserts that ʿAbd al-Malik died before he had the chance to engage the Portuguese:

> digo que, al tiempo que el Rey *vido* su gente ronpida, y *miro* a una parte y a otra, y *vidose* detrás de si sin gente de cavallo, que se avian esparsido por miedo de las lombardas, por algunos dellos ser ydos a pelear, fue tanto su enojo que se puso sobre los estribos y puso mano a la espada; y tomole un temblor que cerro los dientes; *perdio el sentido* y la vida yuntamente. Fue cosa mucho para *ver*, y permision devina. Acudi yo luego, y, viendo que estava muerto, luego de inproviso lo hize echar en la litera, deziendo que estaba desmaiado. Fingi que le daba de beber. Cobrile la cara, porque no *sentiese* la gente tan gran mal.[65]

> I tell you that when the King *saw* his people broken, *looked* this way and that, and *saw himself* with no horseman behind him, because they had dispersed out of fear of the cannons, while others had gone on to fight, such was his rage that he stood up in his stirrups and drew his sword. And a great trembling overtook him so that it locked his jaw. He *lost his senses* and his life at the same time. It was quite a thing to *see*, and by divine permission. I attended him then, and, seeing that he was dead, improvised by having him put in his litter, saying he had fainted. I feigned giving him something to drink. I covered his face, so the people would not *sense* so great an evil.

As the person immediately responsible for the king's health, Valencia recounts this moment using details that place him close at hand, a testimonial position that diverges from Mendonça's deliberate evasiveness. Valencia's expertise and exposure to personal peril give him authority as a witness to this death and enable him to move beyond the limitations of the endangered gaze, assume an interventional gaze, and confront royal death head on.[66] Valencia alone, as one trained to read and interpret what was written on this royal, dying body, is a trustworthy witness who foresees the *denouement* of this plot before anyone else. He accesses latent information contained within the archive of this body and identifies strategies to reanimate it as though it is living in the present. His foresight empowers him to recognize events as they happen and, in the moment of writing, now look back on the sequence of events that led up to that moment of the battle and lead the reader through the moments that foreshadowed it. His perspicacity in interpreting the signs of ʿAbd al-Malik's body lets him give al-Manṣūr the jump on other potential challengers—a moment of anticipation that again demonstrates the doctor's command of the *now* as a moment linked indissolubly to pasts and futures.[67] Rather than allow the disruptive asynchrony of his king's death to overwhelm or overcome him, Valencia capitalizes on the temporal complexity of the royal corpse and actively drags its dead time into synchrony with the present.

Valencia communicates the severity of the dying king's case to al-Manṣūr, who instructs him to keep that information secret and then moves to take power even before his brother's death: "dende aquella ora enpeso a entender en los negocios del reino [and from that hour he began to give orders in the business of the realm]."[68] The temporal problem of succession that beleaguered Sebastian's witnesses in Mendonça's telling was the delay between the royal death and the emergence of a viable heir. Here, with Valencia's help, the presumptive heir anticipates royal death and suspends the body in a state of artificial animation at the right moment: "dende aquella ora" (from that hour). Valencia and al-Manṣūr thus keep the heterogeneous time frames of royal mortality and continuous body politic in simulated sync. Although conscious of the quandaries this royal death poses, Valencia establishes himself as the royally mandated guardian of coveted information about ʿAbd al-Malik, while ensconcing his potentially problematic testimony in the safety of successful intervention. In this way, Valencia facilitates the smooth transition of power from elder to younger brother and serves as the pivot point that links and muddles ʿAbd al-Malik's living past, dead present and al-Manṣūr's victorious future.

If al-Manṣūr is heir to the throne, Valencia claims ownership of his own sensorial experiences and appropriates those of the dead king himself. He designates ʿAbd al-Malik's newly dead corpse as a flesh archive that he is corporeally situated to interpret and whose lacunae and silences he is prepared to cover and fill.[69] Valencia establishes the moment of death as a point of sensorially inflected epistemological transfer, thus highlighting his immersed presence at the center of the action. Valencia is not just endangered; he is also involved. Here, the most literal reading of this passage is straightforward: the king loses consciousness after suffering a seizure and dies immediately. The doctor recognizes that he is dead but devises a solution that keeps other witnesses from joining him in the chaos of this new, untimely reality. Valencia uses visual vocabulary to describe both the king's experience and his own: the king is eyewitness to the impending defeat of his people and sees which factors are contributing to that imminent failure. These testimonial experiences are nested, making Valencia witness to both the king's act of witnessing and the context in which it occurs. ʿAbd al-Malik's act of eyewitnessing is encompassed by Valencia's simultaneous but more expansive visual experience of this moment of the battle: "Fue cosa mucho para ver [It was quite a thing to see]." Valencia seems to absorb the dying ʿAbd al-Malik's own perceptions as an *eye*witness while retaining his own broader, multi-sensory perspective on the scene, and then transmits both levels of information to his reader. Unlike the reticence Mendonça showed in portraying such a moment, Valencia's intervention in obscuring the obscenity of the king's death at the time gives him greater license to subsequently narrate this moment of crisis. While Sebastian's death was improperly managed on several levels, Valencia's careful oversight of this other royal death makes that moment less destabilizing.

Valencia conveys how information passes from ʿAbd al-Malik to himself through the sequence of verbs of sensation that transition from third to first person. At first the king sees his soldiers, looks in all directions, and even observes his own position relative to that of his forces. At the moment of his death, the king's jaw locks, another physiological impediment to his ability to relay orally any of what he has seen that recapitulates the earlier phases of his illness that affected his tongue's capacity to communicate with those around him. In this telling, loss of life is simultaneous with but distinct from loss of one's capacity to witness. By establishing himself as the direct recipient of this sensory information, Valencia suggests that when he witnesses the king's loss of the ability to speak, he assimilates Abd al-Malik's memory and can subsequently testify on his behalf. This reading is reinforced by the ambiguous sentence that follows ʿAbd al-Malik's death: "Fue cosa mucho para ver, y permision devina [It was quite a thing to *see*, and by divine permission]." Valencia's incorporation of the knowledge contained in this flesh archive follows from "he saw" to "it was a thing [for me] to see," which in turn retroactively justifies the act of telling, "digo que." Valencia's more global perspective as witness allows him to absorb the king's perspective into his own and to so perfectly appropriate it that he can now give this emptied out body a new voice.

This unit of firsthand testimony is discursively set apart in historiographical language that comments on the relationship between memory and writing—Valencia witnesses *and* narrates.[70] Valencia demonstrates that he is the principle reliable transmitter for the knowledge extracted from the archive of the king's flesh and subsequently interpreted by conjugating the verb in the first person, "digo que." The doctor's firsthand experience of ʿAbd al-Malik's death thus exists on two planes and in two heterogeneous temporalities. Valencia can precisely identify the place and time at which he obtained this information—recall how the presence of the corpse *hic* anchors the experience of witnessing to a single point of embodied reference. Simultaneously, however, Valencia as chronicler of this body becomes the intermediary between the *here* and *now* of this text and the *here* and *now* of the readerly space and time. His active involvement in establishing and interpreting the archive of ʿAbd al-Malik's dead body unites the multiple temporal registers that the act of narration requires.

Sobchack emphasizes that the detailed documentation of death is only ethically sustainable when the documentarian's gaze is inflected by their active involvement in the encounter: "it literally comes out of hiding; its vision is confrontative."[71] Valencia's urgent involvement responds to this moral imperative—as we have seen, he conveys visual information and offers a verbal and aural experience of ʿAbd al-Malik's death. The doctor relates that he spent the remainder of the battle running between ʿAbd al-Malik's commanders and the king's tent, giving voice to the dead king's orders. Valencia also continues his medical ministrations—repeated and recognizable rituals that reenact these remains as though they can still save the king from his illness. He sustains his effort for hours, reencountering the corpse as though it is still alive: "E, por hirnos por delante, davamos a entender ser mandado del Rei; porque yo me apeava de mi cavallo cada ora, fingiendo que hablava con el [And, we went on ahead, making it understood that it was by order of the king; for every hours I would dismount my horse, pretending to speak with him]."[72] By concealing the king's cadaver and reanimating it with a performance that drags its living past into dead present, the doctor manages to keep panic from spreading among the Maghrebi troops.

Valencia relates that even after the end of the battle, al-Manṣūr encourages him to keep information about the death of his brother a secret: "Acabada la batalla, vino tener a las banderas Muley Hamet, teniendo aviso que el Rey era muerto. E avisome no lo dixese a nadie [The battle being finished, Mulay Ahmad came to the banners, having heard of the King's death, and warned me to tell no one]."[73] At al-Manṣūr's behest, Valencia's ventriloquist performance to reanimate ʿAbd al-Malik's corpse for his subjects continues after the battle:

"Y llamome [al-Mansur] en publico, y dixome que fuese a ver si su hermano estaba en desposicion para poder hablar con el. Y entre y detuveme un poco, y bolvi a salir e dixele que el Rei avia comido y estava reposando [And he called me in public and asked me to go to see if his brother was disposed to be able to speak with him. And I went in and waited a bit, and returned again and told him that the King had eaten and was resting]." The charade continues until al-Manṣūr ensures the creation of a document supporting his accession to the throne; although the most immediate danger of revealing the king's death has been averted with 'Abd al-Malik's forces' victory, the untimeliness of his demise still threatens to unravel the stability of the state. Valencia thus continues to conspire with the heir to drag out the time of death until the gap can be bridged. Al-Manṣūr makes known that his brother is dead only once his inheritance of the throne has been confirmed in writing:

> Ya en este tiempo Cide Mahamet ben Aiça estava escreviendo una carta de como levantavan por rei a Mulei Hamet. Y acabado d'escrevir, mando llamar los Xarifes y alcaides, asi de la cavalleria como de la escopeteria, y les hizo el mismo una habla, deziendoles como su hermano era muerto, y muriera como buen capitan . . . y ellos mismos lo tenian jurado por rey, y agora el era su rey, y que les haria lo que ellos bien verian. Y todos respondieron a una: "que Dios lo exalçase," y le besaron la mano, y lo juraron por rey.[74]
>
> About this time Sīdī Muḥammad ibn 'Īsa was writing a letter declaring how they chose Mulay Aḥmad to be their King. And when the letter was finished, he sent for the *sharīfs* and qadis from cavalry and infantry alike, and he himself made an speech, declaring his brother's death, and how he died like a good captain . . . and how they themselves had sworn him to be their King, and how he was now was their King, and how he would use them very well, as they would see. They all with one voice responded, "that God raise him up," and kissed his hand; and he was sworn their king.

The official passage of power from 'Abd al-Malik to his brother brings the disruptive asynchrony of this monarchy's body natural and body politic back under control. The lifelike simulacrum of 'Abd al-Malik's corpse that has been voiced by Valencia is no longer needed, because his dead body natural has been substituted by al-Mansur's living one. With the accession of al-Manṣūr to the throne as 'Abd al-Malik's rightful heir, Valencia concludes his intervention. The success of this temporal resynchronization is confirmed as the Moroccan leadership accepts the validity of this document with one voice—in effect, marking that the monarchy has recuperated its power of speech and is no longer in need of performative reenactment.

Valencia proves himself to be an expert interpreter of the flesh archive of ʿAbd al-Malik's body. His hermeneutic talent gives him unique insight into multiple temporal frames, past and present, and allows him to manipulate the heterogeneous time frames of body politic and body natural to keep them in sync and forestall the chaos that could have spun out of control when his king died during battle. Valencia constructs himself as an interventional witness, a perspective that justifies his detailed representation of this disruptive royal death and inscribes his gaze as ethical. Valencia presciently recognizes that this corpse cannot, under any circumstances, be *now.* By dragging the living past into the present and knitting it to a more stable future, Valencia artificially establishes ʿAbd al-Malik's corpse's time as *not now*—a temporal performance that strategically absents the untimely corpse until a more opportune moment arises.

Conclusion

The absence left by the untimely death of a king in its asynchrony opens the perfect venue for that powerful body to be reanimated by another voice. If the asynchrony of that death disrupts the delicate temporal balance required to sustain social stability, that problematic corpse cannot be mimetically represented as being *here* and *now* in the text without giving future readers iterative access to this moment of maximally destructive chaos. If such a representation is, in effect, an obscenity, witnesses to the problematic moment of death must respond to this ethical quandary either by denying their own capacity to testify, in effect plugging their ears against to the dissonance of temporal frames falling out of sync, or by themselves externally imposing a lifelike time frame long enough to ward off the chaos of asynchrony. Ventriloquism denies that the living royal body is *there* and *then* and instead insists that its essential functions continue into the *here* and *now.* Such reanimation only compounds the corpse's already temporally slippery status as an archive and reiterates the potential for future activation and revocalization of the enervated and silent flesh that remains after the moment of death. As I will explore in the coming chapter, ventriloquism also reveals and operates on corpses' extant, latent agency as subjects in the world of the living.

3
Vitality
Wounded Narrators and the Living Dead

> Por las causas dichas en el Cap. Precedente se define, y retira el Alma del cuerpo, para el relox de la vida cessando el armonía, y obras de la fabrica corpórea, y lo que era viviẽte razional queda en Cadaver insensible, lo que fue luz en tinieblas, lo que maravilla de naturaleza en cuerpo horrible, espãtable, y fiero.
>
> Due to the aforementioned causes in the preceding chapter [death] is defined as the retreat of the Soul from the body, so that the clock of life ceasing its harmony, and the works of the corporeal fabric, and what was a rational living being remains insensible in the Cadaver, that which was light in the dark, that which was a marvel of nature remains in a horrible, ghastly, and fierce body.
>
> —JUAN EULOGIO PÉREZ FADRIQUE, *MODO PRACTICO DE EMBALSAMAR CUERPOS DEFUNCTOS*

Wounded, deformed, and dead bodies form part of the literal, iconographic, and figurative architecture of Miguel Leitão de Andrade's account of al-Qasr al-Kabir. The presence of these bodies that punctuate the text emerge as entities whose material presence contribute to the epistemological edifice Leitão seeks to construct throughout his account. In addition to the foldout illustrations of the battle analyzed briefly in chapter 1, another image in Leitão's *Miscellânea do Sitio de Nossa Senhora da Luz do Pedrogão Grande* (1629) gives us an entry point to understanding the vital role of the corpse in this text: the frontispiece, an elaborate architectural spectacle replete with Corinthian columns, displays two cousins of the author, visually represented as martyrs. Both relatives are identified by name, relation to the author, and the year and location of their deaths: on the right, Diogo de Andrade, died in Brazil in 1570; on the left, Friar Nicolão Leitão do Rosario, died in Cuama in 1592.[1]

Diogo de Andrade's head is shown still cleaved by a knife whose handle retreats into the shadow cast by the columns and from whose blade drip several drops of blood. The image resonates with the attributes of Saint Peter Martyr, a Dominican friar assassinated with an ax blow to the head who died writing "*Credo in Deum*" on the ground in his own blood.[2] While Diogo de Andrade was eventually canonized as one of a group of Jesuit martyrs, this representation iconographically links him to the Dominican order. On the left, Nicolão Leitão de Rosario's body gushes blood from arrow wounds to his torso and legs—the five wounds to his body iconographically linking his martyrdom with the *cinco chagas* (five wounds of Christ) on the Aviz coat of arms, the dynasty brought to an end by the events Leitão will recount.[3] The figures themselves visually engage with the reader—the staring gaze of Diogo de Andrade is particularly striking, as his empty eyes lock with those of the reader—each actively modeling the spiritual behavior the reader should mimic. Both figures thus intertwine the imagery of martyrdom, Portuguese national identity, and the Leitão family's close relationship with the Dominican order, while continuing to assert their own liveliness well after their deaths.

Another woodcut image by João Baptista displays the author kneeling before the Virgin and presenting her with a copy of the book itself, linking his textual offering to the violent opening display of familial martyrdom. Through this portrait, Leitão makes his body visually available to his audience, a fleshy body upon which they can map subsequent descriptions of the wounds inflicted on it. Leitão's own textually rendered wounds become visually as well as genealogically linked to those of his ancestors, who perpetually bleed out on the cover of his tome. All of these injuries and bodies support Leitão's complex claim to narrative authority, which foregrounds this physical trauma as legible proof of the authenticity of his account. The loss of mobility and access those injuries impose on him, however, also undermines his efficacy as an eyewitness to the very events he claims to have seen.

As we saw in chapter 1, Mendonça relies on the indexical presence of his dead brothers in arms through incantatory repetition to ground his narrative, while Valencia maintains his immediate connection to ʿAbd al-Malik's absent corpse. Miguel Leitão de Andrade and Juan de Silva take another approach. For them, bearing witness to the narrator's own body becomes intimately associated with those corpses. In the first chapter, I argued in answer to the question *Where is the corpse?* that the corpse is the present and material substrate of communication, and, in the second chapter, that in response to *When is*

Figure 3. João Baptista, Detail of frontispiece of Leitão de Andrade, *Miscellânea do sitio de N. Sa. da Luz do Pedogão Grande* (Lisbon: Matheus Pinhero, 1629).

the corpse found? the narrator can avoid violating representative taboos by creating temporal ambiguity around its discovery as corpse. Here the corpse elicits a third question: *Who is the corpse?* These fundamental narratological questions allow us to identify key actors and actants within the story, the objects that populate the worlds in which those actors and actants move and

Figure 4. João Baptista, *Do Autor Mighel Leitão d'Andrada, etat 73* (Lisbon: Matheus Pinheiro, 1629), showing the author offering his *Miscellânea* to the Virgin of Pedrogão Grande.

upon which they act, and how they are situated in those worlds in time and space. The ontology of the corpse that emerges in its presence and absence opens a space in which narrators explore their own status as subject and object in relationship to that corpse. While theorists of the dead often focus on "corpse care" as the primary venue for interaction between the living and the dead, that focus is limited in its representation of the corpse as object and living body as subject. Rather than care for the corpses in his immediate surroundings, Leitão instead showcases his own limitations as agent and simultaneously conceives of those corpses as subjects with agency.

If subjectivity, as Bruno Latour has argued, hinges on the capacity to make things happen, to have efficacy in the world, in whom is that agency and subjectivity invested and where can it be observed? Subjectivity can first be identified in the effect it has, its ability to put other entities into motion.[4] Read in terms of the corpse's indexical referentiality, this definition of subjectivity articulates the action as an index of the actant. The action is *what remains of someone* and can be interpreted back toward its antecedent subjectivity. If identifying an actant is a hermeneutic process, then we must seek agentic capacity by interpreting the semiotics of observable actions and following the threads, linguistic and material, back to their approximate nodes of origin. This chapter and the next proceed from the question, *Who is the corpse?* To ask the question in this way is to answer it already, since to ask *who?* recognizes the corpse's subjectivity—one doesn't ask *who?* about a thing. In contrast, to ask *what?*—as I will do in the final chapter—instead encodes the corpse as object.

Perhaps one of the most commonly shared understandings of corpses is their different ontological status from the living. A paradox frequently encountered in theories of the corpse is the sense that it is *dead matter*, but also that it spills beyond that simple classification into a class of entity that political theorist Jane Bennett terms *vibrant matter*.[5] While Bennett suggests this idea to better understand how human and nonhuman entities collaborate in political ecologies, an awareness of ontological complexity can also be observed in a literary context. The central paradox of the corpse resides in its ambivalent inherence: its status as human and nonhuman, person and thing, animate and inanimate.[6] The complex status of the corpse derives in part from the referential relationship it retains to its own departed subjectivity—the corpse is an index that mediates between here and not here. In the preceding chapters, we saw that this indexicality shows up grammatically in terms of the corpse's absence or presence *here* and *now*. Here that complexity inflects their status as subjects in syntactical and semiotic terms, enabling them to variously appear as objects, as an integral participants in a social world, and as agents with efficacy in the world. Corpse care is a common process that inflects the body as object, which regards it as inanimate. Even so, one of the underlying motivations for corpse care is a recognition of the corpse as social entity—an attitude that reveals a sense of its lingering capacity to act as a subject.

In Leitão's narrative, the corpses emerge as vibrant matter: entities empowered to incite action and movement along useful trajectories. These qualities imbue them with agency that the narrators themselves identify and recognize.[7] Their capacity to action stands in relief, materially and linguistically, to Leitão's limited capacity to make things happen in the world.[8] The narrator's efforts to associate his own injured body with dead ones highlight his recognition of the power of the corpse as actant in early modern economies of knowledge. In other words, the corpse is vibrant matter.

The Text

The corpse appears as vibrant matter in Leitão's *Miscellânea*, thus titled, says its author, "pola diversidade de cousas que nelle vão misturadas [because of the diverse things combined in it]."[9] The text collects poetry and songs, many by other authors, recounts a range of traditions about Portuguese history, all as they relate to the Virgin at Pedrogão Grande, and follows the journey of a character named Galacio with his friend, identified as Miguel Leitão de Andrade, as they return home to celebrate that manifestation of the Virgin.[10] The first six dialogues introduce Galacio and Devoto, describe the different hermitages to different saints in the region around Pedrogão Grande, tell of miracles and sacred objects at the hermitage of the Convento de Nossa Senhora da Luz, recount miracles the Author experienced personally as a child and young adult, and depict the founding of the monastery dedicated to this figure. In the seventh dialogue, the author, a Portuguese veteran of the battle, like Mendonça, presents a detailed account of al-Qaṣr al-Kabīr. He draws upon both personal anecdotes and ones gathered from other captives held in Fez following the Portuguese defeat. He does not, however, present his own story as the definitive report of the events of the battle, instead referring readers to Mendonça's *Jornada de África*. Against a detailed description of Sebastian's corpse, Leitão juxtaposes his own injured and scarred body as vouchsafe of the information he conveys. The tangible proof of his own wounded and scarred body that Leitão offers to his reader lends credibility to his story but paradoxically limits his capacity as witness. Ultimately, Leitão's account is incomplete and unsatisfying in his account of witnessing Sebastian's corpse, but it reveals a nuanced understanding of the corpses he witnesses as vibrant matter, especially the king's corpse, as well of his own complex status as both subject and object.

Leitão was born in 1555 in Pedrogão Grande, in the bishopric of Coimbra, and was living in Lisbon when his book was published.[11] His father died when he was thirteen, and an elder brother, Fr. João de Andrade, cared for him and brought him to study at the University of Salamanca and then to the Spanish court at Madrid. Leitão finally returned to Portugal and the University of Coimbra after his brother was called there by Sebastian's uncle and eventual heir, then Cardinal D. Henrique. At Coimbra, Leitão studied canon law, although his studies were soon interrupted when Sebastian began recruiting men for the African expedition that would culminate at al-Qasr al-Kabir. Leitão joined the *terço dos aventureiros*, the same troop of noble volunteers for which Mendonça fought. In the aftermath of the Portuguese defeat at the battle, he was taken prisoner and spent several years in captivity in Fez. Upon his return to Portugal during the 1580 dynastic crisis, he supported D. António, Prior of Crato, in his claim to Henrique's throne, which led to his imprisonment.[12] Leitão eventually redeemed himself in the eyes of the Spanish-controlled Portuguese throne and later became a commander of the Order of Christ.[13] Through the *Miscellânea,* Leitão gives thanks to the Lady of Pedrogão Grande for his political and spiritual redemption following his imprisonment both at home and abroad.

Most of what we know about the *Miscellânea* and its author comes from the text itself. Leitão cannot have completed it earlier than 1628, since the narrator makes reference to and illustrates the birth of conjoined twins in that year in a town near Leiria.[14] It was printed by Matheus Pinheiro in Lisbon in 1629, with engravings on the frontispiece, two foldout inserts, and a portrait of the author by the Portuguese engraver João Baptista. The sprawling 640-page text is what António Cirurgião calls "uma das obras mais peculiares da literatura portuguesa [one of the most peculiar works of Portuguese literature]."[15] The publication date links it to the initiation in Coimbra of the canonization process of his godfather, Diogo de Andrade, and his fellow Jesuit martyrs in 1628.[16] It is dedicated to the Senhora da Luz do Pedrogão Grande, patron of the monastery in Leitão's hometown near Coimbra, which had been occupied by the Dominican order since its foundation on September 12, 1476.[17] The text incorporates a wide range of media, including dialogue between the two travelers, prose narrative, poetry, epigrams, musically notated songs, and more.[18] It is divided into twenty dialogues, although the dialogic format is unsystematic and frequently gives way to narrative.[19] The seventh and eighth dialogues are dominated by the voice of Devoto, who commemorates the miracles he claims the Senhora da Luz of Pedrogão Grande performed on his behalf.[20] This heterogeneous text, then, combines deep political and religious commitments, with particular dedication to the author's connections to the Dominican order.

Leitão identifies himself as Devoto—"era Miguel Leitão Dandrada, Cõmendador da Ordem & Milicia de N. S. Iesu Christo [he was Miguel Leitão de Andrade, Commander of the Order and Militia of Our Lord Jesus Christ]"—to narrate al-Qaṣr al-Kabīr and his subsequent captivity in Fez.[21] Devoto declares to his companion, Galacio, at the start of his story that his purpose in narrating the battle is not to add to the quite complete version that is available in Mendonça's *Jornada de África,* published by another survivor of the battle more than two decades earlier in 1607, but instead to glorify the Virgin of Pedrogão Grande because of the miracles she performed on his behalf. Like Mendonça, Leitão is also committed to undoing the damage of Conestaggio's account of al-Qasr al-Kabir in *Dell'unione.*

As a veteran, Leitão draws on two related kinds of embodied knowledge that are characteristic of early modern soldiers' writing. To begin with, Leitão affirms his own status as an eyewitness and invokes members of the institutional brotherhood fostered among soldiers in support of that claim to debunk Conestaggio's misinformation.[22] Still available, but as yet untapped, is the redeeming knowledge that Leitão and other survivors can contribute: "contra a honra dos Portugueses de que *eu*, & muytos que ainda são vivos, & nesta jornada se acharão *podemos* ser *testamunhas de vista* [against the honor of the Portuguese that *I*, and many who are still alive, and in this expedition found ourselves, we can be *eyewitnesses*]."[23] Leitão tries to produce a truth both ethical and epistemic by combining his factual intervention with what Andrea Frisch refers to as compurgation, the power of aggregated *ad hominem* witnesses, and marks himself as one of many by using the first-person plural "podemos" (we can be).[24] What as a singular, first-person assertion might be perceived only as an individual alternative viewpoint in plural increases the epistemic legitimacy of the dialogue by signaling Leitão's membership in a group. As Miguel Martínez explains: "An economy of reputation, by which the fame and honor of individual soldiers relied on testimonies, both oral and written, of comrades-in-arms, regulated relations between those who had been killed and those who survived. The impulse to give account of oneself and one's comrades gave way to many front lines that, written from the battlefield, would keep alive the memory of many common infantrymen and their deeds in the republic of soldiers."[25] In such an economy, the unnamed "muytos" are marshaled as eyewitnesses to attest to both Leitão's reputation and the credibility of the facts that he recounts.

A component piece of this fraternity, a key aspect of Leitão's assembled epistemological body, is the king himself. Like Mendonça and other Iberian soldiers, Leitão designates the king as the ultimate source of epistemic justice for soldiers: "Bẽ merecia por certo a lealdade Portuguesa a Sua Magestade mãdar emẽdar estes e outros tais livros [Truly, Portuguese loyalty well deserved that Your Majesty command that these and other such books be amended]."[26] Martínez highlights the fact that many Iberian soldiers involved in early modern Iberian imperialism petitioned directly to the king to rhetorically, at least, circumvent the "lettered officials that stand between him and the king's grace."[27] In a sense, such a rhetorical strategy incorporates the commander in chief, the king, within the circle of soldierly comradeship while definitively excluding from the fraternal order those anonymous administrators whose bureaucratic behavior gets soldiers killed. In this early modern martial rejiggering of medieval compurgation, Leitão simultaneously provides socio-ethical and factual proof.[28] The living Spanish king is not the only royal member of the eyewitness's epistemic assemblages, as the coming chapter will explore in greater detail; even when dead, Sebastian's mobile corpse participates as a vital and vibrant hinge around which each account revolves.

Beyond the efforts Leitão makes to situate himself within a military fraternity and in relationship to his relatives' martyred bodies, he also displays his own injured body to the multiple layers of his audience within and beyond his text. This body, made more materially present to the reader's imagination through its representation in the front matter of the text, undergoes physical alteration over the course of Leitão's story. He renders his wounds present in the text through deictic reference while he reiterates the compurgatory power of soldierly esprit de corps by repeating his participation within a collective that vouches for his ethical and social position:

> Hora eu me fiquei no mesmo lugar, ou por aly se nos deu aquella infausta voz, de ter, ter . . . entre a multidão de mortos, & de miserias que *vos contei*, onde recebi *estas* duas feridas *que me vedes nesta* cabeça (não falando na terceira que recebi sendo menino que *vos contei*) & outras tres *nesta* perna esquerda.[29]

> Now I stayed in the same place, or there where was given that unlucky call to "fall back, fall back" . . . among a multitude of dead, and of miseries that *I told you* of, where I received *these* two wounds *that you see in this* my head (not to speak of the third that I received as a boy as *I told you*), and another three in *this* left leg.

Displaying his wounded body and distinguishing between which wounds pertain to this moment of witnessing shores up both the ethical and the epistemic basis of Leitão's narrative through the tangible, corporeal details that ratify his physical participation at the event.[30] The body as a major source of textual authority is a significant feature of the early modern soldiers' republic of letters, wherein: "the exposure of the injured body, whether in writing or in flesh and bones, is a privileged mode of relation between the veteran and his society or the state: bodily deprivation, disease, wounds, and hunger contributed to legitimize the voice of the returning and petitioning veteran."[31] Leitão asks his reader to identify with his injured body in a visceral way, to contemplate the "affective, bodily instrument of the real."[32] The gesture submits the information presented as composing a flesh archive whose information can be verified through a close interpretation of this body.[33]

Despite the support they provide for Leitão epistemologically, his wounds become ontologically problematic because they obstruct his ability to keep witnessing the events he narrates. While the wounds support a multipronged claim to narrative authority, their presence also advertises vulnerabilities in Leitão's physical and ontological agency. At the nadir of the battle, a disembodied voice calls for the Portuguese retreat. Even as Leitão emphasizes his status as a witness to this moment, he concedes that his participation at that moment was limited to utter paralysis among the innumerable dead. Leitão cannot identify the agent of the voice that called on the Portuguese to fall back; the narrator attributes this key action to a passive subject—the unlucky voice *was given*. Here, the dissipation of Leitão's agency becomes discernible in the grammatical fibers of his story. The blurring of the lines that demarcate living and dead force us to reexamine the categories to which we assign these entities, which in turn gives us new language with which to discuss the power and the grammar of the dead.

Dead and Vibrant Matter

As illustrated by the epigraph for this chapter, medical professionals like Pérez Fadrique and Montaña de Monserrate explain the moment of death in mechanistic terms—a clock that ticks its last, the extinguishing of light in the dark. Nevertheless, these clear-cut definitions of death did not map onto popular beliefs about the whereabouts of the soul in the moments, hours, or even days following death. Examining a long-held French royal commitment to the division of the corpse in multiple burial sites and related practices in other parts of Europe, Elizabeth A. R. Brown argues that widespread medieval royal and noble European burial practices point to a belief that the dead retained ties to the world of the living long after death: "The practice of division reveals a general unwillingness to admit that after a person's death the body did not, in some sense, live on, or that, after death, earthly ties with family and friends did not endure. Why else the desire to have the body buried next to particular loved ones or in particularly cherished places—or indeed the belief that the dead body could continue to serve the soul by attracting prayers on its behalf?"[34]

These terrestrial, ambiguous attitudes toward the inflection point between life and death were also reflected theologically in the renewed commitment to the cult of the saints at the final convocation of the Council of Trent in June of 1564, a meeting dominated by Iberian clergy and of great interest to Philip II of Spain.[35] Central to this renewed devotion to the cult of the saints were ongoing discussions about how to verify the authenticity of saints and their relics.[36] Even as the Church systematized and centralized the processes by which an individual was beatified and canonized over the course of the sixteenth century, those processes affirmed and upheld the ideas at the core of the veneration of the saints—the value of the saints as intercessors and patrons for their living and dead devotees and the link they sustained between heaven and earth. The cult of the saints presumed the continued efficacy or animacy by holy corpses in the world of the living.

Early modern Iberian understandings of the interpenetrated realms of the living and the dead also manifested in key political processes. Unlike the French or English monarchies, medieval and early modern Castilian kings did not celebrate a coronation ceremony. Instead, an heir was selected and ritually sworn in (*jurado*) well before the old king's death, which allowed him to automatically assume the throne on the death of his predecessor. The passing of the old king was publicly marked through ceremonies of *exequias*, rituals that commemorated the king's transition to the hereafter and recapitulated the burial of the royal corpse *in absentia* throughout his realms. Once the old king's death had been observed, the new monarch would be acclaimed in other public ceremonies that confirmed his accession to the throne. Although legally these ceremonies were not necessary for the new king to rule, Carlos Eire acknowledges that "a monarch remained somehow 'imperfect' until acclaimed in public ceremonies."[37] Philip III's coronation inverted the usual order of the process and was acclaimed in a private ceremony as king of Spain after Philip II's painful and drawn-out death but before the old king's public funeral and exequies were celebrated.[38] Eire argues that this new process smoothly transferred power from father to son "by making it ritually impossible to question the king's status once his father was 'fully' dead."[39] If orthodox Catholic doctrine and medical texts alike affirmed the immediate sundering of the connection between body and soul upon the subject's demise, the inversion of acclamation and exequies highlights the belief in a deeper interpenetration of terrestrial and celestial realms: "Philip III gained ritual recognition as king while his father was still symbolically present, hovering over Madrid, as it were, while waiting for his funeral honors."[40] While the cult of the saints was predicated on the capacity of the holy dead to intervene on behalf of the living in heaven, and early modern testamentary and funereal practices point to an understanding of the limited intercessory powers the living had on behalf of the dead, Philip III's accession to the throne points to the inverse of that vector of intervention: the assumed efficacy of the dead on behalf of the living in earthly matters.

One path for theorizing the capacity of inanimate or nonhuman objects to have efficacy in the world or tend to persist can be found in Jane Bennett's concept of vibrant matter, which gives us the language to reconcile this contradictory state. The idea of vibrant matter attends to the "painful nagging feeling that something's being forgotten or left out" of subject/object binaries.[41] This framework for understanding of agency as the effect of *ad hoc* configurations of human and nonhuman forces is powerful for the corpse, an ontologically ambiguous entity defined by its lingering agency after death. Bennett argues that recognizing that subjects and objects exist along an expansive and heterogeneous spectrum discloses the agentic capacity of nonhuman bodies and asserts the "strange ability of ordinary . . . items to exceed their status as objects and manifest traces of independence or aliveness."[42] The framework for vibrant matter hinges on several core concepts: Latour's *actant*, defined as something, human or nonhuman, that has efficacy in the world, can do things, or can make things happen; Spinoza's *conative bodies*, or bodies with an "active impulsion or the trending tendency to persist"; and Deleuze and Guattari's *assemblage*, which are networks or confederations of ontologically diverse elements whose cooperative power is greater than the sum of their parts.[43] Bennett's insistence on the vitality of matter regardless of where it falls in that range is critical for understanding the power of corpses, whose disconcerting presence, neither wholly object nor fully subject, consistently subverts and corrodes clear classification.[44] The notion of vibrant matter reminds us to recognize "the curious ability of inanimate things to animate to act, to produce effects dramatic and subtle," a power that is unmistakable in the corpse.[45]

Attention to the corpse as object, or exclusively dead matter, is best exemplified by the practice of corpse care "with a material object as centerpiece."[46] Corpse care consists of actions taken for the benefit primarily of the living and represents a process through which the present living select, manipulate, and inscribe their past, cordoning the dead off to establish order among the living.[47] Considered grammatically, corpse care can be defined as a set of activities in which the living human retains all agency and subjecthood and performs actions upon the dead body as an object.[48] Under such circumstances, the relative animacy (what linguists term "prominence" or "inherence") of the corpse is low.[49] Thus in a hierarchy of animacy, the corpse receiving care from the living is treated as *inanimate*, the inert recipient of the action of transitive verbs.[50] These activities may also protect the survivors from the pain of seeing the corpse abandoned or even desecrated, as we will explore further in chapter 5. Although corpse care is focused on the dead body, it rigidly inflects the corpse *as object* and reflects how living agents strive to survive the pain of mourning through predictable and regulated customs, to formulate their relationship with the dead going forward, and to prevent the return of the improperly attended dead as revenants.[51] Even considered from this objectifying activity, persistent anxieties about haunting and ghosts are only the most obvious indication that a binary between the corpse *as object* and the living *as subject* inadequately addresses commonsense understandings of living and dead bodies. Attending to the ways the corpse acts as animate subject in the world of the living rather than as inanimate object brings into sharper focus what it is about corpses that allow their shades to continue living among us.

Corpses are inherently referential objects—specifically, indexes—that communicate complex spatial and temporal information. That indexicality derives from its ontological status: the corpse "engages our sympathy *as an object which is* an index of *a subject who was*."[52] Vivian Sobchack extrapolates from that referential relationship to mark a clear contrast between animate and inanimate, living and dead, and deny the corpse as a process of transformation.[53] That indexical framing nevertheless undermines the very ontological binary it is intended to erect: the corpse is an unstable entity because it is in a state of ongoing flux between *object that is* and *subject who was*, not least because of the biological processes of decay. If a corpse indexes *a subject who was*, it also holds onto and references the residues of subjectivity, shimmering as still-vital material. The constantly changing state of a decomposing corpse, which requires a continuous reassessment of its ontological status that, *pace* Sobchack, changes the experience of corpses as simple objects. If subjectivity manifests itself in action as remains, as traces or residues, that agency does not exist as a binary and does not immediately dissipate at the moment of death.

Corpses exist in a gray realm, neither only subjects nor only objects, a quality that manifests and operates in text through the syntax and semiotics of its representation. In grammatical terms, a subject or actant, either individual or collective, is the driving force that acts as the subject of verbs, that has semantic and syntactical efficacy.[54] The agent has the power, sometimes violent, to turn other things into objects by acting on them or making use of them. It is an observed linguistic feature of Romance and Semitic languages, *inter alia*, that subjectivity and objectivity do not exist grammatically in a binary but are instead arrayed relationally.[55] Even the state of being on the receiving end of action encompasses a wide spectrum of animacy and markedness. The agency that can be expressed through action by actors along the gradient of animacy is also reciprocal: "The power of a body to affect other bodies includes a 'corresponding' and 'inseparable' capacity to be affected."[56] In one example from Spanish, that array is marked by the selective use of the "*a personal*," which imposes a prepositional buffer between the action of a transitive verb and an animate direct object.[57] Grammatical structures like the *a personal* recognize and hardwire into language the sense that ontological status is contingent, labile, and context-dependent. As expressed through text and in language, matter can thus be both subject and object simultaneously; it articulates across a broad range of animacy and determinacy and should be distinguished locally because of this potential variability.

The notion of the corpse as vibrant matter resonates with anthropologists' and archaeologists' recognition that the corpse is a social entity that retains agency even in death. Observing the corpse elicits a broad range of psychological and physiological reflexes—fear, anger, sadness, nausea, revulsion—visceral, affective responses that some anthropologists argue are provoked by the "emotive and affective potency and efficacy of bone as material, and bones as uneasy, ambivalent subjects/objects."[58] This sense of the agency of the dead expands Deborah Posel and Pamela Gupta's intervention on "the dualistic life of the corpse," which they define through a vision of the corpse as both material object and signifier of broader political, cultural, and social endeavors.[59] In contrast, Cara Krmpotich, Joost Fontein and John Harries unfurl a more capacious sense of a corpse's liveliness: "The crucial outcome of considering the agency of bones as deferred human agency and as material objects or 'non-human actants' is the destabilization of any easy boundaries between persons and things, subjects and objects, actions and reactions."[60] These anthropologists stress that the materiality of the dead is not incidental to their agency but is a concomitant and irreducible aspect of their efficacy.[61]

Reading the corpse as "vibrant matter" reconfigures what can be said about the corpse and how it is said, a shift that emerges syntactically as the corpse emerges into prominence, moving from accusative toward nominative, from objecthood toward subjecthood.[62] That ambiguity disconcerts the living. We generally prefer to objectify corpses and retain a clear binary between living and dead. Nevertheless, the corpse confronts the living, forcing them to come to terms with their own complex position on the spectrum between living and dead and to identify more closely with the corpse.

Wounds on Display

For narrators to reckon with corpses *as actants*, they must first recognize the limitations of their own agency as actors in the world. A narrator's openness to that greater ontological complexity becomes apparent when they center attention on their own severely limited physical capacities and, even more strikingly, when they identify affectively with the corpses themselves. If Leitão's narrative passivity aligns him with the dead, as suggested earlier, at other moments he identifies even more explicitly with them, signaling his proximity to them on the spectrum of animacy.

In one case, he describes one corpse he contemplated at length after being injured, a body that is flagged as particularly significant because of its affiliation with the Dominican order whose martyrs have been depicted on the cover:

> Iazia hum frade de São Domingos diante de mim de barriga morto, & com a mão & braço esquerdo estendido pera diante, o qual vendo: me lembrei da minha criação, & padres de nossa Senhora da Luz, & me encomendei muyto a esta Senhora, fazendo minhas contas, pedindo perdão a Deos, tendo a ja feita de lha de dar logo por me não passar por pensamento aver, ou poder escapar com vida, . . . & não saber das feridas se erão mortais.[63]

> There lay before me a Dominican friar, dead from a wound in his belly, and with his left hand and arm extended out before him. Seeing this, I remembered my upbringing, and the fathers of Our Lady of Light, and I commended myself greatly to this Lady, making my accounts, and asking God for forgiveness, taking it for granted that I would have to do it [ask God for pardon] later, because it didn't occur to me that I would be able to escape with my own life . . . and not knowing if my wounds were mortal.

The passage briefly but vividly conveys the image of the friar's corpse, and those few details impart information about how he fell and died. As we would expect from the foundation of indexical presence delineated in chapter 1, this corpse establishes a common ground from which its observer can pivot toward interpretation. The gesture, itself a residue of the dead body's lingering attachment to life, prompts Leitão to seek out and interpret this index's antecedent. Considered in terms of its referentiality within the text as a material object, this friar's martyrdom at the hands of their enemies certainly relates him to his compatriots depicted on the frontispiece, themselves killed in their mission to spread Christianity throughout the Portuguese global empire. The combined effect of his hermeneutic response to the corpse's indexical and affective gesture is that Leitão associates it with other Dominicans among whom he spent his childhood at the monastery of the Senhora da Luz and the manifestation of the Virgin to whom the *Miscellânea* is dedicated and to whom Leitão is devoted. Following the dead friar's gesture toward himself prompts him to appeal to the Virgin in his time of need, to ask for her intercession in what is presented as a particularly corporeal predicament, and to render an account of himself to God. He needs the impetus of the residual energy of this dead body to send him farther down the gradient of bodily capacity toward death. Although the exchange of positions of agency is subtle, this passage opens up a world in which an inversion or flattening of our expectations for the agency of ontologically heterogeneous beings is possible.[64] The wounds Leitão shows to his reader thus not only give him the right to proclaim himself witness but also highlight his awareness of his limitations as an operator in the sphere he was witnessing. Leitão's status as both object and limited subject positions him to identify with and recognize the residues of subjectivity latent in the dead who surround him. He counts among the dead, completely immobilized in a fixed place; he has been reduced to vibrant matter, even as one of his dead companions exhibits a surprising degree of agency.

In the preceding passage, Leitão responds to the corpse's affective power and identifies with it. Again, we see the "body's *capacity* to affect and to be affected"[65] and bodies' "strange ability . . . to exceed their status as objects and manifest traces of independence or aliveness."[66] The traces of the Dominican's last fall remain in his body's posture, which stretches and reaches out to those around him, activating "those intensities that pass body to body (human, nonhuman, part-body, and otherwise)."[67] Read thus as vibrant matter, this corpse emerges in prominent subjectivity, retains clear efficacy as an actant, and independently expresses itself toward other bodies in the world.[68] The captivating power of the corpse produces concrete effects on its observer: the dead friar's exhortatory gesture immediately animates Leitão to a strong affective response and ritual behavior.

The reversal of subject and object is particularly conspicuous in Leitão's passivity as the helpless recipient of this body's affective force. Observing the friar's corpse underscores Leitão's own relative loss of prominence at the moment that he is faced with the material results of death. The inanimacy he attributes to himself at this moment is particularly striking: Leitão relates viscerally with this inanimate thing, links his own wounds with those of the dead man, and is contaminated—existentially, semantically, and syntactically—with that thing's status *as object*. He recognizes himself not as subject but as an object at the mercy of external forces, emanating from his perception of this dead body. Aware of his own injuries, he projects the future of the other body's wounds onto his own, in effect collapsing *those* other wounds into *these*, his own, wounds. He thus takes his own death as a *fait accompli*—"tendo a ja feita" (taking it for granted)—that all he can think to do is administer his own last rites to himself. Leitão's affinity for this body elicits certain responses from him but does not allow him to reassert his agency as a living subject. Instead, he migrates closer toward a status that further ingrains him as object.

Efficacy of Corpses

Despite his expectation that he will soon die, Leitão survives the battle, only to be taken prisoner by the victors, his physical incapacity compounded by his loss of legal freedom. He is brought to the enemy camp and left in a tent with other wounded combatants, all identified as "Mouros." His wounds severely limit his agency as eyewitness to the most important corpse of the event he witnessed: he says that he saw the Portuguese king's remains with his own eyes. The corpse of the Portuguese king manifests as even more vital matter by exhibiting greater mobility than Leitão's body is capable of.

Although the Dominican corpse is significant for Leitão's own spiritual well-being and sense of mortality, and it counts among the martyrs venerated in the *Miscellânea*, it is clear that it held little value from a strategic or historical standpoint. The other corpse he recounts seeing, however, is without a doubt the most significant claim of his text, historically speaking. He describes in detail the scene of the royal corpse's discovery:

> O dia depois da batalha, estando eu na tenda com os feridos companheros Mouros, seria pellas oito ou nove horas da manhãa, ouvi em todo o Arrayal dos Mouros grandes algarazas, festas e disparar de seus tiros. E veyo de fora a mim meu amo, que Abderehamen se chamava, & pegando em mim pera me levantarme disse. Abeçor Soltan Abecor Soltan, do que eu nada entendiendo, me disse hum dos feriados, que era Mouro dos de Granada, dize tu Amo, que vayas a ver tu Rey, que va por alli. E levandome pera detras da tenda, vejo passar diante de mi espaço de cinco ou seis varas, o infelissimo Rey Dom Sebastião muyto interissado, & de bruços atravessado em hua sela, vestido em hum gibão de Olanda branco, calções de raxa arenosa, em hum cavalinho castanho & Sebastião de Resende seu moço da Camara do serviço nas ancas dele. O qual deveo tirar de sobre as fronhas que então se costumavão, os ditos calções & despir o gibão pera cobrir o corpo de seu Rey, que jà achou nuu, e despojado como logo todos o forão dos Alarves, nem levava camisa nem cousa na *cabeça, & pernas*, mas polla grande dor, & magoa me não dar lugar me não cheguei mais a levantarlhe o rosto, pera o ver bẽ como o meu amo quisera, & por também não ser tido na conta, & confirmar a que os Mouros fazião de mim, do que depois, & ainda agora me acho muito pesaroso, & arrependido.[69]
>
> The day after the battle, I was in the tent with my wounded Muslim companions, it must have been about 8:00 or 9:00 o'clock in the morning, when I heard in the whole Muslim camp great rejoicing, celebrations, and shooting of guns. And my master, whose name was 'Abd al-Raḥmān, came from outside to me, and, grabbing me to get me up, said, "Abeçor Soltan Abecor Soltan." Since I understood none of this, one of the wounded, who was one of the Granadan Muslims, told me, "Your Master says that you should go to see your King, for he passes by there." And taking me behind the tent, I see pass before me at a space of five or six *varas*, the most unhappy, moving figure of King D. Sebastian, who was borne face-down on a saddle, dressed in a doublet of white linen and breeches of sandy, rough cotton, on a small brown horse with Sebastian de Resende, his chamberlain, on its hindquarters. The latter must have doffed the clothes that he then wore, the aforementioned breeches and doublet, to cover the body of his King, which he had found nude and despoiled like they all were by

> the Arabs, wearing neither shirt nor anything on his head nor legs. But due to the great pain and injury not permitting me, I did not succeed in raising my face to him, to see him well like my master wanted, and for also not being taken into account, and confirming what the Muslims made me do, of which later and even now I still find myself regretful and repentant.

Again, Leitão highlights his contracted subjectivity, which can now be discerned in corporeal, legal, and linguistic realms. As in the previous scene with the Dominican's corpse, Leitão relates his own physical limitations due to injury. As in the earlier scene of battle, Leitão lies prone, a position from which his master has to rouse him so that he can serve as witness. Ultimately, these injuries and the resulting pain limit his efficacy and block the most basic actions he might want to carry out. Furthermore, the narrator reiterates his own legal subjugation to his "amo" (master), 'Abd al-Raḥmān, both in his own voice and through the direct discourse of his interlocutors in the scene, who identify him in terms of his relationship *as object* or possession belonging to an active subject. Finally, Leitão is unable to engage independently with his master because of linguistic limitations; he cannot discern what actions his master is ordering him to take without the intervention of another wounded man. Although none of these factors is striking in the context of the aftermath of a battle, in conjunction they convey Leitão's profound impotence.

The very grammar of the text also evinces Leitão's objectification through the repetition of the first-person object pronouns "mim" and "me." In his captivity, Leitão not only loses legal power over himself, but he also experiences a fundamental crisis of subjectivity that is reflected in the very valences of his discourse. He no longer serves as the subject of transitive verbs.[70] Rather, he is now the direct object of other actors' object-oriented actions: "veyo a mim" (he came to me); "pegando em mi" (grabbing me); "me levantarme" (to get me up); "me disse" (he said to me). It is certainly to be expected that a wounded prisoner would have less agency than an able-bodied, free soldier, but the linguistic emphasis on Leitão's weakness prepares the reader for the climax of the scene. His helplessness is such that he can fulfill neither the function his master demands of him in the moment nor the expectations the reader has for a narrator: he can neither confirm nor deny that he recognized his dead king's face because his injuries prevented him from reaching the corpse in time to bear useful witness to it. This is not simply obstructionist rebellion against his new master's orders. On the contrary, he still regrets the corporeal limitations he experienced at the time that impeded his efficacy as witness: "mas polla grande dor, & magoa me não dar lugar me não cheguei mais a levantarlhe o rosto [But due to the great pain and injury not permitting me, I did not succeed in raising my face to him]." His capacity for efficacy in the world, however, is not sufficient to his needs, even with the collaboration of other agents in his immediate surroundings.

If Leitão is physically and grammatically immobilized, Sebastian's body is on the move. As chapter 4 will explore in greater depth, this mobility is due to its cooperative participation in an assemblage with other living and nonhuman agents that carry it along a trajectory that passes Leitão by but does not bring him into its orbit.[71] Initially, it is unclear whether Sebastian is living or dead. When he fails to understand his master's orders, another occupant of the tent translates them for him: "me disse hum dos feriados, que era Mouro dos de Granada, dize tu Amo, que vayas a ver tu Rey, que va por alli [one of the wounded, who was one of the Granadan Muslims, told me, 'Your Master says that you should go to see your King, for he passes by there']." That limited information leaves open the possibility that Sebastian has only been captured, is still alive and moving under his own power as the active subject of the motion verb.[72] In the subsequent sentence, that ambiguity remains when Leitão recounts that "E levandome pera detras da tenda, vejo passar diante de mi espaço de cinco ou seis varas, o infelissimo Rey Dom Sebastião [And taking me behind the tent, I see pass before me at a space of five or six *varas*, the most unhappy, moving figure of King D. Sebastian]." It is at this point that Sebastian's animacy is more clearly marked, when it becomes apparent that he is, in fact, not solely responsible for his own movement, but is relying on other entities: "muyto interissado, & de bruços atravessado em hua sela, vestido em hum gibão de Olanda branco, calções de raxa arenosa [who was borne face-down on a saddle, dressed in a doublet of white linen and breeches of sandy, rough cotton]."[73] The earlier action verbs are now complemented by the narrator's use of passive participles to describe actions that have been done to Sebastian's body: he is borne, he has been dressed.[74] Our expectations for Sebastian's efficacy in the world are suddenly reduced by the realization that, rather than witness a royal procession, Leitão instead is watching the dead and despoiled body of his king be brought by. Even so, the liveliness of this corpse still exceeds that of its narrator. The momentum that carries the body by the tent emphasizes its active power exceeding that of the still-living Leitão.

The confused temporality of this key moment of the narrative enhances the liveliness of Sebastian's matter. Although Leitão sets the scene on the day after the battle, that is, in the distant past, he does not maintain the narrative in the past tense. He begins stating clearly in the preterit that he heard great festivities—"*ouvi* em todo o Arrayal" (I *heard* in the whole camp)—but his description of his own circumstances is chronologically ambiguous. His own position, marked in succession by the phrases "estando eu na tenda" (I being in the tent) and "levandome pera detras da tenda" (taking me behind the tent), as well as the time at which it happens, "seria pellas oito" (it must have been/ it must be about 8:00 o'clock), could be read as taking place either in the past or the present, and are only marked as past by their relationship with the verb that follows them, "ouvi." The most important event, the moment at which Leitão sees the king's corpse, is clearly in the present tense—"*vejo* passar diante de mi" (I *see* pass by before me)—and also encodes the corpse as the subject of the infinitive verb *passar* (pass by). Semantically, Leitão makes the text reenact the obscene presence of a dead king's body on the move. This inflection makes this moment subject to perpetual reenactment. The text makes the active parade of Sebastian's corpse through the military camp indexically proximal, revivifying this moment that can be accessed continually in this way.[75]

If action is in turn an index of the actant, in effect this preserves the mobile, vital matter of the royal dead body just out of reach on the page, waiting to be reanimated along with the images of his dead soldiers. Critically, the corpse and other actants in its orbit retain sufficient efficacy to remain mobile on a dynamic trajectory that remains beyond Leitão's reach, relegating him to the inadequate state of immobility. As we will see in the next chapter through Silva's narrative of his relationship with the same corpse, Sebastian's body persists as a repository of agency that can attract other bodies to it and make things happen—in other words, as vibrant matter acting in an assemblage.

4
Assemblage
Recovering Diplomatic Power with Corpses

> Es pues la muerte de naturaleza quando dexando de ser el compuesto se aparta el Alma del cuerpo pues no vive el cuerpo, mas que mientras tiene unión con èl Alma, y su muerte no es otra cosa, que una separación de los dos, con la qual cessan todas las acciones vivientes.
>
> Thus, natural death is when there ceases to be a compound because the Soul departs from the Body that is no longer living, but which meanwhile has a union with the Soul, and its death is nothing but a separation of the two, with which all living actions cease.
>
> —JUAN EULOGIO PÉREZ FADRIQUE, *MODO PRÁTICA DE EMBALSAMAR CUERPOS DEFUNTOS*

The correspondence among Philip II of Spain, Philip's secretary Gabriel de Zayas, and Juan de Silva, Spanish ambassador to Portugal from 1576 to 1578, indicates a deep concern for the Mediterranean implications of Sebastian's African enterprise. Silva's unsuccessful efforts to persuade Sebastian to sign the treaty between Philip and the Ottoman sultan, Murad III (r. 1574–95), which would have established the Maghreb as off-limits politically for both Spain and the Ottoman Empire. The primary complaint in this Spanish discussion of the events on the ground is Sebastian's myopic focus on local concerns: he seeks to regain Portuguese forts on the African littoral lost decades earlier, restore Portuguese honor, and satisfy his own personal ambition of participating in a crusade by pursuing this expedition, ignoring the broader implications of those actions. This portrayal of Sebastian in Silva's letters as impulsive, immature, and unrepentantly locally focused is one that has pervaded the scholarship on the battle since the beginning of the twentieth century.[1] This portrait of Sebastian increases Silva's own prominence at the Portuguese court by highlighting his utility within this setting and in collaboration with other actors around him. Silva's carefully negotiated position begins to fall apart when he departs with Sebastian's expedition to North Africa in June 1578 and comes crashing down around him two months later when he is wounded at al-Qaṣr al-Kabīr. Rather than determine the itinerary of the diplomatic assemblage that he has worked to convene at the Portuguese court, he becomes dependent upon another agent whose lesser social status and greater efficacy after al-Qaṣr al-Kabīr rankles Silva. This agent, Andrea Gasparo Corzo, mediates between Moroccan and Spanish officials to bring the dead Portuguese king's body back to the Iberian Peninsula.[2] Silva's association with this itinerant corpse becomes the central focus of his subsequent correspondence.

The same royal corpse also appears as vibrant matter in assemblages in a collection of letters that Silva wrote to the Spanish king and his privy council.[3] Although Silva experiences many of the same events as Portuguese narrators, he consistently adopts a perspective oriented toward the consequences to Spain of these events. While Mendonca's and Leitão's concern for Portuguese honor at times constrains their willingness to criticize their own leaders, Silva's professional perspective sheds a different light on the same events. In addition to a view of the preparations at the Portuguese court for the battle, Silva gives the reader access to another perspective on the complex relationships between the living and the dead. Silva is wounded at al-Qaṣr al-Kabīr, and his subsequent communications reveal his growing awareness of the implications his wounds have for his autonomous agency—of his own vulnerability as object as well as subject. Like Leitão, Silva recognizes Sebastian's mobile dead body as vibrant matter but then acts on that recognition in a new way. He seeks to cooperate with this dead body and other living bodies to stay within the corpse's orbit as it is translated back to safety on the Iberian Peninsula.

In the months leading up to al-Qaṣr al-Kabīr, Silva mediates between royal bodies and his royal patron, emphasizing this service in hopes of gaining greater financial support. In his telling of the events leading up to the Portuguese departure for Morocco, Silva emphasizes his immediate access to the body of the dying former Portuguese Queen Regent Catherine, which serves as an anchor for his narrative credibility.[4] His actively negotiated relationship with this body attests to the importance of his role as official witness and mediator in the diplomatic assemblage. After he is injured at the Battle of the Three Kings, however, Silva loses his capacity as mediator and is able to emphasize his access to authority and agency only by collaborating with the agents recovering the corpse of Catherine's grandson, Sebastian, to the Iberian

Peninsula. Like other narrators of the event, he observes, represents, and avails himself of the proximal evidence of mortality. These royal corpses become bodies of knowledge whose powers of mobility and tendencies toward subjectivity Silva observes and whose agency he taps into by collaborating with them in assemblage. Despite the lack of efficacy that he has over the trajectory of Sebastian's corpse back to the Iberian Peninsula, Silva insists on one access point to power: his proximity to that important corpse.

As shown in chapter 1, the indexical presence of the corpse provides a stable ground of interaction between narrator and reader that vouches for the authenticity of his account. In contrast to Mendonça's present and static corpses that create a common ground for narrative, the "here" of Silva's account is itinerant, a fact that presents complications for a narrator who has been at pains to emphasize his own diplomatic impotence. Silva relies on other actants within the assemblage as a source of agency to compensate for his helplessness and fulfill his need to stay in the presence of the mobile corpse. The vital complexes of bodies that he joins orbit around the repository of power of Sebastian's corpse and cooperate to determine a mutually beneficial trajectory. Through language that reiterates his dependent relationship on these other bodies, living and dead, Silva delineates the ontologically diverse assemblage that eventually returns him to the Iberian Peninsula. The assemblage a narrator creates with corpses unearths the interplay of that distributed agentic power within and through mosaicized alliances that form among nonhuman and human, vital and inert bodies.

Assemblages of Service

In 1538, Silva began his life of service to the Spanish royal family at age six as a page to the future Philip II. In late 1575, Silva received a commission from Philip to monitor Sebastian as the new Spanish ambassador in Lisbon. As ambassador for Spain in Portugal, Silva was expected not only to "burnish his prince's image" and project the power of Spain in the Portuguese court, but also to be Philip's eyes on the ground.[5] The dynamics that governed early modern diplomacy have been studied extensively from a historical perspective, and I do not mean to replicate that work here. Instead, I want to build on it to understand how early modern royal service functions semiotically in terms of the assemblage—a complex of independent or semi-independent bodies that confederate or congregate to enhance their power—and how Silva conceives of his service to the Spanish crown in terms of his spatial relationship to an evolving, mobile confederation of agents that includes significant royal bodies.[6] The dynamics of service that undergirded early modern diplomacy inscribes

Silva as a semiotically significant actant within an evolving assemblage, a prominent participant as long as he could demonstrate his utility as an information-gathering actant within the cooperative dispositif, or institutional, administrative, and knowledge oriented apparatus.

Assemblages, a concept closely related to the Foucauldian notion of dispositif, form out of complementary abilities or capacities that its human and nonhuman elements bring to a nonhierarchical collective to gain efficacy in the world.[7] Impotent or less potent on their own, with more and less "structured modes of individuation within the group subject," the different members share competences with the collective to the group to benefit from their symbiotic relationship.[8] Despite its basis in cooperation, however, an assemblage at least partially preserves the independence of the participant members. It retains its heterogeneous nature, which in turn fixes its finite life span—the semi-independent members can remain within one another's orbits for only so long. Assemblages thus take advantage of the symbiotic dynamism of their grouping to move toward or away some shared destination or starting point, metaphorical or literal. The purpose of that symbiotic relationship is conceived of as emerging along a *trajectory*, "a directionality or movement away from somewhere even if the toward-which it moves is obscure or even absent."[9] The notion of trajectory will be crucial for discussing Silva's participation in an assemblage because it gets at both the fixed temporality of the cooperative and its spatiality. The assemblage's trajectory follows an itinerary of its efficacy as a group, leaving a trace, an index, of the places in which it had power and authority in a series of locales, all of which were designated as "here."[10] Moving forward, I am interested in the cooperative capacities of the assemblage, how their efficacy manifests in and through space, and the traces that are left of that cooperation.

Service to Philip's state, diplomatic and otherwise, depended on competent actants cooperating in symbiosis to achieve a mutually beneficial goal. Folger has demonstrated that colonial writings in the early modern state "are produced as a reaction to a strategic bureaucratic apparatus of astounding dimensions. In other words . . . the *relación* presented to the authorities, as well as the more or less chaotic historiographical works of 'amateurs,' must be seen in relation to a larger *dispositif*, a 'scriptural economy.'"[11] On Folger's argument, then, agents like Silva were empowered to write but only so long as they were subject to the broader colonial assemblage. In 1611, Sebastián de Covarrubias would define "servir" and its derivative concepts as follows: "vale obedecer a otro, y hazer su volũtad, y unos sirven libremẽte dando gusto a otros, y estos sirven con su volũtad; otros sirvẽ forçados como los esclavos, y otros en una mediania, alquilandose, o haziendo concierto con la persona a quien sirvẽ, como son los criados a los señores [means to obey another, and do their will; and some serve freely giving pleasure to others, and these serve with their own will; and others serve forced as are slaves; and others somewhere in the middle, renting themselves, or making an agreement with the person whom they serve, as are servants to masters]."[12] In other words, entering into service required relinquishing one's independent will and submitting it to another's, especially when that service was enforced or contracted. Especially considering Silva's focus on the compensation he hoped to earn by serving the Spanish king, his service was certainly not undertaken only to bring his king pleasure, but rather falls in Covarrubias's middle category of contractual service that entailed relinquished autonomy. Read in terms of assemblage, Silva agreed as contracted emissary from Philip's court to subject his individual agency to the group subject of the Spanish crown. Although as ambassador he was endowed with more agency than were other actants within the Spanish imperial bureaucracy, Silva's service nonetheless operates within a tightly interlaced network of agents collaborating toward a shared end.[13]

Silva's participation in the assemblage of early modern diplomacy involved extended and intimate interactions with both his dispatching monarch and the hosting court. Certainly, the ambassador maintained the trust of his dispatching monarch by transmitting consistent and credible information back home, but the intimacy of that relationship was deeper since privileged courtiers and ambassadors served as surrogates for their royal masters in their duties. Organological metaphors of state meant that ambassadors were used to participating as semi-independent agents within a political assemblage, which extended the king's body into international spaces.[14] The administrative dispositif "both subjugates and empowers the subject, as an obedient servant of the King and as an official representative of the sovereign, respectively."[15] These posts thus served to extend the person of the dispatching king into more geographical space through the ambassador as a member of the royal assemblage.[16]

Finally, in semiotic terms, Silva's presence in Portugal is indexical. An index is a mediator—it points from a thing that is "here" to a thing that is "not here." Or, to recall Margaret Schwartz's useful definition of the index first cited in chapter 1, the ambassador's material existence at court bears "a referential relationship to an absent subject. They are a kind of medium that connects" these different worlds: the *origo* from which Silva enunciates and the space of reading in which his information is received.[17] His position enables him to constitute narrative, to transpose his experience of "here" in Portugal back to Spain.[18] Unlike that of a corpse, however, indexical capacity is not hardwired into Silva's material but is instead defined and maintained through his service to the absent royal subject. In other words, Silva is a different kind of corporeal index than a corpse—his corporeal presence at the court "here" in Portugal is a trace of or indicates the presence "over there" of his dispatching king in Spain. Unlike a corpse, however, he is a meaningful, material index only so long as he can carry out his duties. According to the outgoing Spanish ambassador to Portugal, Juan de Borja, Silva's earliest task was to establish a working relationship with the Portuguese king and his ministers.[19] While resident diplomats were designated eyewitnesses who observed and testified on behalf of their dispatching monarchy, they still had to negotiate their position at both dispatching and receiving courts.[20] Their success mediating information was grounded in their physical presence and direct access to critical knowledge in cooperation with other entities at court. Silva maintains his own referential discourse in two ways: as emissary from Spain, he stands in for and refers to the Spanish court; as mediator from Portugal to Spain, his sustained access to information and networks "here" at the Portuguese court allows him to project this context back to Philip and his ministers for their consideration and action. His role in this assemblage is can thus be most productively distilled down to his indexical function.

As Silva's letters as well as correspondence from his contemporaries who served as diplomats at other European courts show, another piece of that assemblage were the royal bodies with which he was expected to sustain contact in their resident courts. Knowledge of these royal bodies was critical for gauging political stability and marking the efficacy of the reporting agent, in part because physical access to the king reflected one's status in the monarchy.[21] The Aviz court, long closely linked to the Habsburg Castilian court by ties of marriage and geographical proximity, held similar attitudes toward access to the king's body.[22] Access to the king's *aposento* and private spaces pointed to one's position at Iberian courts, since social and political privilege correlated with access to the physical body of the king.[23] Leitão offers a contemporary explanation of the importance of that kind of access: "aquelle corpo do Rei, com todos os que lhe assistem, officiaes e grandes e menores, morando onde elle mora, como Igreja todo o corpo. . . . Corte vem de cruore, s., sangue, porque o que mais nelles se pratica, se encaminha a carne e sangue [that body of the King, with all that attend him, officials and grandees and minor [nobility], living where he lives, like a Church the whole body. . . . Court comes from *cruore*, definition, blood, for however much else in them is practiced, it leads to body and blood]."[24] The metaphor of the court as a body coursing with blood perfectly mirrors the matters of body and blood that it governs. Proximity to the royal body was, nevertheless, power with constraint: "The nearer one stood to the ruler, the greater influence one had as a broker, but the narrower was one's room for maneuver."[25] In other words, these royal bodies and the information that inhered to them formed a critical piece of the diplomatic assemblage in which Silva participated.

Less studied as key members of courtly assemblages were other royal bodies: those whose presence and significance at court extended beyond their deaths. Carlos Eire argues that even common corpses relied upon networks of responsibilities and obligations that made the living accountable for the fate of the dead.[26] Even more significant to the living were the bodies of kings—still compelling to those mediating information about them in death as in life; all the more referential as an "inherently communicative object" as "a convenient vehicle for religious and monarchical propaganda."[27] Eire has documented ritual and funeral rites in the Habsburg court that emphasize the symbolic significance of the royal corpse politically and socially: royal exequies that extended and recapitulated the royal burial throughout the Iberian globe; the construction and organization of the Escorial as royal mausoleum; the collection of relics collected near or even in contact with the dying king; the unique ordering of funeral honors for the dead king and acclamation rituals of his successor.[28] All of these rites conceived of the presence of the king's corpse as crucial for sustaining political stability, since the dead king continued to play an active role in tidying up the transition of power from old to new king.[29] As alluded to in chapter 3, when Philip II died, the acclamation of Philip III took place before the royal exequies for his dead father. The ritual recognition of Philip III while his father's corpse was still physically present and not yet interred smoothed out the disruptiveness of the interregnum: "This enhanced the acclamation by making it ritually impossible to question the king's status once his father was 'fully' dead."[30] In other words, the smooth transition of power in the interregnum depended upon the cooperation of an assemblage formed by the kings' terrestrial bodies and other frequently referential bodies—ambassadors, relics, monks, and so on.

I am not the first to suggest that a corpse can form a critical part of an assemblage—Schwartz defines the corpse as "an assemblage of multiple elements, some of which are human and some of which are not."[31] Because dead bodies are "indisputably *there*, as our senses of sight, touch, and smell can confirm," they stubbornly persist, and force the living to acknowledge and relate to them, as I explored in chapter 1.[32] That persistent presence inclines corpses to form temporary and long-term cooperative relationships with the living. Building on the argument from chapter 3, we can see that if seemingly dead and material things retain agency autonomously, that agency can only be augmented and bolstered in partnership with other human and nonhuman actants. Such collaborative enterprises can be theorized in terms of the assemblage and conative substances that accumulate in confederate bodies.[33] These related concepts are particularly useful for understanding the ways in which living and dead bodies work together to determine the trajectory of the group.[34]

Schwartz focuses on a modern assemblage of living, dead, human, and nonhuman elements that attend to the dead's posthumous needs. Her understanding of that assemblage is composed of elements like human flesh, bacteria, the molecular and chemical makeup of the dead organism, embalming fluid, and even the living humans who inject that fluid. But other kinds of human/nonhuman assemblages draw on the agency of all members of that cooperative group, dead and alive, to achieve goals more expansive than corpse care. In fact, the corpse is capable of forming more varied assemblages that exceed Schwartz's workaday, temporary team of elements whose sole purpose is to lay that corpse to rest. Schwartz also highlights the relationship between this assemblage and the corpse as index, noting, "These technologies are important, but they interact or assemble with a thing that is already inherently communicative because it is referential."[35] Assemblages with corpses take on the corpse's own referential potential, including their tendency to generate a shared frame of reference that valorizes information shared about and through them. Bearing in mind these bodies' subjective capacity explored in chapter 3, as well as their referential qualities, here I will expand on the role of assemblages in moving and communicating with the living and dead alike.

Diplomatic Assemblage at Home

Silva, a "consummate courtier" who was brought up from an early age in the royal courts of Charles V and Philip II, understood these intricate politics of access and proximity.[36] Transmitting information about royal bodies thus carried implications for important matters of state. It also speaks to the trusted position of the diplomat conveying that information—Silva's role in this assemblage is as a conduit for information. The emphasis that Silva places on his intimate access to the body of the Queen Regent doubly emphasizes his credibility as an eyewitness—his very presence in the most private quarters of a royal personage point to his exalted position at court, and therefore his credibility as a trustworthy official, and his demonstrated physical knowledge of that body acts as a touchstone for the veracity of what he reports.

In the two years leading up to al-Qaṣr al-Kabīr, Silva created space for himself at the Portuguese court to act as an agent with what in the preceding chapter we termed *prominence* or efficacy in that administrative apparatus—prominence that is legible both through his actions and the language in which he narrates. Although he complains regularly about the financial demands of his position, a constraint characteristic of Philip's statecraft that kept his surrogates on a tight leash, Silva nonetheless affirms the position of trust and access that he builds at the Aviz court by recounting the key negotiations in which he engages with Sebastian on Spain's behalf.[37] Most tellingly, he conveys communications among the royal family members at the Portuguese and Spanish courts and demonstrates his intimate access to the body of the dying and dead Catherine of Portugal, Philip's aunt, Sebastian's grandmother and sometime regent. MacKay suggests that Catherine, who served as queen regent to Sebastian until 1562, was loyal to Spain, "whose ruler, Philip (her nephew and one-time son-in-law), was her constant correspondent and one of her few remaining relatives."[38] Silva's concern for her health thus maps onto Spanish interests within Portugal at this time, since her demise would mean the loss of an important ally to Castile in the Portuguese court. Moreover, the ambassador's access to the innermost chambers of a queen's apartments and knowledge of a royal female body indicated his exclusive and trustworthy access to the most confidential secrets of the Portuguese monarchy.[39] These interactions underscore the importance of Silva's agility as an agent—in both diplomatic and ontological terms—dedicated to his king's service; he serves as a prominent actor within this diplomatic assemblage that carefully manages a royal corpse.

In his letter of January 6, 1578, Silva emphasizes his agency in culling and reporting information about Catherine's illness by affirming the volition he exercises in providing Philip with these details: "A último del pasado avisé á V.Maj.^{d} particularmente de la indispusicion de la reina; y por ser cosa que tanto cuidado dará á V. Maj.^{d}, me parece que debo advertir á menudo del progreso de su enfermedad [On the last day of last month, I notified Your Majesty particularly of the indisposition of the queen; and as this is something that will much preoccupy Your Majesty, it seems to me that I ought to give frequent news of the progress of her illness]."[40] Here Silva establishes and negotiates his own position and the terms of his service to Philip; as an autonomous agent of the king, he determines not only what information he dispenses to his master and how, but even decides which details will be most interesting or concerning to Philip. To return to Covarrubias's definition of service, in this passage, Silva seems to be striving towards exercising his own will, toward the class of service that "sirven libremẽte . . . con su voluntad" (serve freely . . . with their own will), rather than only adhere to an agreement with Philip to do the king's will.[41]

Intimate knowledge of a royal body gives Silva the political capital to raise himself from a clearly defined relationship of master and servant, as had been established on Silva's assumption of his duties, to one of greater parity, from which he predicts the Spanish monarch's own concerns and interests before the king himself is aware of them. His anticipation of Philip's desires confirms him as a semi-independent member of the royal body itself—if his role is to substitute the king as his representative at the Portuguese court, then his service extends not only to physically enacting that royal presence, but also to knowing where royal interests lie. Silva's prediction of Philip's concern for the queen's health is confirmed by a letter the king sends to Silva on February 10, in which the king explicitly requests information about his aunt's illness: "aunque confio en Nuestro Señor que los beneficios le habrán sido de provecho, pues, si hubiera habido algun accidente en contrario, me lo hubiérades escripto, como era razon y decis que lo haríades [although I am confident in Our Lord that the benefits will have served her well, as, if there were to have been some chance event to the contrary, you would have written to me about it, as would have been correct and as you say that you would do]." Rather than cut Silva down for his presumptuousness in anticipating his royal wishes, Philip confirms that Silva accurately foresaw his will, and expresses his expectation that he will continue to do so with further developments: "me lo *hubiérades* escripto, como era razon y decis que lo haríades [*you would have* written to me about it, as would have been correct and as you say that you would do]."[42] Philip thus accepts Silva's characterization of his prominence and independence within the diplomatic assemblage and encourages him to continue in that vein.

In subsequent communications dispatched approximately once a week between January 6 and February 12, Silva emphasizes in ever more detailed terms his access to Catherine's declining body. On January 29, Silva writes to tell Philip of treatments the queen has undergone that have improved her prognosis: "Su Al.[za] se ha ido hallando mejor de la hinchazon de la pierna, que es lo que mas se ha temido, y la mejoría deste accidente se ha continuado de manera despues de la purga, que ya casi no le temen los médicos [Her Highness has gone on improving from the swelling in her leg, which is what they have most feared, and the improvement from this accident has continued in such a way since the purgative that now the doctors almost do not fear it]." Most apparent in this passage is the intimately detailed knowledge of the queen's body to which Silva has access. Not only does he know what treatments she has undergone, but he is also familiar with the status of her swollen leg and the extent to which the treatments have mitigated that swelling, a part of the female royal body most male courtiers would never see. On February 11, Silva writes to Philip that Catherine's health has taken a turn for the worse, and that her physicians expect that she will die before the end of the day. His knowledge of the slightest details in her health is still on display, obtained when he is called to her bedside in the early morning hours: "Ha comido y reposado: está quieta; pero flaquísima, y el pulso en el brazo derecho casi no se percibe: en el derecho le tiene [She has eaten and rested. She is quiet, but gaunt, and the pulse in her right arm is almost imperceptible, while it can still be found in the right one]."[43]

Silva's intimate familiarity with the royal body does not stop when the queen succumbs to her illness, but instead persists beyond her final moments. On February 12, the ambassador writes again to Philip to confirm her death:

> La noche pasada ántes de las dos horas plugo á Nuestro Señor llevar á la reina, dándole un fin gloriosísimo y santísimo, muy conforme á su vida. Sobrevínose la muerte mas arrebatadamente que se pensaba, aunque era combatida de tantas enfermedades; porque desde el último aviso que envié á V.M.[d] no se habia ofrecido en su disposicion novedad de importancia.[44]

> Last night before two o'clock, it pleased Our Lord to take the queen, giving her a most glorious and saintly end, very much in keeping with her life. Death overcame her more violently than was expected, although she was beset by so many illnesses; for since the latest news that I sent to Your Majesty her disposition had not offered any new developments of importance.

Although much of his report is taken up by platitudes that speak to the newly deceased queen's moral rectitude, elements of this passage evince intimate awareness of the circumstances of her demise, including a specific time of death, and a set of expectations for her prognosis, which are then upset by the violent and sudden way in which she dies. Silva's understanding of Catherine's death is demonstrated through the detail with which he can narrate the sequence of events that led to her demise:

> A la noche le vino un crecimiento grande que le respondia á cuartana, y destos habia tenido tres menos rigurosos. Este último la apretó de manera que le quitó juntamente la habla y el sentido y los pulsos. Ungiéronle con gran priesa, sin acuerdo ninguno. De allí adelante hasta la mañana, se fué descubriendo el pulso y le tornó enteramente el sentido y tambien la habla con alguna dificultad.[45]

> At night, a great fit overtook her that corresponded to a fever, and of these she had had three weaker ones. This last took her in such a way that she lost the ability to speak, her senses, and her pulse all at once. They rubbed her rapidly, but without any regaining of consciousness. From there forward until the morning, gradually her pulse returned, as did her consciousness, and her ability to speak, with some difficulty.

The fine detail with which he recounts her final moments signals his access, which emphasizes his prominence in both social and agentive terms. The detail of the account further implies that Silva was in conversation with the queen's private physicians. His access to the private physicians establishes a chain of transmission that Silva can document: the physicians touched the nearly defunct queen's body by rubbing it to revive her, an act that was either narrated to Silva in short order or that the ambassador himself saw take place. His role as a witnessing actor in this collective of human agents surrounding Catherine's body, including the physicians who have themselves come in physical contact with this royal body. The authority of that presence suffuses Silva's telling of Catherine's passing.

Silva's final words on the queen are of his intention to send Philip her final will and testament: "Como se entienda la particularidad de su testamento, la enviaré á V.M.[d] [So that the particularity of her testament may be understood, I will send it to Your Majesty]."[46] Silva establishes himself as a link between royal, corporeal presence, textual production, and transmission. Silva doubles down on the credibility of what he transmits in implying his witnessing of a royal death, his presence before a royal corpse, and then also establishes his access to secondary witnesses of that body. The doctors have touched and interacted with the royal corpse, and then transmitted their knowledge of that body to Silva, making him a secondary and important legal witness to that interaction. Silva then sets that account down in writing, both in his letter to Philip and in the queen's final will and testament, which he transmits to the Spanish king. Silva's prominent role in this complicated assemblage of agents has been established and confirmed through his ongoing contact with Catherine: his position as royal intermediary serves a concrete, legal purpose that generates the appropriate documents recounting her death.

Silva's knowledge of Catherine's ailing body, as well as these other moments in his letters demonstrate and support his position as Philip's intermediary. This status enables him to maneuver with independence at the Portuguese court and to anticipate his royal master's wants and needs.[47] This agency characterizes Silva's writing even when he departs Lisbon for North Africa with Sebastian's fleet and continues with their journey through Cádiz, Tangiers, and Arzila. The diction of his correspondence frames Silva not as a passive observer on the sidelines but as an active participant in the network of agents serving Spain's interests. When he is injured at al-Qaṣr al-Kabīr, however, Silva's capacities as agent, both narratively and semantically, dissipate, and his communications to the Spanish court cease.[48]

Impotence

On October 4, 1578, after more than two months of silence, Silva resumes his missives to Philip, pleading pardon for his silence and blaming injury and captivity for interrupting his duties. Silva's postbattle letters betray much less urgency than did those leading up to August 4, 1578—the intervals between them are much longer, coming weeks apart, rather than days or hours. He focuses entirely on two subjects: his recovery from a musket wound in his arm sustained at the battle, and the return of Sebastian's body to the Iberian Peninsula. The tenor of these letters is also conspicuously changed. If before August 4 Silva acts as the primary mediator of sensitive intelligence in his letters to Philip, afterward his letters are redundant, often communicating what Silva recognizes to be information that the king already has. This transition is also marked by an increasing reliance on externally authorizing agents—prior to August 4, Silva emphasizes his own participation in the events; after that date, Silva focuses on details about his injured body and Sebastian's corpse and narrates his reliance on external agents to achieve goals. In many ways, Silva's newly complicated agency mirrors Leitão's: the injuries on his body are evidence of his presence at the events he narrates, but they also reduce his social, linguistic, and ontological prominence within the assemblage of service.

Like Leitão, rather than obfuscate his physical shortcomings, Silva actually emphasizes the injuries he has suffered and reiterates the diplomatic and testimonial impotence he now experiences through the very semantic structure of his expressions.[49] Silva can no longer point to his efficacy as Philip's surrogate; instead, he recognizes that he is subject to the whims of other agents within a Mediterranean network. The disruption of his agency is inflected grammatically: he no longer uses active verbs in first-person singular or plural, but instead almost exclusively refers to himself as the direct or indirect object of transitive verbs. In his first two letters to Philip after the battle, both dated October 4, 1578, Silva narrates his weakness with correspondingly passive language: "Sabe Nuestro Señor que si algun cuidado humano me ha dado pena despues que estoy así doliente, ha sido no hallarme en esta ocasion vuelto con alas á Portugal, porque me parescia que pudiera ser embajador de servicio en esta ocasion [Our Lord knows that if some human care has made me suffer as I am thus in pain, it has been to not find myself returned on wings to Portugal, because it seemed to me that I would be an ambassador of service on this occasion]."[50] Rather than serve as principal mediator of information about the situation unfolding around him, he is instead reduced to an object: his status as ambassador is not recognized as motivation for his freedom, but rather he is reduced to a gift to be given by one monarch to another. Silva is acutely conscious of his loss of prominence in his diplomatic role, of his lost inability to act as an "embajador de servicio" (ambassador of service), or, in the words of Covarrubias, "obedecer a otro, y hazer su volũtad" (obey another, and do his will).[51] Beyond his professional failings, Silva's loss of efficacy becomes apparent through the very language he uses to describe it. Rather than express active desire or narrate his efforts to return to Portugal, Silva characterizes himself repeatedly as the object of other agents' actions: "enviar*me* libre" (set *me* free); "hacer presente *de mí*" (make a gift *of me*); "ha sido no hallar*me* . . . vuelto con alas á Portugal" (it has been to not find *myself* returned with wings to Portugal). That lost prominence is particularly acute in his influence on his own trajectory; movement back to Portugal is conceivable only in the fantastic terms of flight. Silva's rhetorical passivity is most revealing when contrasted with the bustling activity of the letters written before August 4. On June 25, Silva describes his interactions with the Portuguese king himself in extremely active terms: "*Yo dije* al rey por el camino todo lo que *entendí* que convenia á su servicio, hasta aventurar á que pensase que lo decia de miedo [Along the way, *I told* the king everything that *I understood* to be convenient to his service, even venturing so far that he might have thought I said it out of fear]."[52] This earlier rhetoric characterizes Silva's prominence in the Portuguese court. After August 4, 1578, however, Silva succumbs to his injury and betrays that incapacity through his verbal inflection.

Having situated his own body and reduced efficacy, Silva reports on the recovery of "el cuerpo del rey" (the body of the king), which has also been brought "here," "á esta frontera" (to this border) to do the work of mediating between the *here* of enunciation and the *there* of epistolary reception.[53] The ambassador situates himself as copresent with the body with the deictic "este":

> Parecióme acompañar *este* cuerpo, como quiera que el mio estuviese, y así me hice traer en hombros de moros por *estas* sierras: que de otra manera no pude venir, porque mis heridas aun no lo sufren, mas espero en Dios que hecha cierta diligencia en mi cura en llegando á España, quedaré en dispusicion de ir á servir á V.M. sin mas dilacion.[54]

> It occurred to me that I should accompany *this* body, whatever the state of my own, and so I had myself brought on the shoulders of Muslims through *these* mountains: for by no other means could I come, because my wounds will still not stand it, but I trust in God that if I am diligent in my recuperation upon arriving in Spain, that I will be well disposed to serve Your Majesty without further delay.

The first short phrase—"parecióme acompañar este cuerpo," it occurred to me that I should accompany this body—does complex work. Yet again, Silva is framed as the passive object of a verb: it occurred *to him* that he might accompany the corpse. Although the verb *parecer* (to appear; to seem) and its variants are common idiomatic expressions that Silva uses with some regularity in his letters, his use of it in this way is unusual.[55] Normally, Silva deploys the most common meaning of the expression to hedge an impression that he relates to the recipient of the letter, either out of politeness or to convey doubt. For example: "Parecíame justificación muy digna de Su Mag.[d]" (It seemed to me a justification most worthy of His Majesty), "no parece conveniente" (it does not seem convenient), "al rey le parecerá que" (it will seem to the king that), "que me parece muy justo" (which seems fair to me).[56] The usage is consistent with Silva's assertive agency and liveliness across his prebattle correspondence—it appears as part of a judicious assessment of the circumstances on the ground, material and psychological. In contrast, in the letters written immediately after al-Qaṣr al-Kabīr, expressions with *parecer* consistently take on a passive valence that diminishes its object's agency, as also seen in an earlier reference to Corzo: "le pareció [a un Andrea Corzo] pedir al rey merced del embajador para enviarme libre, y aunque el rey se lo concedió por escrito, lo tornó a revocar, diciendo que mas queria hacer presente de mí á V. M.[d] en su nombre [it occurred (to one Andrea Corzo) that he should ask the king for diplomatic immunity to set me free, and though the king conceded it in writing, he then revoked it, saying that instead he wished to make a gift of me to Your Majesty in his name]."[57] In this instance, even as Silva acknowledges Corzo's service on his behalf, he makes light of the merchant's own agency in the matter—"le pareció" (it occurred to him)—and minimizing his status in the network serving Philip—he is "un Andrea Corzo" (one Andrea Corzo), not an entity Silva acknowledges as worthy of the monarch's notice and recognition.

The impetus that pushes Silva to associate himself with Sebastian's powerful body comes from the nominal clause "acompañar este cuerpo" (accompany this body), which functions as an external operator that still encompasses Silva's needs and limitations. Forces associated with this body, thus, can make something happen—Silva's translation from one place to another—that Silva as member-actant of the assemblage cannot make happen on his own. The spatiality and temporality indexed by "*estas* montañas" (*these* mountains) is destabilized by the framing of the port of Ceuta as *here* on *this* frontier. Unlike the fixed, stable *here* of Silva's diplomatic post in Lisbon, the origo from which Silva enunciates is defined in relationship to "*este* cuerpo" (*this* body). *This* mobile corpse thus emerges as the singled fixed index that establishes temporary rafts of mutually intelligible fields of interpretation along its itinerary through Morocco, supplanting Silva's previous referential service.

Silva grapples especially with his own loss of narrative power and agency in letters that report on efforts to recover Sebastian's corpse back to the Iberian Peninsula. On December 11, 1578, Silva relates the active role played in this mission by Corzo. Silva observes that Corzo succeeded in regaining the heretofore captive and politically crucial corpse of the dead Portuguese king:

> Últimamente llegó Andrea Corzo á Alcazarquivir con órden de traer el cuerpo del rey . . . el cual habia Muley Hamete concedido *a V.M.* para que le pasásemos en Castilla, y de allí *dispusiese dél V.M.* como fuere servido. Llegado un fraile que llevaba *una carta de V.M.* Pidiendo se diese por rescate a los portugueses, respondió que le tenia concedido *á V.M.*, y que de la misma manera le hubiera dado si fuera vivo y le tuviera en prision, y que pues *V.M. le pedia* para Portugal.[58]

> Recently, Andrea Corzo came to al-Qaṣr al-Kabīr with orders to bring the body of the king . . . which Mulay Aḥmad had conceded *to Your Majesty* so that we could cross with him into Castile, and from there *Your Majesty could dispose of him* as best served you. A friar came bringing a letter from *Your Majesty* which asked that he be given in redemption for the Portuguese. He responded that he had conceded it *to Your Majesty*, and that in the same way he would have given him over if he were alive and he had him in prison, and that *Your Majesty* asked it for Portugal.

Silva stakes his corporeal, political, and narratorial recovery on Sebastian's royal body. He demonstrates his understanding of Philip's interest in recovering Sebastian's corpse by emphasizing the utilitarian benefit of the body as a physical object. Silva does not suggest that Sebastian's body has been recovered out of a sense of familial or spiritual duty. The diction of this passage, which recalls moments in Silva's correspondence before the battle that focused on his talent for service to the king, reestablishes the terms of this epistolary correspondence—all actions communicated in some way need to prove their usefulness to Philip: "de allí dispusiese dél V.M. como fuere servido," as best may serve you. Nevertheless, even as Silva demonstrates that he understands the importance of Sebastian's body to the Spanish king, he leaves himself as agent out of the equation. Before al-Qaṣr al-Kabīr, Silva did not hesitate to anticipate the desires of his master nor to position himself perfectly to fulfill those. Now he is far less certain what those desires might be with respect to Sebastian's corpse, an ambiguity betrayed by his speculative use of the future subjunctive "como fuere servido," as you might be served.[59] Furthermore, the utility of this dead body also serves to highlight Silva's corresponding loss of efficacy on Philip's behalf.

Silva fails to furnish the king with any new information in narrating the steps taken to carry out this task. As Philip is aware, his intermediary Corzo has already secured the passage of Sebastian's body to Portugal, a fact that Silva can be sure Philip knows, since it is a courtesy that the new Moroccan sultan, al-Manṣūr, has conceded to the Spanish king.[60] When reduced to the information that Silva attempts to report in this missive, the uselessness of his testimony is apparent. He notifies Philip of the steps the king himself has taken through other agents to secure the corpse of his nephew: Philip wrote a letter asking al-Manṣūr to return Sebastian's corpse to Castile; a friar brings a letter from Philip to the Maghreb; al-Manṣūr states that he has already conceded this favor to Philip. Before the battle, Silva articulated power in the Portuguese court. Now, the same prominence no longer inheres to him, and he must rely more heavily on other members of the assemblage.

The Itinerant Corpse

Since Sebastian's corpse is useful but on the move, Silva must constantly signal his proximity to it so he can profit from its power. Before his injury, Silva had sufficient vital force that he could independently keep up with the changing settings he sought to narrate. Now, however, Silva is so enfeebled by his wounds that he cannot travel unassisted nor autonomously influence his trajectory, and thus must seek to ally himself with other bodies to keep himself within the orbit of the royal corpse. These symbiotically operating bodies work in concert along this vector from al-Qaṣr al-Kabīr to Ceuta and eventually toward the Iberian Peninsula. Silva has lost his singular, individual agency and must now define himself *in relation to* other communal entities. He situates himself as part of an assemblage, the entirety of which has agency and whose indexical power derives in large measure from the royal body it serves.

Other members of the assemblage include those who act to translate Silva's and Sebastian's bodies back to the Iberian Peninsula. One key member of the collective is the merchant and possible renegade Corzo.[61] In addition to redeeming Silva and recovering Sebastian's corpse, Corzo, his brothers, and other members of their family served as a network of informants throughout the Mediterranean who used the cover of commerce in service of the Spanish king.[62] In what seems to be a rather snobbish attempt to downplay his debt to this liminal figure, Silva dismissively refers to him as "un Andrea Corzo" (a certain Andrea Corzo) and credits the reach of Philip's power with his release from captivity in Larache, implying that this power effectuated itself through Corzo rather than deriving from any initiative the man could have taken on his own:

> y fuí llevado á Alarache, donde he estado como digo; mas la grandeza de V. M.[d] basta á remediar con su sombra mayores miserias, y ainsí fué que deseando un Andrea Corzo (de quien entiendo que tiene V. M.[d] noticia) hallar cualquiera ocasion de servir á V. M.[d], le pareció pedir al rey merced del embajador para enviarme libre.[63]
>
> and I was brought to Larache, where I have been as I say; but the greatness of Your Majesty suffices to remedy with its shadow the greatest miseries, and so it was that a certain Andrea Corzo (of whom I understand Your Majesty is aware) desiring to find any occasion to serve Your Majesty, it occurred to him to plead diplomatic immunity to the king [al-Manṣūr] to set me free.

Silva first underscores his own passivity—"*fui* llevado" (I was brought)—while conceding that Corzo has usurped his power by repeating the verb "servir" (to serve). He repeats the passive expression he uses elsewhere to describe his own weakness—"le pareció" (it occurred to him)—to narrate the actions Corzo took to have Silva moved to Larache. The difference, of course, is that while Silva does, in fact, lack efficacy, Corzo's activity as a subject is discernible through the resulting motion he effectuates—Silva is moved from captivity in Fez to Larache.[64] Whereas Silva has lost his capacity to serve Philip, Corzo has taken concrete steps to serve as Philip's agent with his old acquaintance al-Manṣūr to liberate Silva and release him into the orbit of Sebastian's corpse.

The cooperation of other agentic entities is what facilitates Silva's itinerary: the mobile bodies of the Muslims whose shoulders carry Silva over the Atlas Mountains; "*estos* caballeros portugueses" (*those* Portuguese horsemen), perhaps the same that the anonymous Moroccan chronicler claims Philip will later burn at the stake for transmitting unwelcome news; a friar; Corzo.[65] Like Mendonça, Silva regularly points to his surroundings with proximal deixis: "Hallé *aquí* en Ceupta una carta de V.M.[d] [I found *here* in Ceuta a letter from Your Majesty]."[66] Although it would be easy to dismiss the beginning of his letter as phatic—*here I am in Ceuta*—this and the other deictics that cluster with Silva's and Sebastian's bodies denote a concern for corporeal presence that exceeds mere social pleasantries. The particular emphasis on copresence with the royal body exceeds that found at other points in Silva's correspondence. For example, on June 29, Silva writes from Cadiz to let Zayas, noting only, "Hallámonos en Cádiz con una gran armada en número de velas y mayor en cualidad [We found ourselves in Cadiz a great armada in number of sails and even more so in quality]."[67] His presence, though implicitly in the place mentioned, is not pinpointed indexically. Unlike Mendonça, Silva's surroundings are in constant flux as a function of the epistolary, diplomatic context in which his narrative emerges. Returning again to the letter cited in the previous section:

> Parecióme acompañar *este* cuerpo, como quiera que el mio estuviese, y así me hice traer en hombros de moros por *estas* sierras: que de otra manera no pude venir, porque mis heridas aun no lo sufren, mas espero en Dios que hecha cierta diligencia en mi cura en llegando á España, quedaré en dispusicion de ir á servir á V.M. sin mas dilacion.[68]
>
> It seemed to me that I should accompany *this* body, whatever the state of my own, and so I had myself brought on the shoulders of Muslims through *these* mountains: for by no other means could I come, because my wounds will still not stand it, but I trust in God that if I am diligent in my recuperation upon arriving in Spain, that I will be well disposed to serve Your Majesty without further delay.

He notes the geographical location of his own body with respect to a changing background constantly rendered present: "así me hice traer en hombros de moros por *estas* sierras: que de otra manera no pude venir [and so I had myself brought on the shoulders of Muslims through *these* mountains: for by no other means could I come]."[69] He has passed through "*estas* sierras" on the shoulders of "moros," but his ongoing presence in a particular topographical space is defined by being on the move. His body requires other agents to reach its destination and depends on the infrastructure of a trans-Mediterranean assemblage. Silva highlights the temporality as well as the spatiality of this journey when he remarks that he has been unable to depart Ceuta because bureaucratic documents have been delayed "hasta agora" (until now). Silva thus indicates his presence "here" and "now" at a particular location whose specificity varies over the course of the letter, but in geographical proximity to the various agents of a cooperative group.[70]

Reiterating his relative passivity within this collaborative relationship, Silva juxtaposes his own body and the royal corpse: "Parecióme acompañar este cuerpo, como quiera que el mio estuviese [It seemed to me that I should accompany this body, as though it were my own]." The corpse's own itineracy emerges as one of the forces that enables Silva's own movement through space. Its gravitational pull is so strong that the conceptual and semantic borders between the dead body and Silva's injured one begin to collapse. The syntactical subject "acompañar este cuerpo" (accompany this body) establishes Sebastian's body as the antecedent of subsequent masculine referents. In the next clause, however, Silva uses the masculine pronoun "mío" to gesture not to the expected antecedent of Sebastian's body but instead to his own. This semantic collapse represents his body as meaningfully indistinguishable from Sebastian's dead body and explains why the trajectory *this* body follows determines that of *mine*.

Furthermore, this passage suggests that the assemblage whose efficacy ensures Silva's homeward momentum will also affect his efficacy as ambassador. Rhetorically, Silva draws a parallel between the relative utility to Philip of the Portuguese king's dead body and his own maimed one. As suggested earlier, Silva indicates that he is keenly aware, as were Corzo and al-Manṣūr, of the value of Sebastian's body to Philip—the Saʿdī sultan concedes Sebastian's body to his uncle not for mortuary honors nor out of respect for the dead, but specifically so that Philip can "dispusiese dél . . . como fuere servido [dispose of it as it may serve him]." Unlike Silva's, Sebastian's body is one significant enough to Philip that he has personally taken steps to ensure its recovery to the Iberian Peninsula. In linking his own body to the useful royal dead body, Silva makes his case for his own utility to the Spanish sovereign, whom he petitions for permission to convalesce in Seville, so that he "quedaré en dispusicion de ir á *servir* á V.M. sin mas dilacion [will remain disposed to go *to serve* Your Majesty without further delay]."[71] Here, Silva relies on the same concept of service to propose that the recovery of his body would allow him to serve the Spanish king like the royal corpse is expected to. Just as the translation of Sebastian's corpse from the Maghreb to the Iberian Peninsula will activate that latent posthumous utility for Philip, so, too, Silva implies, will his own return to Castile reanimate his service to Philip, reconstituting him from a passively transported body back into an efficacious and active agent working on Philip's behalf. The conceptual link between these two passive bodies is clear—Silva implies that both his own and Sebastian's bodies will achieve greater prominence working on Philip's behalf with their return to the Peninsula.

Ironically, Silva identifies the issue at hand when he foregrounds Corzo's service to the crown: while Silva can no longer act in Spanish interests, Corzo has interceded successfully with Moroccan agents on both Philip's and his ambassador's behalf. Silva's injury and subsequent captivity exposes his epistemological, not to mention political and social, weakness in this geographical space. The ambassador's dependence on Corzo reveals the merchant to be the primary mediator for Philip across the Strait of Gibraltar rather than Silva. This summary of Corzo's actions synthesizes the complicated, multilateral ransom economy that linked Spanish and North African actors on both sides of the Mediterranean.[72] He has cooperated as an integral member of the assemblage in which Silva's and Sebastian's bodies are members and has helped generate the momentum that returns them painfully back home.

In Silva's letters written following al-Qaṣr al-Kabīr, the ambassador evinces a complex framework of passivity, presence, and cooperation that centers on the royal corpse. An assemblage constellates around that body, and includes other members—Silva's wounded arm, shoulders of Muslims who bear Silva and the corpse over the Atlas Mountains, anonymous agents, and a renegade. All of these actants apply forces that determine the trajectory of Sebastian's corpse back to the Iberian Peninsula, and its impact when it arrives there—movement that would never have taken place without the impetus generated by the corpse itself. While Leitão's representation of his own infirmity in some senses abides by generic expectations for veterans' accounts of their travails, Silva's insufficient competence as a result of his wounds can be compensated for only through the partnership he forms with other human and nonhuman actants. Silva's narrative of this collaborative effort to the parties who will determine the extent of his restoration as a more independent agent proves to be an innovative approach that recognizes the force of the corpse as vital and agentive matter. In many ways, Silva's answer to the question *Who is the subject?* is that it is an assemblage of vital matter, including corpses, that holds him back from oblivion.

5
Erasure

Corpse Desecration for Narrative Control

wa-yawma yuḥsharu ʾaʿdāʾu llāh ʾilā l-nāri fa-hum yūzaʿūna ḥattā ʾidhā mā jāʾūhā shahida ʿalayhim samʿuhum wa-ʾabṣāruhum wa-julūduhum bi-mā kānū yaʿmalūna wa-qālū li-julūdihim lima shahidtum ʿalaynā qālū ʾanṭaqanā llāhu llādhī ʾanṭaqa kulla shayʾin wa-huwa khalaqakum ʾawwala marratin wa-ʾilayhi turjaʿūna. (Q 41:19–21)

One day, God's enemies will be ushered toward the fire, distraught and bewildered. As they approach it, their hearing and vision and skin bears witness against them, revealing what they had been doing. They address their skins, "How can you bear witness against us?" They answer, "God has caused us to speak, as God causes all things to speak for God created you in the first instance and you inevitably revert back to God!"

One of the most gruesome images of corpses in all of the accounts of Wādī al-Makhāzin is the flayed and stuffed skin of al-Mutawakkil, which after his defeat at Wādī al-Makhāzin perambulates the city of Marrakesh on his uncle's orders. The prolonged public display of al-Maslūkh, "The Flayed One," as al-Mutawakkil's straw-stuffed skin came to be known, vividly exemplifies the phenomenon of the state's public exercise of exemplary violence in early modern Morocco while simultaneously manipulating corporeally based knowledge.[1] Before being desecrated, al-Mutawakkil's corpse is recovered from the waters of Wādī al-Makhāzin, across which he had tried to flee when it became clear that his and Sebastian's allied forces would lose. He and his companions, who, according to Moroccan narrators, included the Portuguese king, drown in their flight. As al-Manṣūr's forces sort through the corpses of those fallen on the battlefield, they recover these two bodies from the river and take measures to identify and take charge of them.

The preceding chapters have grappled with how narrators deal with corpses from positions of weakness or incapacity: Mendonça falls back on naming the dead to cobble together proof of his own and his companions' bravery, even as Valencia desperately covers up of 'Abd al-Malik's inconvenient death. Meanwhile, Leitão exposes his scarred leg and head to his reader as abject proof of his story's credibility and Silva desperately brings himself in close proximity with a months-old royal corpse in hopes of appropriating some of its epistemological power. However, the composition of the text of al-Maslūkh's flayed skin from al-Mutawakkil's desecrated body emerges from al-Manṣūr's newly attained position of dominance and power, and thus it opens up a wider array of creative possibilities for how to manipulate and represent this corpse, using its fleshly remains as a medium of expression.

The treatment of al-Mutawakkil's corpse is a case of what anthropologists call "necroviolence," a term coined by Jason De León that refers to the hostile defilement, division, disappearance, or other violent manipulations of human remains.[2] Such practices capitalize on beliefs about the link between the material dead body, bodily dispositions, and moral, social, and religious identity.[3] The public exercise of such violence communicates lasting messages with "a text whose support is the body" about the ultimate fate, social and spiritual, of those subjected to it.[4] By refusing to ask *who*? and instead asking *what is the corpse*?, necroviolence strategically generates a grammar of the corpse that makes it exclusively the object of other agents' transitive activity. Corpse desecration is a process that morally and semantically erases the subjectivity of its victims and then justifies itself by generating what in affect theory is termed an *object of threat*, an invisible but ever looming menace whose future peril justifies preemptive action against it in the present.[5]

The necroviolence directed toward al-Mutawakkil's corpse successfully creates a controlled corporeal text designed to be read as an object, rather than an unruly subject. Passive, mediated, and active necroviolence to explore how these practices move a corpse from vibrant matter to violently managed object, from subject to object. The passive and mediated forms are a manifestation of biopower that disrupts narrative by obscuring culpable actors and preventing survivors from progressing through the grieving process by generating complete accounts of the victim's death.[6] In contrast, the active form not only makes its agents visible but actually empowers those agents to reproduce and reappraise the corpse as object and justifies their actions as preemptively neutralizing a future menace. Active necroviolence makes its agent visible and empowers them to erase all subjectivity from the corpse. The flayed skin is left as an emptied-out referent, an immediate textual object that indexes the dynamic object of threat that moves perpetually out of sight but just on the horizon, menacing.

As we will see, these corpse-centered actions operate as creative necroepistemology in two versions of the story. Our primary focus is on the *Tārīkh al-dawla al-Saʿdiyya al-Takmadārtiyya*, one of the major chronicles of the Saʿdīs, the Moroccan dynasty whose internal dispute led to al-Qasr al-Kabir. This episode is taken up and transmitted in a later chronicle: Muḥammad al-Ṣaghīr ibn al-Ḥajj al-Ifrānī's *Nuzhat al-ḥādī bi akhbār mulūk al-qarn al-ḥādī* (A Stroll through the Leaders and Chronicles of the Kings of the Last Century) (first quarter of the eighteenth century). Necroviolence is a deliberate erasure of the subject and transformation of the corpse into an object of threat that must, by the same logic, be converted into propagandistic text and then promulgated as a message through dismemberment or destruction. The public flaying of al-Mutawakkil by the new Saʿdī monarch marks him as a pariah in al-Manṣūr's reconstituted kingdom, but more important, does critical narrative work by composing it as a well-controlled textual object. The careful management of al-Mutawakkil's corpse from the moment of its discovery in the waters of the river through its disgrace before the citizens of Marrakesh does more, however, than simply mark him as an outsider. Ultimately, the desecration of this body strategically creates a public text from the mutilated cadaver that tightly manages the story of al-Mutawakkil's defeat, like those that irrupted into the gaping void left by Sebastian's disappearing body.

The Texts

While the obsessive Portuguese contemplation of the Battle of Wādī al-Makhāzin was not matched on the southern edge of the Western Mediterranean, the event nevertheless garnered significant notice by the major Moroccan chroniclers and intellectuals of several generations. For some, Wādī al-Makhāzin was the defining movement not just for the reigns of ʿAbd al-Malik and al-Manṣūr, but for the entire Saʿdī dynasty. During the reign of Aḥmad al-Manṣūr's grandson, Muḥammad Shaykh al-Aṣghār (r. 1636–55), an unidentified Fezzi scholar wrote *Tārīkh al-dawla al-saʿdiyya al-takmadārtiyya* (Chronicle of the Takmadartī Saʿdī Dynasty), which recounts the major events of the dynasty, dedicating a significant portion of the text to Wādī al-Makhāzin.[7] *Tārīkh al-dawla* has received some attention as a minor historical source from scholars interested in establishing the ideological agenda of the Saʿdī dynasty and the contemporary responses to that agenda, but its literary discourse has been neglected, and here I will study the chronicle as a literary artifact.[8]

Tārīkh al-dawla was a key source for al-Ifrānī's definitive chronicle of the Saʿdī dynasty, *Nuzhat al-ḥādī*, and itself drew on some of the most important earlier annals of the dynasty, including ʿAbd al-Azīz al-Fishtālī's *Manāhil al-ṣafā fī-akhbār al-shurafā'* (Clear Fountains of Chronicles of the Sharīfs) (before 1621) and Aḥmad ibn Muḥammad Ibn al-Qāḍī's (1552–1616) *al-Muntaqā al-maqṣūr ʿalā ma'athir al-khilāfat Abī al-ʿAbbās al-*Manṣūr (Limited Selection of the Legacy of the Caliphate of Abu Abbas al-Manṣūr) (ca. 1587–90). It stands out from the three other major chronicles for its frank and generally negative appraisal of the Saʿdīs, unlike al-Fishtālī's and Ibn al-Qāḍī's panegyric chronicles, which were commissioned by al-Manṣūr to combat Ottoman ideological attacks on the independent Moroccan state.[9] The chronicle condemns the Saʿdīs for failing to wage jihad, a critique also levied at their predecessors, the Waṭṭāsids.[10] Of particular interest is the detailed account of Wādī al-Makhāzin that makes up the bulk of its pages. The anonymous historian also implicitly rejects al-Manṣūr's claims to the caliphate, reserving the caliphal title of "Commander of the Faithful" for the Ottoman sultan and avoiding this honorific when he refers to any of the Saʿdī sultans.[11] Evariste Lévi-Provençal argues that this is the chronicler's strongest ideological blow against the Saʿdīs, as it represents a broader rejection of Saʿdī legitimacy, which was predicated on their *sharīfi* status.[12] As a member of the Fezzi ulama, the anonymous chronicler was not likely to view the dynasty in a favorable light for historical and geographical reasons, not least because of abuses the city suffered at the hands of certain leaders of the dynasty.[13] Evidence for this can be found in the vitriol the anonymous historian directs toward one of the earlier rulers, Muḥammad al-Shaykh al-Mahdī (r. 1524–44 in Marrakesh, 1549–57 all Morocco), and toward al-Manṣūr's son, Muḥammad al-Shaykh al-Ma'mūn (r. 1613–24), who distinguished himself as governor of Fez by oppressing the city's ulama in the final quarter of the seventeenth century. Nevertheless, the chronicler is less critical of al-Manṣūr and gives him credit for the economic prosperity the sultan brought to Morocco, in large measure through ransoming Christian captives taken at Wādi al-Makhāzin.[14]

There are three editions of *Tārīkh al-dawla*. The earliest publication came in French translation (1924), by Edmond Fagnan, of a manuscript copy of the chronicle in the Bibliothèque Nationale in Paris as "Sur la dynastie Saʿdienne," and was followed by an edition by Georges S. Colin of a manuscript of the chronicle held by the Biblioteca Nacional in Madrid and published as the *Chronique anonyme de la dynastie Saʿdienne* (1934). In 1994, ʿAbd al-Raḥīm Benḥādda published an edition of *Tārīkh al-dawla al-Saʿdiyya al-Takmadārtiyya* that more closely hews to the BNF manuscript that Fagnan translated but also endeavors to incorporate some of the differences of the BNF manuscript, as well as two manuscripts held by the Bibliothèque Nationale du Royaume du Maroc.[15] This chapter relies on Benḥādda's edition because of his philological thoroughness but occasionally cites passages from Colin's edition where the Paris manuscript gives more detail about a given moment.[16]

Al-Ifrānī's history, meanwhile, would eventually supplant both the anonymous chronicle and al-Fishtālī's *Manāhil al-ṣafā* as the most widely referenced history of the dynasty, because it is easier to read than al-Fishtālī's work and more readily available than *Tārīkh al-dawla*. Hunwick wryly notes that al-Fishtālī is "difficult to work with, being written in the pompous ornate style of the belle-lettrist and designed to flatter the vanity of al-Fishtālī's royal patron."[17] One of *Nuzhat al-ḥādī*'s roles in Moroccan history was to distill al-Fishtālī's arcane panegyric into more accessible, lucid language. Its translation into French by Octave Houdas in 1888–89 made *Nuzhat al-ḥādī* one of the chronicles of early modern Moroccan history that was most widely disseminated among European Orientalist scholars of the late nineteenth and early twentieth centuries. Like the anonymous Saʿdī chronicle, *Nuzhat al-ḥādī* has principally been treated by historians of the Maghreb and sub-Saharan West Africa as a source for reconstructing political and military events, tracing chains of transmission and authority through intellectual networks, or discerning Alawite attitudes toward their Sadi predecessors' policies, architecture, and leadership style.[18]

Mercedes García-Arenal reminds readers of both *Tārīkh al-dawla* and *Nuzhat al- ḥādī* to bear in mind the literary conventions dictating the portrayal of powerful figures. Thus, she emphasizes the extent to which literature and life were mutually imbricated—just as their chroniclers styled representations of rulers after preexisting models, so did rulers use the same literary precursors as prototypes for how power could and should be exercised.[19] García-Arenal's emphasis on the intersection of power and literature in the *Tārīkh al-dawla* highlights the need for a more nuanced understanding of the chronicle as a text whose conformity to and deviation from such conventions indicates not just its ideological stance vis-à-vis the Saʿdīs but also an awareness of the rhetorical power to be derived from manipulating them. The epistemological underpinnings of such rhetoric are of most interest, regardless of the extent to which the text transmits reliable fact; by treating *Tārīkh al-dawla* and *Nuzhat al-ḥādī* as the objects of literary rather than historical analysis, these chronicles can be analyzed as *adab*, which can be defined broadly as "the literary areas . . . belong[ing] to the domains of the secretaries (*kuttūb*), the poets, philologists, and the ulama."[20] The chronicling author would have been expected to avail himself of the full range of rhetorical and oratorical devices in order to accomplish his ideological purposes and demonstrate his own erudition; those deployed in the *Tārīkh al-dawla* have gone largely neglected.[21]

Necroviolence

Corpse desecration, disappearance, mutilation, and other related practices are among the corpse-centered activities that most disturb the living. Such ritualized and violent forms of disrespect toward the dead violate social taboos and invite widespread censure and approbation. Anthropologist Jason De León coins the term necroviolence to describe "violence performed and produced through the specific treatment of corpses that is perceived to be offensive, sacrilegious, or inhumane by the perpetrator, the victim (and his or her cultural group), or both."[22] Despite this shared horror of corpse abuse, it also comprises a category of behavior toward the dead that has been observed, represented, and studied transhistorically in both historical and literary contexts as diverse as the *Iliad*, the Hebrew Bible, the Ottoman Empire, the early modern French penal system, Nazi Germany, and the present-day US-Mexico border, to name only a few.[23] The scholar who narrows her focus to the premodern Mediterranean is still spoiled for choice of examples of necroviolence, as the cases mentioned throughout this section will illustrate.[24] The forms it takes and the reasons for which it is deployed are as diverse as the contexts in which it is found.

A vector of necroviolence can be directed toward the living: deterring behavior, demonstrating military might, or inflicting psychic pain on survivors. It is most frequently directed at the dead themselves, however, and aims to deny them burial rites, impede their passage to an afterlife, or continue punishment and humiliation after death. Although images of corpse desecration can invoke images of uncontrolled violence—a rampaging Achilles who hurls insults and stones in equal measure at Hector's exposed body—the scholarly literature indicates that such impetuous aggression is not the only nor the most interesting manifestation of these practices.[25] As with other kinds of ritual violence, some of the more powerful and interesting cases arise are when these actions are purposeful and strategic.[26]

At its core, necroviolence arises from the exercise of power and germinates alongside other techniques that regulate and discipline human bodies across society. The term thus invokes Achille Mbembe's idea of *necropolitics*, which interrogates Foucault's concept of biopower for its tendency to paint all forms of violence with the same brush.[27] Mbembe calls for a closer look at the state's power over life and death, highlighting the instantiation of biopower in the exercise of sovereignty that controls the living by wielding death. In other words, necropolitics is when the sovereign state exercises and demonstrates its power through its authority to kill people.[28] Here, Mbembe's use of the prefix "necro-" is slightly misleading, in that the thrust of his concept is still aimed at the living: the living are killed to manipulate the behavior of those left behind. It is here that a growing number of scholars have stepped in to continue to theorize the fate of the dead after the moment of death.[29] Deborah Posel and Pamela Gupta point out that necropolitics continues postmortem as dead populations are disciplined to further consolidate power and shape modern biopolitics.[30] Consistent with disciplinary agendas, much of the work that considers the role of the dead in cultural, economic, and sociopolitical terms asks what happens to a population at large when sovereign power acts on corpses.[31] Less carefully considered, however, has been the literary and textual valences of that violence: What happens to knowledge and its transmission through the corpse itself under those circumstances, and how does this violence manifest in and as language?

Necroviolence in its passive or mediated state is identifiable by what it disrupts: care for the dead in accordance with social norms and expectations for a good death.[32] It can be perpetrated by individuals, groups, institutions, or states, but many of these perpetrators rely on similar techniques. Under a regime of passive necroviolence, survivors might struggle to access the recently deceased person's body to prepare it for burial, enact mourning rituals, or even identify it. Impeding such care for the dead, which can reflect their social or political status, denies the humanity of that individual or their community more broadly.[33] All of these actions can have ramifications for the dead person's afterlife, their community, and posthumous processes like transitions of power that depend upon a positively identified body. Imposing an intermediate agent like time, environment, or scavenging animals can obfuscate how someone died, whose body has been desecrated, or even that they died at all.[34] The silence and erasure such mediation imposes have consequences for the creation of history and what stories can be narrated in the aftermath of the violence.[35] If no one person can be blamed for the corpse desecration, such cases can allow blame to revert back to the victim himself or his community, shielding culpable parties behind ambiguity and trapping survivors in an ambivalent state.[36] Grammatically speaking, it is only half the story—it gives us the corpse as object without a guilty subject to take responsibility for that objectification.

While necroviolence can be mediated or left to passive processes, active, deliberate violence on the dead human body makes up a dramatic and significant subset of this phenomenon. These spectacular actions can include exposing or displaying naked bodies, severing and separately displaying their body parts, permanently dismembering their body, or burying them in unconsecrated ground. Active corpse desecration departs from its passive and mediated variants because, rather than shield culpable parties from the shame of their actions, it embraces the shock value of corpse desecration and takes full advantage of the strong reactions it provokes. It thus most decisively demonstrates its perpetrators' biopower over the living and the dead: they can kill at will and their power is so undisputed that they can also do what they wish with the resulting corpses.[37] If passive or mediated desecration speaks to the impotence of the dead person or their community, active necroviolence clearly makes additional statements about the power of the perpetrators: they deny the dead membership in their community, signal a change of leadership, terrorize defeated populations into submission, or punish beyond death.[38] The public display of body parts like heads and skins, if properly contextualized, enables the public to identify certain powerful bodies and attest to their death.[39]

These gruesome displays activate multiple categories of disgust as an affective response: manipulated dead bodies are made into viscerally repugnant objects that provoke "core" or "material" disgust and are marked as morally contaminated objects whose transgressions warrant their expulsion from the boundaries of the community.[40] Grammatically, that power is exerted by parties who take responsibility for these atrocities on corpses that have been violently and definitively classified as objects. Understood in terms of Peircian semiotics, necroviolence justifies its actions on the *immediate object*—the object as it stands at a given point in a semiotic process—by conflating the immediate with the *dynamic object*, the object of the sign at the end of a semiotic process.[41] Desecrated corpses are converted into objects of disgust, subhuman, inanimate, animalistic, and utterly repugnant. The process of objectifying and dehumanizing these corpses serves to justify this brutality in ethical terms.

Turning to the vocabulary of affect theory, necroviolence produces an *object of threat* that invited its own desecration. An object of threat invites precautionary violence in the present because a terrible future can be read in it. This sense of foreshadowing of emerging but unfulfilled danger justifies preemptive action, regardless of the "actual facts" that emerge in the aftermath of that action. Preemptively responding to a threat requires us to imagine the future and presently unknowable outcome of a series of events that, if we act appropriately, will never come to pass.[42] This cyclical, nonlinear temporality can also be understood semiotically. The immediate object that is eliminated in the present stands at an evolving, emerging point in the semiotic process. As an index, it refers back to past events that have led to its existence in the present, and it also points to the unrealized threat in the future. And yet, because it relies on the menace of the future threat to justify itself, the object of threat can never fully annihilate all traces of the immediate object. In transforming the immediate object into a new manifestation of itself, the new immediate object retains residues of its past self that warranted the preemptive action in the first place and points to a new or yet more distant dynamic object in the future. By redirecting the observer's attention toward the threatening future, agents of necroviolence exploit the complex signification of the desecrated corpse in the present to explain, justify, or otherwise obfuscate ethical culpability.

Necroviolence, whether active, mediated, or passive, ultimately works on behalf of a regime that produces its own objects of threat in enemy corpses and then neutralizes them. Chapter 3 theorized the power of the corpse as vital matter—the tendency of corpses to retain agency and subjectivity after the moment of death and to make things happen. The success of body mistreatment as strategy is the other side of this coin. The lingering subjectivity of a corpse, its potential efficacy as an actant in the world is shaped into a self-renewing, foreshadowed future threat that perpetrators of necroviolence recognize and neutralize. It is a mechanism that devastatingly objectifies the peril of the reawakened, agentive dead body. Its brutal processes can most productively be read as a response to the final question of this book: *What is the corpse?* Formulating the question as *what?* rather than *who?* takes for granted the erasure of subjectivity that this treatment perpetrates and relies on to justify itself. When the corpse can be indelibly rewritten back into the discourse of authority as the object of threat, it inscribes its own annihilation at the hands of power.

Recovering Royal Remains

When we consider the management of al-Mutawakkil's corpse from its discovery after the battle, the building blocks of its destruction can be discerned early. Al-Mutawakkil dead warrants greater cause for concern than he did while alive. While ʿAbd al-Malik and Sebastian garner the lion's share of the chronicler's attention in his report of the battle itself, al-Mutawakkil figures primarily in terms of his relationships to other actors. Nevertheless, the careful management of his corpse from the final moments of the battle immediately identifies this corpse as a potential object of threat to the stability of al-Manṣūr's new regime. Although in some ways the recovery of al-Mutawakkil's corpse abides by normative death rituals, his retrieval from his watery grave reveals him and constructs his remains as pointing to a potential threat that must be contained. When experts recuperate that corpse, they ensure that no piece of him can go unaccounted as a first step in the process of necroviolence.

Unlike some of the cases of passive corporeal mistreatment that De León describes, in which corpses are subjected to the natural taphonomic processes of the desert, the active necroviolence depicted in the *Tārīkh* diverges from normative corpse care soon after the moment of al-Mutawakkil's death.[43] This temporal delay leaves open other possible endings in which al-Manṣūr could have buried his nephew with honor, and the rupture with those conventions of the good death retroactively classifies the deposed king's body as an object of threat. And yet, the felt reality of the threat this body poses forecloses those possibilities. The process by which al-Mutawakkil's body is recovered from Wādī al-Makhāzin anticipates that process by which it is flayed and composed as an object of threat, and so the incipient processes of care for the corpse resonate with impending violence. The operative logic of necroviolence ultimately imbues the episode with "powers of self-causation."[44]

Al-Mutawakkil is found drowned in the river alongside his ally, having failed to ford it while trying to retreat once their defeat became evident: "wa-ammā mawlāy muḥammadun wa-l-sulṭānu al-naṣārā wajadūhumā (kadhā) al-ʿawwāmūna bi-l-ghawṣi bi-l-mawḍʿi alladhī bi-izāʾi al-qanṭarati wa-akhrajūhum [And with respect to Mulay Muḥammad and the king of the Christians, swimmers discovered both of them by diving in the water in the place that was facing the bridge, and took them out.]"[45] In contrast with the Portuguese sources, which recount that Sebastian dies in battle after foolishly plunging back into the breach, this source instead tells of an ignominious death marked by retreat and incompetence.[46] The discovery of these drowned royal bodies is not happenstance. The skills of specialists, *ʿawwāmūna bi-l-ghawṣ*, literally "swimmers good at diving," are enlisted to find, identify, and extract these royal corpses from a particular place. From the perspective of the anonymous Moroccan chronicler, the priority is the access of the appropriate people to those bodies, their positions both at the moment of discovery and of burial, and how they are handled. Mendonça and Leitão relate that the royal bodies are uncovered and distinguished from piles of other bodies by men intimately familiar with the identity or body of the king. In contrast, the anonymous chronicler shows that they are found unattended in their watery grave and pulled out by those skilled at looking for something in a particular environment.

The identity of the royal corpses is taken for granted; at issue at this moment in the text is the specificity of the place in which they are found. Of paramount importance to the anonymous chronicler's description of the finding of these royal bodies is their position. The divers find al-Mutawakkil and Sebastian in an individual and specified place: "Bi-l-mawḍʿi alladhī bi-izāʾi al-qanṭarati" (the part of the river that faces the bridge). The term *al-mawḍaʿ*,

or location, becomes important in the passage that immediately follows, in which the chronicler describes the manner in which these corpses are treated in burial. In this first passage of discovery, however, the term refers to the place in which they are found as unmistakable and unique—"al-mawḍaʿi alladhī bāzāʾu" (the place, that which faces). The narrator uses not an indefinite noun—*mawḍaʿan*, a place—but a definite article, *al-*, followed by a demonstrative pronoun, *alladhī* (that which), which further refines the absolute specificity of the expression. The corpses' location is most important and well known.

Absent the preemptive logic of an object of threat, documenting this body's position could be read in terms of location-specific customs that structured the treatment and burial of the dead body throughout the Islamic world. Attention to a corpse's position is a transhistorically consistent feature of Islamic burial practice that distinguishes Muslim graves from those of different religious groups.[47] Normative burial practices read significance into the direction bodies faced and dictate that bodies be buried facing *qibla* (*tawjīh al-mayyit*).[48] Furthermore, knowledge of the place of someone's death in some Islamic contexts was, and continues to be, related to a concern for rapidly interring a corpse.[49] Care to ensure a quick burial in part relates to what happens to the soul in the days following death, a period referred to as *sabiʿa*, or the seven days in which the corpse is interrogated by angels, Munkār and Nakīr, and required to prove that he or she is a true Muslim, a process referred to as *fitnat al-qabr* (trial of the grave).[50] A timely burial, which in modern Islam has been formalized as a twenty-four-hour period, also carried geographical implications: "Islamic tombs mark a time and a place, like a threshold object signifying the person's transition from life through death to the life beyond, especially since Islamic custom encouraged the dead to be buried on the spot where they died."[51] Read as part of a ritual of intercession, recording the place and circumstances of a person's death might document the particular site at which al-Mutawakkil's soul was subjected to interrogation and punishments of the grave, and signal to living visitors to that place where they could intercede actively with God in favor of the deceased.[52] The one exception to the injunction for a rapid burial as dictated by the major jurists, including Mālik and al-Shāfiʿī, is drowning. In such a case, Ibn Rushd remarks that "delay in burying him is recommended (in the [Mālikī] School) for fear that he might still be alive and that excessive water in his body may have made signs of life in him less obvious."[53] The chronicler documents the exact location of Sebastian's and al-Mutawakkil's bodies, which might simply indicate an interest in the precise, watery location at which these two people crossed the threshold between life and death.

This doctrinally focused reading begins to fall apart, however, when we consider that the corpse of al-Mutawakkil is not buried where it was found, but instead is subjected to violent partition and a translation of nearly 310 miles (500 km) to the southwest. Despite some parallels between these religious and legal expectations and how the two royal cadavers are treated, they do not fully account for what the chronicler chooses to convey in this passage. He displays no concern for whether the drowned bodies of al-Mutawakkil and Sebastian could still show signs of life, as recommended by Ibn Rushd, but rather narrates the immediate containment and control of those bodies. The importance of this site and the explanation for the delay in burying al-Mutawakkil seems to do with more terrestrial concerns. If, rather than attempt to fully account for al-Mutawakkil's flaying on strictly legal or eschatological terms, we instead consider the epistemological power of this corpse, the information the chronicler provides his reader begins to snap more clearly into focus.

Another account of the moment of discovery in al-Ifrānī's *Nuzhat al-ḥādī* supports reading this moment in terms of the logic of an object of threat. Al-Ifrānī elaborates on the account offered in the anonymous chronicle and recounts that, in addition to Sebastian and al-Mutawakkil, a third body was found among al-Manṣūr's enemies in the waters of Wādī al-Makhāzin: that of Abū ʿAbdullah ibn ʿAskar, a Moroccan historian and intellectual who had accompanied al-Maslūkh on his retreat:

> wa-mimman wujida fī al-qatlā ʾabū ʿabdi llāhi bin ʿaskar ṣahibu dawḥati al-nāshiri fa-ʾinnahu ḥariba maʿa al-maslūkhi wa-kāna min biṭānatihi wa-dakhala maʿahu bilāda al-rūmi fa-wujida mayyitan bayna qatlā al-naṣārā ṣarīʿan wa-takallama al-nāsu fī ʾamrihi ḥattā qīla ʾinnahu wujida ʿalā shimālihi mustadaraban li-l-qiblati.[54]

> Among the dead was also found Abū ʿAbdullah ibn ʿAskar, author of *Dawḥat al-nāshir.* He had accompanied the Flayed One (al-Maslūkh) in his flight and had gone with him to Christian lands in the capacity of a courtier. His cadaver lay amidst those of the Christians. About this have been recounted different things, among which is that his body had been found lying on its left side, with its back turned to *qibla.*

The disposition of the corpse anticipates the future preemptive action that should and will be taken against these corpses. As in the anonymous chronicler's account, al-Ifrānī describes in detail the three-dimensional spatial arrangement of Ibn ʿAskar's body: it was found lying on its left side, among nonbelievers, and, most damningly, with its back to *qibla.*[55] This position facing away from *qibla*, the orienting axis around which Muslim piety revolves, means that he was always already damned. His body rejects a salvific orientation, literally turning its back on the Muslim faith, anticipating the soul's condemnation in the afterlife.[56] Alongside this condemned body is also found al-Mutawakkil's, whose own fate is foreshadowed onomastically: al-Ifrānī uses the epithet "al-Maslūkh" to refer to al-Mutawakkil before his death, linguistically anticipating the eventual flaying that forecasts his corpse's eventual desecration. His courtier's body's physical disposition also anticipates his master's eventual embodied, public condemnation. Al-Manṣūr did not simply deny him Muslim burial out of cruelty but preemptively removed the threat posed by an unruly corpse that had already damned itself by collaborating with the enemy.

The chronicler identifies the first witnesses of the dead bodies: the swimmers are explicitly identified as the subject of the verb *wajada*, to find. The unique skill set of these divers qualifies them to speak to the manner in which the royal corpses were disposed at the moment in which they are found. These are not just skilled swimmers—the term *ʿawwāmūna* can specifically refer to people who are accomplished in navigating the surface of the water two-dimensionally—but *ʿawwāmūna bi-l-ghawṣ*, swimmers skilled at venturing beneath the surface of the water, and thus witnesses particularly adept at understanding the position of a body three-dimensionally within the water. In declaring the specialized skill set of the first witnesses of these royal corpses, the chronicler establishes the expertise undergirding the information he transmits about these corpses. The specificity with which he narrates the discovery of the bodies effectively communicates a line of corporeal custody from the river to the divers to those whom al-Manṣūr subsequently orders to flay the skin from al-Mutawakkil's corpse. Tracking the hands through which these two important bodies passed crisply focuses the reader's attention on the reliability and authority of the chronicler's information.

Beyond logging the expert witnesses to the royal corpses, the chronicler also leaves no doubt as to whose bodies were recovered. This comes in stark contrast with the Portuguese chroniclers, who concede varying and sometimes substantial degrees of equivocation about the identity of Sebastian's body after it has been extracted from the unidentified masses of rotting flesh with which these latter chroniclers report it lay. As we have seen, this confusion among the first witnesses of this royal dead body fosters uncertainty in narrating and authorizing this critical moment. Here, no such doubt nor disorder is permitted. With his use of a dual pronoun (*humā*), the chronicler precisely indicates that these were the only two bodies recovered by the divers in the river: "wa-ammā mawlāy muḥammadun wa-l-sulṭānu al-naṣārā wajadūhumā (kadhā) al-ʿawwāmūna bi-l-ghawṣi bi-l-mawḍʿi alladhī bi-izāʾi al-qanṭarati wa-akhrajūhum [With respect to Mulay Muḥammad and the Christian king, swimmers discovered *both of them* by diving]."[57] The divers' recovery of these important remains was targeted, professional, and meticulous. Correspondingly, the account of the discovery of al-Mutawakkil's and Sebastian's bodies beneath the bridge—the same bridge that ʿAbd al-Malik so presciently had his soldiers destroy the night before the battle—reflects an interest in geographical specificity that resonates with but surpasses the aforementioned Maliki norms regarding the treatment of corpses.[58] As shown before, the recorded location of where these two specific bodies were found is precise almost to the point of being reproducible if some doubting person wished to check. Such precise documentation of the place in the river does not lead to their burial in this place, as we might expect given the doctrine on this point, but instead indicates the chronicler's concern for establishing a clear chain of custody for these important bodies.

After the battle, the chronicler focuses on the potentially disruptive power of this corpse by relaying how al-Mutawakkil's dead body is managed, identified, and contained. Specialists are sent out to find out where those bodies are, what state they are in, and how they can be efficiently recovered and interred. The chronicler's preoccupation with the particularities of who should find and deal with these royal corpses, and the state in which those corpses are discovered does track with broader cultural concerns with the normative treatment of the dead, but in the context of this body's posthumous desecration must also be read as the careful handling of a possible threat. Al-Manṣūr and his supporters are thus able to manage the narrative about them that subsequently will be transmitted to future generations.

The Flayed One

Corpses have a lingering capacity to act as subjects and to act in cooperation with other entities well after the moment of death. Given the power of the corpse to signify, generate community, or act as a repository for independent narratives, that capacity represents a threat to those for who would prefer that the dead person's demise represent a clean break or rupture with the past. For al-Manṣūr and his allies, the deaths of both competing sultans at Wādī al-Makhāzin cleared space for a new kingdom united under al-Manṣūr's leadership, much as the death of Sebastian opened up the possibility of an Iberian Union under Philip II's leadership. As seen in the preceding chapters, however, Philip's hopes for a united Iberian kingdom were undermined by the uncertain fate of his nephew's body, which led to rampant speculation that someday

Sebastian might return to restore Portugal's independence. As victor, al-Manṣūr had no intention of allowing such a disruptive force undermine his claims to power. Ordering that his nephew's body be flayed allows him to decisively demonstrates his political power and attempt to cut off any challenges that might take root in his rival's unruly body.

Immediately after recounting the discovery of al-Mutawakkil's and Sebastian's bodies in the waters of Wādī al-Makhāzin, the chronicler describes how al-Manṣūr orders the public desecration and careful disposal of al-Mutawakkil's remains:

> Fa-amara al-sulṭānu mawlā aḥmadu bi-salkhi jildi ibni akhīhi mawlā muḥammadin wa-ḥashwihi tibnan wa-arsalahu ilā murrakashi fa-ṭuyyifa bihi bihā li-yuʿāyanahu al-nāsuʿalā tilka al-ḥālati wa-dufinat juththatuhu wa dufina man māta miman kāna maʿahu min ʿuṣāti al-muslimīna wa-dufina sulṭānu al-naṣāriyyi bi-mawḍiʿin muʿayyanin li-yaʿrifa ʿinda al-iḥtiyāji ilayhi.[59]

> The Sultan, Mulay Aḥmad, ordered that the skin of his nephew, Mulay Muḥammad, be flayed and stuffed with straw. And he sent it to Marrakesh, and had it circumambulated around the city so that people would have to face it in that state, and they did take a warning from it. The rest of al-Mutawakkil's corpse was buried, as were those belonging to the disobedient Muslims who died alongside him, and the Christian king was also buried in a particular place so that it would be known whenever there was a need for it.

Initially, the purpose of this public act of desecration would seem obvious: dividing the dead body into parts denies al-Mutawakkil ritual incorporation into a diachronic community, validation as a true believer or even human.[60] The central necroviolent action—represented by the verbal noun *salkh* (flaying), verb *salakha* (to flay), and passive participle *maslūkh* (flayed one)—is not lexically specific to humans. Rather, it is most commonly used to describe actions directed toward goats or sheep. To recall the terminology of chapter 3, the transitive verb *salkh* most frequently operates on targets of subhuman animacy. In contrast, al-Manṣūr emerges as an active participant in these proceedings. He takes a personal and active interest in the fate of his nephew's body—the command for the flaying and subsequent display in Marrakesh comes directly from him. The juxtaposition of the taboo act of corpse abuse and the foregrounding of al-Manṣūr's familial relationship with al-Mutawakkil compounds the enormity of this act; this violence is not impulsive or irrational, but deliberate and strategic.[61] Unlike flaying as an element of butchering, however, here the goal is not the production of a food item, but rather the humiliating process itself and the textualization of skin whose public display employs a rhetoric of social order and exemplary punishment. The process of objectifying al-Mutawakkil as al-Maslūkh, of transforming *him* into *it* exemplifies the process of necroviolence not just in terms of the exercise of political power, which it does, but also in grammatical terms. The reduction of a corpse to a *what?* is a necessary part of the process of necroviolence.

Al-Maslūkh is objectified in the very grammar of its representation on the page of the chronicle. The originating agent who enacts necroviolence is clearly designated as al-Manṣūr, who is the only subject of the key verbs that recount the flaying and public humiliation of al-Maslūkh: *amara* (he ordered that) and *arsala* (he sent). Even the action of flaying, conveyed as a verbal noun (*maṣdar*) *salkh* (the flaying), retains al-Manṣūr as the effective subject of the sentence, instead of identifying a new subject who carries out that flaying. The action of this verbal phrase ultimately reaches al-Mutawakkil through a series of possessive relationships that buries him deep in a construct phrase: "the flaying of the skin of the son of his brother." This series of genitive relationships has the effect of imposing distance between al-Manṣūr as actor and the ultimate object of his actions: the son of his brother. It deeply embeds that dead subject *as object* in the background, grammatically bracketed in the margins.[62]

Al-Maslūkh is also rendered grammatically as an object following his flaying: the grammatical construction of his name (*al-maslūkh*, that which was flayed) is the *ism al-maf'ūl* (passive participle) of the dehumanizing action of the verb (*salakha*, he flayed) that composed him as a dehumanized object. Portraying this body as a passive participle emphatically completes of the process of converting the cadaver into a textual object. This textual object becomes mobile, but, unlike Sebastian's corpse in chapter 3, it does not move under its own steam; it is consistently acted upon by passive verbs—*ṭuyyifa* (it was circulated around the city); *dufinat juththatuhu* (his corpse was buried). In these cases, as the object of the passive verb (in Arabic, *al-maf'ūl alladhī lam yusamma fā'iluhu*; the patient whereof the agent has not been named), al-Maslūkh's objectification is confirmed verbally.[63] Thus, this corpse is not just represented as a textual object whose skin reports its own creation and speaks of the threat it once posed but is persistently rendered as object within the interstitial grammar of the text. The violence of al-Manṣūr's actions, which denies al-Mutawakkil's very humanity, is possible because of that grammatical distance.

If the language that portrays his body's desecration curtails al-Mutawakkil's privileges as a human, that linguistic objectification is expanded and condoned by the legal implications of his actions while he was still alive. Al-Mutawakkil's status in his community is complicated by his alliance with the Portuguese and Spanish against other Muslims.[64] How and why certain members of the Muslim community would be disavowed or excluded from the community for collaborating with non-Muslims was a major legal question for Muslim scholars during the sixteenth and seventeenth centuries, particularly in those jurisdictions adjacent to Portuguese and Spanish presidios along the Mediterranean and Atlantic littoral.[65] Some prominent Maghrebi jurists maintained a hard-line position that those Muslims who chose to remain under Christian dominion in proximity to Muslim lands were apostate.[66] Religious and political leaders, in particular, were held to a higher standard for their economic and political interactions with Christians, are censured for committing apostasy, and, under some circumstances, may be seen as forfeiting their lives and property for that collaboration.[67] By this standard, al-Mutawakkil would have been considered an apostate, a legal status similar to that of a nonbelieving aggressor, a position that would have had consequences for his corpse's treatment.

Notwithstanding al-Mutawakkil's effective apostasy through his alliance with Christians against Muslims, prescriptive Māliki law would have frowned upon the mutilation of his body as an acceptable mode of punishment.[68] In his book on *khilāf*, a discipline that scrutinizes differences of opinion among Muslim jurists, *Bidāyat al-mujtahid*, Ibn Rushd (Averröes, 1126–1198) argues that an apostate or non-Muslim body deserves the attention of the believer only if it inconveniently reasserts its presence with its stench. He states that, according to the Mālikī rite at very least, Muslims have no obligation to tend to the corpse of a nonbeliever, not even that of a relative: "About the bathing of a disbeliever by a Muslim, Mālik said that a Muslim is not to bathe a disbelieving father, nor is he to make a grave for him unless he fears the decay of his body, in which case he may bury him." Mālik's position is notably harsher than al-Shāfiʿī's, who, according to Ibn Rushd, suggests that "there is no harm if a Muslim bathes and buries his next of kin who are polytheists."[69] By this standard, then, it would seem that *passive* necroviolence such as abandoning or exposing a disbelieving body is permissible under some circumstances. Even so, in the section regarding rules of jihad, Ibn Rushd clarifies that the absence of responsibility does not extend to permission to disrespect or mutilation (*muthla*) of the body, even if it belongs to a nonbeliever.[70] This is to say, all of the major Muslim legal schools whose thought Ibn Rushd examines—the Mālikī, Shāfiʿī, Ḥanbalī, Ḥanafī, and Ẓāhirī schools—agree that under no circumstances is it acceptable for a victor to commit *active* necroviolence by mutilating the bodies of his enemy, regardless of the actions or beliefs of that enemy. At least by the norms established in the wide set of legal positions reviewed by Ibn Rushd, then, al-Manṣūr's flaying of al-Mutawakkil's corpse falls well beyond any accepted standards for the violation of an enemy's body.

Despite nearly universal condemnation of corpse desecration by the major schools, the fact remains that such practices were widespread in the medieval and early modern Islamic world. Contemporary sources extensively document public violence and corpse abuse in Morocco and the Islamic Mediterranean during the sixteenth century.[71] In both Fez and Marrakesh, a key feature of this spectacle of violent punishment was the practice of *tashhīr* (to make notorious), which consisted of parading criminals throughout the urban landscape to make public their shame and wrongdoing.[72] Lange speculates that rituals of public violence in medieval Islam, rather than worry about injunctions against *muthla*, were in fact deliberately constructed to remind victims and spectators of eschatological imagery. Mediano eloquently argues: "In the course of its exercise of violence, authority creates a discourse: it produces a text whose support is the body. This is a pedagogical discourse: it teaches and, by using indelible marks to do so, becomes part of memory. Its references, its composition, and its allusions become part of a common language, intelligible to all."[73]

In Islamic eschatology, depictions of punishments of the grave abound in graphic representations of bodily torture and suffering in which parts of the body itself—hands, legs, ears, skin—will testify against the hypocritical believer (Q 77:35).[74] These visceral portrayals of embodied pain, fragmentation, and punishment all threaten the hypocritical Muslim with expulsion from the community and shame made legible through their very own body parts. The chilling image of flaying is explicitly invoked by the Quranic description of Judgment Day that serves as this chapter's epigraph, in which sinners' bodies and senses are made to testify against them before hellfire:

> wa-yawma yuḥsharu ʾaʿdāʾu allāhi ʾilā al-nāri fa-hum yūzaʿūna ḥattā ʾidhā mā jāʾūhā shahida ʿalayhim samʿuhum wa-ʾabṣāruhum wa-julūduhum bi-mā kānū yaʿmalūna wa-qālū li-julūdihim lima shahidtum ʿalaynā qālū ʾanṭaqanā allāhu alladhī ʾanṭaqa kulla shayʾin wa-huwa khalaqakum ʾawwala marratin wa-ʾilayhi turjaʿūna (Q 41:19–21)

> One day, God's enemies will be ushered toward the fire, distraught and bewildered. As they approach it, their hearing and vision and skin bears witness against them, revealing what they had been doing. They address their skins, "How can you bear witness against us?" They answer, "God has caused us to speak, as God causes all things to speak for God created you in the first instance and you inevitably revert back to God!"

Here, the body and tools of witnessing themselves become textual objects that bear independent witness against the enemies of God. Lange argues that a key feature of Islamic eschatological suffering is that it is "eminently public": "In the eschatological imagination, the punishments of hell are carried out in the open, they are fully visible to the eye of the beholder." Lange contends that such public ignominy is formulated to demolish the victim's "right not to be slandered and not to have one's sins revealed to the public[, which] is a major concern of Muslim law and ethics." On this argument, that structure not coincidentally mimics Quranic models for exposing and shaming sinners and generates a text on the body of the criminal that is meant to be read and internalized by the audiences witnessing these public rituals. The notoriety produced through such public disgrace and shame is thus an integral feature rather than a side effect of both eschatological imagery and their structurally similar counterparts in public punishment and humiliation.[75]

The language that characterizes al-Maslūkh as subhuman reduces him to an object that does not deserve concern as a full subject, imposing linguistic and ethical distance between his contemptible remains and the righteous ruler who orders their desecration. Although al-Mutawakkil's entitlement to postmortem care in accordance with normative Muslim jurisdiction is called into question by his legal status as an apostate, by the dictates of prescriptive Māliki law, even that diminished legal status does not justify the mutilation of his corpse. Despite what such prescriptive edicts might have said, spectacles of public shaming of criminals, living and dead, were widespread in sixteenth-century Morocco. These spectacles capitalized on well-known Quranic images of bodily torture and suffering to make these criminal bodies testify to their own deserved public dishonor. The contradiction between widespread legal standards and historical practice is thus resolved by the logic created by the punishment itself: the humiliated or desecrated body is rendered subhuman and justifies its own humiliation with the resonances generated between the contours of its punishment and images of divine justice. Al-Manṣūr is thus exonerated for his arguably extralegal treatment of his nephew's corpse, since that treatment merely exercises in the lived world the eschatological fate that awaits this traitor in the afterlife.

Object of Threat

The circumambulation of al-Maslūkh embraces the shock value of corpse desecration to highlight the political and ethical power wielded by those who flayed him. It excludes him from his community and underscores his utter defeat. That flayed skin also does important textual work: providing material upon which a new, unthreatening narrative can be written. A dead body, particularly a politically significant one like al-Mutawakkil's, poses a clear and present narrative danger through its propensity for forming assemblages with other bodies, living and dead. The ritual violence committed against al-Mutawakkil's potent corpse creates a new textual object whose display neutralizes the object of threat in the future and the contained remains in the past to which it refers. Seen through this lens, al-Manṣūr's treatment of his nephew's corpse is an effort to control of all aberrant narratives that could have emerged or could emerge from this royal body and threaten his claim to power.

Returning to the passage that describes al-Mutawakkil's flaying, necroviolence manifests not just as a political and social tool, but as a textual process undergirded by grammatical logic:

> Fa-amara al-sulṭānu mawlā aḥmadu bi-salkh jildi ibni akhīhi mawlā muḥammadin wa-ḥashwihi tibnan wa-arsalahu ilā murrakashi fa-ṭuyyifa bihi bihā li-yuʿāyanahu al-nāsuʿalā tilka al-ḥālati wa-dufinat juththatuhu wa dufina man māta miman kāna maʿahu min ʿuṣāti al-muslimīna wa-dufina sulṭānu al-naṣāriyyi bi-mawḍiʿin muʿayyanin li-yaʿrifa ʿinda l-iḥtiyāji ilayhi.[76]

> The Sultan, Mulay Aḥmad, ordered that the skin of his nephew, Mulay Muḥammad, be flayed and stuffed with straw. And he sent it to Marrakesh, and had it circumambulated around the city so that people would have to face it in that state, and they did take a warning from it. The rest of al-Mutawakkil's corpse was buried, as were those belonging to the disobedient Muslims who died alongside him, and the Christian king was also buried in a particular place so that it would be known whenever there was a need for it.

As seen in Quranic images of Judgment Day, al-Mutawakkil's skin is separated from him and forced to bear witness against him in this world. The flayed skin is circulated as a text to be read and interpreted publicly: "wa-arsalahu ilā murrakashi fa-ṭīfa bihi bihā li-yuʿāyanahu al-nāsuʿalā tilka al-ḥālati [and al-Manṣūr sent it to Marrakesh, and had it circumambulated around the city so that people would have to face it in that state]."[77] The prospect of facing this disgusting object "in that state" conjures a full sensory onslaught of what that experience would entail: the sight of contorted features, stretched orifices or knife wounds distorting its appearance; the stench of rotting flesh not cleaned away; the sounds of flies buzzing nearby. And yet, evasive practices like looking away or plugging the nose and ears are not available because the face-to-flayed-face encounter is mandated—the visceral revulsion this thing provokes is the intended response. That material disgust is intended to map onto and mingle with moral disgust: here is certainly an outcast to be reviled, an object of disgust.[78]

The act of flaying also creates a textual object whose lesson can be read on the material of the flayed skin.[79] A permeable boundary between private and public, self and other, the skin becomes meaningful and legible as a membrane that records incidents of interaction.[80] The power of the skin as a textual object is that it retains those previous moments of dermography, but it also invites present and future interventions.[81] The clearer the remnants of the originating violence are and the more extreme that violence was, the more the resulting textual object reminds the viewer of the threat it posed to warrant its own violent composition. Flaying becomes the preemptive action that diverts the threat an unruly corpse can present and promulgates the message that justifies that violence. This kind of dermography produces skin with latent potentiality for further writing: by promulgating this flayed text, al-Manṣūr labels al-Mutawakkil's corpse as the source of a potential and unspecified future threat and rewrites its story before it can fulfill that potential. He establishes a synechdocal and indexical relationship between the skin and the other bodily remains by fragmenting this potentially unruly corpse and isolating just one piece of it for public consumption. The skin, with a controlled message that condemns al-Mutawakkil, stands for the partitioned whole, and refers to the now-controlled danger that the dead body once posed.

The temporal relationship among these different elements is critical for understanding al-Maslūkh as a threat. The present of this passage is the moment of reading and interpretation—the public apprehends and deciphers the preemptive action against the immediate object, which refers to it as an object of threat. The immediate textual object itself circulates in all its disgusting materiality throughout Marrakesh, serving as a clear and present reminder of the threat that the whole from which it was stripped could have posed. Al-Manṣūr dictates its reception. The assembled citizens of Marrakesh are commanded to and, crucially, do stand in judgment of and learn from the lesson inscribed on al-Mutawakkil's skin. Under al-Manṣūr's orders, this corporeal text has been relocated to the center of his power in Marrakesh specifically so that the people of that place must physically confront it: *li-yuʿāyanahu*, so that they would see it with their own eyes. Not only must they look at the flayed, stuffed body that is to be displayed in a particular way, they must actually learn something from it: *wa-yuʿtabirūna bihi* (and they did consider it). This consideration comes not just at the behest of the sovereign, an imperative that would have been expressed in the subjunctive case: *wa-amara an yuʿtabirū bihi* (and he ordered that they learn a lesson from it). Instead, it comes in the indicative, which demonstrates that not only does al-Manṣūr desire that the people of Marrakesh observe the corpse of al-Mutawakkil, but that they actually do look at it and internalize what it communicates.

Here, al-Manṣūr's mandate contributes to the operative logic of the regime of object of threat. The flayed skin documents the alert that led to its own creation: considering this dehumanized object in the midst of its humiliation dictates that the public interpret it as referring to a neutralized object of threat. Accurate uptake of the lesson by the diegetic audience of the text that al-Manṣūr wishes to publicize is indicated by the chronicler's comment that the audience did, in fact, consider the corporeal text as it was presented, and that from thenceforth al-Mutawakkil became known as al-Maslūkh. The temporal and semiotic significance of this moment are intertwined. The material presence of this immediate textual object is confirmed by the present actions of its observers, whose receptivity to the lesson communicated through the immediate object indicates that they have adopted the logic of the system of an object of threat. The temporally cyclical logic continues to play out; the present reception of the immediate object is inflected by the possible future to which it refers and continues to be linked. The threat is neutralized by the interplay between the mandated hermeneutic response to the textual object in the present and the future menace to which that textual object refers. Future versions of al-Maslūkh will hew to al-Manṣūr's interpretation of him because of the successful uptake of the message of the flayed body by its first observers.

The signs that linger on this bodily text quickly slip into an alternate or conditional future that has been circumvented. Even as al-Manṣūr has created a text out of al-Mutawakkil's potentially deceptive skin and sent it to Marrakesh to be contemplated, he also attends to what remains of that body. The chronicler reports that every bit of the dead king's body has been accounted for and controlled: "wa-dufinat juththatuhu wa dufina man māta miman kāna maʿahu min ʿuṣāti al-muslimīna wa-dufina sulṭānu al-naṣāriyyi bi-mawḍiʿin muʿayyanin li-yaʿrifa ʿinda al-iḥtiyāji ilayhi [And al-Mutawakkil's corpse was buried, as were those belonging to the disobedient Muslims who died alongside him, and the Christian king was also buried in a particular place so that it would be known at the point at which there would be a need for it]." Even as he tracks and controls the gruesome puppet of his nephew's flayed skin, al-Manṣūr also monitors what remains of his flayed body (*juththatuhu*) by stockpiling what remains of the flayed cadaver. The corpse is buried in a specific place, *bi-mawḍaʿin muʿayyinin*, so that it may be retrieved if "*ʿinda al-iḥtiyāji ilayhi*" (there were a need for it).[82] The potential utility of these doubled remains is anticipated in this process. Their indexical potentiality is seemingly limitless; just as al-Mutawakkil's original mortal remains have been divided and one piece has been made use of to justify that preemptive violence, so too can these stockpiled remains be endlessly partitioned into subsequent immediate objects that refer to dynamic objects of threat, continuously justifying violence against the remaining material of the royal corpse.

While the early treatment of al-Mutawakkil's corpse in some ways complies with Islamic sensibilities and expectations for how to handle corpses, it becomes clear that the chronicler does not narrate how al-Manṣūr and his officials manage this body in order to document that compliance. Instead, the public ritual of violence that is enacted on al-Mutawakkil's corpse restricts its ability to present alternative narratives or form assemblages with other entities. The dangerous future against which al-Manṣūr and his agents are protecting is multilayered and constantly evolving. Even if they have succeeded in converting al-Maslūkh into propaganda, constant vigilance of other body parts is necessary under the logic of necroviolence. The flayed skin as a textual object foreshadows the threat that its creation neutralized. Ambient fear resonates between and through these temporal spaces and justifies the brutal violence employed to neutralize the threat posed by the potentialities contained within al-Mutawakkil's whole corpse.

Conclusion

Objectifying dead human bodies as objects of disgust, as seen in the treatment of al-Mutawakkil's dead body, subjecting them to the question of *what*? rather than *who*? is an active and brutal denial of their lingering, vibrant subjectivity. Al-Mutawakkil's flaying objectifies him as materially and morally repugnant. The means by which he is humiliated in effigy resonates with eschatological imagery in which body parts testify against the rest. Circularly, this disgusting object justifies its own public humiliation and punishment because, if his skin is publicly testifying against him, he has already been condemned. In effect, this is a subhuman object that does not warrant the consideration other humans, Muslim or no, can expect under the law. That objectification can be found in the very grammar of the account of his flaying confirms the power of this active necroviolence: al-Manṣūr is identified as perpetrator of this brutal act while other actors' participation is elided; al-Maslūkh is shown to be the passive object of such violence that it is reduced to its name.

Some of the dead bodies we have seen up to this point have been frustratingly unruly. They have the potential to derail their army's almost certain victory, to go missing, to decompose too quickly, or, at a minimum, require careful management to produce desired outcomes. Immediately after his death, al-Mutawakkil's disgraced body retains the same potential for such unruliness. What is notable in the representation in *Tārīkh al-dawla* of the overthrown ruler's posthumous care is the new monarch's absolute unwillingness to tolerate such cadaverous disorder and his creativity in solving this problem. Through necroviolence, al-Manṣūr imposes absolute discipline on the message al-Mutawakkil's body can send. The ruler's efforts to erase corpse-based knowledge sets out to neutralize the power of the corpse in its absence as well as its presence. The success of al-Manṣūr's strategy is borne out both in the immediate public consideration of his message and, most tellingly, the onomastic objectification of al-Mutawakkil's disgraced body as "al-Maslūkh" (the Flayed One) in the ensuing chronicles of the dynasty.

Epilogue

Caravaggio's Saint Thomas plunges his finger into Christ's side, probing its depths for proof of the Resurrection. The Capela dos Ossos in Evora, Portugal, literally and liberally adorned with human remains, frankly warns its visitors: "Nós ossos que aqui estamos pellos vossos esperamos" (We bones that are here for yours await). Vesalius's dissections of criminals corrected long-accepted mistakes in Galenic anatomy, establishing the human corpse as a source of verifiable truth. Hamlet contemplates the skull of old Yorick, and there finds insights into death as equalizer. The Counter-Reformation interest in death, dying, and the human body has long been seen as a fundamental feature of early modern European culture, represented vividly in painting and sculpture through the iconography of hourglasses, skulls, the Grim Reaper's scythe, and skeletons. Vesalius's dissections are heralded as first steps toward modern medicine, evidentiary science, and the Enlightenment.

Less well studied have been the innumerable corpses that litter the literary texts of the same period. These bodies, whether hiding in the Inca Garcilaso de la Vega's memory of the Andes after the Spanish conquest of the Incas or as alluded to in chapter 3, swinging uncomfortably close to Sancho's and Don Quixote's heads as they cross from Castile and Leon into Aragonese territory, have largely been passed over in favor of other moments. Nevertheless, they hold the key to understanding one of the most urgent concerns for early modern narrators—how, in a quickly expanding and incessantly mutable world, to establish truth where old standards of certainty no longer held stable. The human body emerges as a tool for establishing a relatively fixed point of reference that connects moments of witnessing, narrating, and reading. This common thread in which a witnessed body is linked with a narrating body and reconstituted before a reading body lends support to the fabric of the narrative, and it establishes a foundation from which future narration can be built. The narration of the Battle of al-Qaṣr al-Kabīr is grounded in the bodies of those who fought there. In particular, in the telling of this event, corpses are used as evidence of the credibility of the account being offered to the reader. Through images of these corpses, the empathetic reader is drawn into bearing textual witness to the events being told and is recruited as an ally to the narrator's cause. The body anchors and confirms the events of the past as the narrator transmits them, and forms the epistemological bedrock from which the reader, now another witness, can pivot to relate the tale to new audiences.

While a number of scholars have documented a shift toward eyewitnessing in early modern historiography, which emerged in part as a result of Spanish colonization of the Americas, this shift evolved within broader epistemological concerns that also affected the Western Mediterranean. Despite the differences in intellectual background and provenance of the texts that I study, there is common ground in which Arabic, Spanish, and Portuguese eyewitnesses establish certainty and narrative credibility through access to the dead body. This is a story of bodies in moments of mutual engagement. Narrators bring corpses into their accounts to engage with not just textually but also materially, and they present the bodies described in their accounts in engagement with their own particularly physical bodies. The embodied presence of the narrator within the text emphasizes his status as an eyewitness and highlights the value of knowledge obtained in person over derivative information acquired from secondhand sources. The interactions between the narrator's body and those within his text anticipate the interactions between the narrator and the intradiegetic audience of his account, or between the material text and its extradiegetic reader. In each of these cases is the sense that the presence of a body grounds and in some way validates the story being told. The epistemological power of the human body derives at least in part from its power to inspire empathy in its viewer. It stands as tangible proof that the reader or the audience can examine carefully to establish the validity of what has been said.

The royal body, already the subject of much scrutiny in presence and absence, becomes a particularly powerful hinge between witnessing and testimony. If ordinary bodies of named and unnamed soldiers help to anchor or even generate the texts that narrate their deaths, the bodies of kings take on a particular potency that must be managed. Already liminal and compelling figures with intimate ties to their subjects, the presence of the king's body in the narrative speaks to the narrator's exclusive knowledge of valuable information. The fact of his access to a royal body alone attests to his trustworthiness and character. At al-Qaṣr al-Kabīr and in its aftermath, the premium on information about royal corpses—both how they died and what happened to the bodies posthumously—augments the prestige and authority that the presence of such bodies bestows upon a particular narrative. In the telling of the battle, Sebastian's, ʿAbd al-Malik's, and al-Mutawakkil's cadavers become focal points for explaining the movements of forces on and off the battlefield, the Portuguese defeat (or Moroccan victory, depending on who tells the story), and the transfer of power in the days following the event as news trickles out about what has happened. In all cases, the royal corpse becomes a text to be read, interpreted, and disseminated to a wider public. The gravity of its material substance grounds the credibility of the reports derived from it.

This book has studied bodies as they are made into texts to be read. They serve as authorizing agents that attest to the credibility of what their narrators have said and written, but they also come to exist as texts that must themselves be read and decoded. Marrakesh's contemplation and interpretation of al-Mutawakkil's flayed corpse, a reading that is carefully monitored and controlled by his successor, is one such corporeal text whose particular story is meant to be read, interpreted in the terms established by the narrator, and passed on to future audiences. Through this process, the flayed corpse comes to stand as a point of reference against which any deviating retellings can be compared and corrected. Whereas al-Manṣūr certainly writes and endeavors to widely propagate a particularly controlled text with the body of al-Mutawakkil, he still holds on to the rest of the dead man's body, as if anticipating a future need to refer to it. The body comes to stand as the point of transition from witnessing to narration, and again from narration to reading. As an object to which the narrator can refer to back up his account, the body in its materiality imparts a certainty that invites readerly consideration.

Even in the twenty-first century, bodies have not lost their power of narrative and authority, as examples from the wars in Iraq and Afghanistan vividly illustrate. Seymour Hersh's hotly disputed alternate narrative of the killing of Osama bin Laden, which dismisses the official White House version of the event as something out of Lewis Carroll, relies upon sources who had access to genetic material from the al-Qaeda leader's body—incontrovertible proof that the CIA had the right guy.[1] While the provenance of inanimate things like yellowcake or weapons of mass destruction have proven to be distressingly and detrimentally equivocal, the identity, fate, and disposal of the most sought-after body of the first decade of the twenty-first century presented comforting evidence of the success of the American intelligence system.[2] Hersh's account is disruptive in part because it calls the fate of that important body into question. Where the official story reassures the American public that bin Laden's body has safely sunk to the bottom of the Indian Ocean, Hersh points to the absence of images and documents corroborating that tale and suggests that bin Laden, even in death, continues to elude our grasp. If we believe him, somewhere in the Hindu Kush mountains lie the pieces of an uncontrolled body waiting to be reconstituted into a new text.

Since March 2020, we have continued to witness the importance of the dead human body in a world wracked by epistemological uncertainty. Since the outbreak of the coronavirus pandemic, the death toll worldwide has reached more than six and a half million lives.[3] Mass burials on Harts Island, where New York's unclaimed dead have been buried for the past 151 years, increased fivefold in April 2020—a fact that was documented in great detail with aerial footage of anonymous undertakers clad head to toe in white hazmat suits moving identical coffins into a massive trench.[4] Despite this concrete, material evidence of the failures of public policy in the face of an unprecedented global disaster, documented through indexical media like photography and film and widely disseminated in print and online media, the Trump White House doubled down on the "alternate facts" that created a narrative to exonerate the administration of blame for these deaths, even seeking to literally reduce the body of evidence of their culpability by artificially keeping testing numbers down in the early days of the outbreak.

Even as the body count of lives taken by COVID-19 continues to tick ever upward, another death toll devastates this country and exposes deep and troubling truths about the history and lived present of this country. The Black Lives Matter movement has gained support and momentum in vocally resisting the necropolitical power of the American police state. Protests in the wake of only the most recent murders of Ahmaud Arbery, George Floyd, Breonna Taylor, and too many others have surged in part in response to the rising visibility of the indexical evidence of the state's arbitrary exercise of deadly power over black bodies made possible by cell phone videos.[5] Even so, the ambiguous capacity of these documents of moments of death and recently dead bodies to attest to some objective truth continues to be called into question, as police departments and unions, recognizing the power of these representations, do everything in their power to keep them from reaching the public eye.[6]

All of these corpse-oriented activities recognize and respond to the devastating power of the corpse to make trouble for the living. Indeed, in many ways, BLM identifies and resists a regime of necropolitical and necrocapitalist power that has inflected American, transatlantic, and transoceanic spaces since the inception of European colonialism in the fifteenth centuries.[7] John Buesterien argues, "By the end of the sixteenth century, the economy of the Spanish empire exerted the foundational cornerstones of capitalist networks in Asia,

America, and Africa and the case of uprooting Africans as part of the economy of the Atlantic triangle was nothing short of the emergence of the business of death."[8] The business of death was an all too well-rehearsed practice within the Mediterranean basin throughout the early modern period, and the manifold manifestations of those economies shaped and took shape in the textual representations of the corpses that fell by the wayside. If this book has shown nothing else, it is that those bodies that have been passed by or condemned to the oblivion of history still have the propensity to rise up and make themselves heard among the living.

Acknowledgments

First and foremost, I want to thank my dad—my first, last, and best reader. You, more than anyone else, have watched this project evolve from its very inception. You've read and edited multiple drafts on a moment's notice. Your own quiet but insatiable intellectual curiosity has been a source of constant pride and inspiration to me.

Thank you to my mom: your love and talent for learning languages, travel, and reading has made my own life path possible. Had it not been for your enthusiasm for me to travel to Spain and Latin America from an early age and to learn Spanish in those places, I would never have been able to pursue my academic career. Your love and always enthusiastic support mean everything to me.

I am extraordinarily grateful to Lisa Surwillo for your support in all things academic and professional. Your exceptional mentorship, scholarship, and teaching set a very high standard, indeed, which I can only hope to emulate with my own students. My thanks also to Roland Greene, for your unfailing and enthusiastic support of me and my project, at all hours, and in all places. To Alexander Key, whose thorough critique of endless drafts made the dissertation a much better piece of scholarship, and whose sense of humor and humility have constantly reminded me of the importance of being a complete human as well as an ambitious academic. To Leyla Rouhi, for showing me that this was a path that I could take, and for supporting me throughout my journey along it.

To Jamie, who since my very earliest days reading has fostered my love for books and words. You've taught me the joys of plundering libraries and bookstores for a great read, of reading Shakespeare aloud while waiting for dinner, and of a deeply felt vocation for teaching. To Bill for filling my bookshelves and applauding my love for them.

To my brilliant friends who have supported me and inspired me throughout graduate school and into our early years in this profession—Lucy Alford, Michaela Hulstyn, Frances Molyneux, Rachel Stein, Leif Weatherby, Caroline Weist, and Matt Handelman. To Melissa Kagen, for serving as consigliere and enthusiastic supporter of all things corpses since 2016. To the rest of our writing group—Caroline Egan, Natasha Tanna, Lyle Skains—for keeping me on track and for generously reading drafts in all states. To Kurt Werner for his punctuation consultations. To Ariela Marcus-Sells for reading early Arabic translations and being a sounding board in the first days of this project.

Colleagues at Washington and Lee, both during my appointment there and in the years since, have been invaluable friends, readers, and interlocutors. The MESA young faculty working group (Kameliya Atasanova, Matthew Chalmers, Kerry Sonia) was profoundly supportive in their enthusiastic and kind critical readings of early drafts of the introduction and chapter 5. Antoine Edwards was an inestimable resource for all things Arabic and a welcome fellow traveler in the final days of editing. Ricardo Wilson's feedback on drafts of the proposal was pivotal for identifying and refining the core ideas that I present in this book, as was the generous professional and personal support he afforded me in navigating the complex world of academic publishing. My thanks, too, to Stephen McCormick, Ellen Mayock, and Seth Michelson for nurturing me as one of your own during my time in Virginia.

During the final years of the writing process, colleagues at the College of the Holy Cross, especially Sarah Klotz, Ana Ugarte, and my colleagues in the Spanish department, were enthusiastic and supportive of my work. Katelyn Knox's advice on proposing and academic publishing was critical for getting this project to press. So, too, were readers of later introduction and chapter drafts, especially Heather Dubrow and Emily Colbert Cairns. My participation in the Mediterranean Seminar brought productive feedback at a critical moment and a generous intellectual community during the pandemic, especially from Fred Astren, Brian Catlos, Sharon Kinoshita, Mark Meyerson, and David Wacks. Jesús Velasco's Iberian Connections seminar put me in touch with other like-minded scholars like Chad Leahy, Felipe Valencia, Noel Blanco Mourelle, and others whose generosity and brilliance has touched my thinking about this project and the field at large. My thanks to Tom Lay for your support and guidance throughout the publication process, as well as to the staff of Fordham University Press for your diligent work that brought this project into its final form.

The publication of this book was made possible through the generous support of the American Comparative Literature Association with a Helen Tartar First Book Subvention Award, granted in 2021. Further publication support came from the College of the Holy Cross through a Publication Award. Initial research for the book in Lisbon was made possible through a grant from the Fundação Luso-Americana para o Desenvolvimento for research at the Biblioteca Nacional de Portugal. Subsequent work at the Archive General de Simancas was funded by a Lenfest Summer Research Grant from Washington and Lee University

And, last of all, to Tyler, Pan, and Kali: your support and love have been a constant source of joy and confidence. Without you in my life, the final years of graduate school and first years of my professional life would have been much sadder and lonelier, indeed.

Notes

Preface

1. MS Escuela Pías de Zaragoza 11, published as "El diálogo de Jesucristo con la calavera," in Miguel Ángel Vázquez, *Desde la penumbra de la fosa: La concepción de la muerte en la literatura aljamiada morisca* (Madrid: Editorial Trotta, 2007), 158–64. All translations of non-English texts in this book are mine, unless otherwise noted.

2. Vázquez identifies these features of Muslim eschatology as constants in Islamic literature dealing with death that date back to only two centuries after the foundation of Islam with Ibn Abī Dunyā's *Kitab al-mawt wa kitāb al-qubúr,* ed. Leah Kinberg (Haifa: Qism al-Lughah al-ʿArabīyah wa-Ādābihā, Jāmiʿat Ḥayfā, 1983). Vázquez, "Hacia un paradigma de la muerte en el islam: El musulmán ante la muerte y los tratados escatológicos de Ibn Abį al-Dunyā," in *Desde la penumbra de la fosa*, 17–40.

3. "El diálogo de Jesucristo con la calavera," 161.

4. Giorgio Agamben, *Nudities*, trans. David Kishik and Stefan Pedatella (Stanford, CA: Stanford University Press, 2010), 37–42. The quotations in this paragraph are at 38 and 40.

5. Ibid., 40.

6. "El diálogo de Jesucristo con la calavera," 158.

7. Irene Silverblatt describes Inca cultural politics as "battles over bodies [that] also became battles over histories," an apt description of the broader phenomenon I study in this book. "Imperial Dilemmas, the Politics of Kinship, and Inca Reconstructions of History," *Comparative Studies in Society and History* 30, no. 1 (1988): 83–102. On how Erauso's duels form part of a convincing performance of gender and an essential aspect of Erauso's narrative persona, see Elizabeth Spragins, "Cuerpos, cuernos, and espadas ceñidas: Sedimenting Gender through

Violence in *La monja alférez*," *ConSecuencias* 1, no. 1 (2019): https://ejournals.bc.edu/index.php/consecuencias/article/view/11769.

8. María de Zayas's stories "La inocencia castigada" and "El traidor contra su sangre" vividly depict the torments of at least three women at the hands of male relatives and lovers. "Desengaño quinto" and "Desengaño octavo" in *Desengaños amorosos*, 7th ed., ed. Alicia Yllera, 265–92, 369–401 (Madrid: Cátedra, 2009. See also Lisa Vollendorf, "Reading the Body Imperiled: Violence against Women in María de Zayas," *Hispania* 78, no. 2 (1995): 272–82; H. Patsy Boyer, "The War between the Sexes and the Ritualization of Violence in Zayas's *Disenchantments*," in *Sex and Love in Golden Age Spain*, ed. Alain Saint-Saëns, 123–45 (New Orleans: University Press of the South, 1999).

9. Elaine Scarry, *The Body in Pain: The Making and Unmaking of the World* (New York: Oxford University Press, 1985), 14.

Introduction: Necroepistemology

1. Some contemporary chroniclers render ʿAbd al-Malik's name with an alif—ʿAbd al-Mālik. I retain the fatḥa rather than the alif, since that is how the sources closer to that figure write the name.

2. Most Portuguese and Spanish sources refer to the battle as "the Battle of Alcácer"—a corruption of the name of a nearby town, al-Qaṣr al-Kabīr. Other names for the event include the Battle of the Three Kings, the Battle of Qasr al-Kabir, the Battle of Ksar al-Kébir, and the Battle of Wadi al-Makhāzin.

3. Josiah Blackmore, "Imaging the Moor in Medieval Portugal," *diacritics* 36, nos. 3–4 (2006): 35–39.

4. Fernão Mendes Pinto's *Peregrinação* provides particularly rich ground for such images. Long passages of this key text are filled with descriptions of "the overpowering stench of dead bodies" (302), "diabolically bloody sacrificial rite[s]" (226), and even "treasure house[s] of the dead" (223), to name only a few. *The Travels of Mendes Pinto*, trans. Rebecca D. Catz (Chicago: University of Chicago Press, 1989).

5. Stephen Cory, *Reviving the Islamic Caliphate in Early Modern Morocco* (New York: Routledge, 2013), 8; Mercedes García-Arenal, *Ahmad al-Mansur: The Beginnings of Modern Morocco* (Oxford: OneWorld Press, 2008), 22; Richard Smith, *Aḥmad al-Manṣūr: Islamic Visionary* (New York: Pearson Education, 2006), 23.

6. Chantal La Véronne notes a long connection between Andrea Gasparo Corso, who appears in chapter 3 as a key intermediary figure, and ʿAbd al-Malik dating to at least the 1560s, "Les frères Gasparo Corso et le chérif Moulay ʿAbd el-Malek (1569–1574)," in *SIHM: Archives et Bibliothèques d'Espagne* III, 157–65 (Paris: Paul Geuthner, 1974). Cervantes himself praised ʿAbd al-Malik for his knowledge of European languages and his predilection for European customs in *Los baños de Argel*. García-Arenal, *Ahmad al-Mansur*, 26–27. Ottomanists assert that ʿAbd al-Malik was installed in the Moroccan throne as an Ottoman client, although

the extent to which that influence continued into al-Manṣūr's reign is certainly debatable. In *Osman's Dream: The History of the Ottoman Empire*, Caroline Finkel follows Hess's position that al-Qaṣr al-Kabīr was effectively a proxy war between the Ottomans and Habsburg Spain (New York: Basic Books, 2007), 169. See also Andrew Hess, *The Forgotten Frontier: A History of the Sixteenth-Century Ibero-African Frontier* (Chicago: University of Chicago Press, 1978), 96–99.

7. Diogo Barbosa Machado, *Bibliotheca Lusitana histórica, crítica e cronológica* (Ridgewood, NJ: Gregg Press, 1962). Cited in Ruth MacKay, *The Baker Who Pretended to Be King of Portugal* (Chicago: University of Chicago Press, 2012), 7–8.

8. Scholars estimate that as much as 50–60 percent of Lisbon's population of 100,000 died in less than a year from this outbreak of the plague. Michael N. Pearson, "First Contacts Between Indian and European Medical Systems," in *Warm Climates and Western Medicine: The Emergence of Tropical Medicine, 1500–1900*, ed. David Arnold (Amsterdam: Rodopi, 1996), 20.

9. António Dias Farinha, "Introdução," *Crónica de Almançor Sultão de Marrocos (1578–1603)* (Lisbon: Instituto de Investigação Científica Tropical, 1997), xlv. Al-Manṣūr would seek to avoid strife in the next generation by clearly naming one of his sons as heir to the throne. Cory, *Reviving the Islamic Caliphate*, 32. La Véronne registers Andrea Gasparo Corso's arrival at the Portuguese court soon after al-Ghālib's death to solicit support against al-Mutawakkil's accession to the throne. Strikingly, although Sebastian would eventually ally himself with the nephew against the uncle, in 1574 there is evidence that he gave financial support to his eventual opponent to dethrone his nephew. "Les frères Gasparo Corso," 165.

10. Hess, *The Forgotten Frontier*, 96.

11. Weston F. Cook, *The Hundred Years War for Morocco: Gunpowder and the Military Revolution in the Early Modern Muslim World* (Boulder, CO: Westview Press, 1994), 244; Cory, *Reviving the Islamic Caliphate*, 8; Abū Fāris ʿAbd al-ʿAzīz al-Fishtālī, *Manāhil al-ṣafā fī maʾ āthir mawālīnā al-shurafāʾ* (Rabat: Maṭbūʿāt Wizārat al-Awqāf, 1972), 41–48; García-Arenal, "Los andalusíes en el ejército saʿdī: Un intento de golpe de estado contra Aḥmad al-Manṣūr al-Dahabī (1578)," *Al-Qanṭara* 2 (1981): 187–88.

12. MacKay suggests that following his 1578 treaty with the Ottoman Empire, Philip saw that involving himself in a Moroccan dynastic dispute would overtax his resources. *The Baker*, 11.

13. Cook, *The Hundred Years War for Morocco*, 246; García-Arenal, *Ahmad al-Mansur*, 10; Mercedes García-Arenal, *Fernando Rodríguez Mediano, and Rachid el Hour, eds., Cartas Marruecas: Documentos de Marruecos en archivos españoles (siglos XVI–XVII)* (Madrid: Consejo Superior de Investigaciones Científicas, 2002), 13. Letters exchanged among Philip, his ambassador to Portugal, Juan de Silva, and his secretary, Gabriel de Zayas, reveal the Spanish king's concerted efforts to reach diplomatic equilibrium in the Mediterranean with the Sublime Porte, an equilibrium that al-Mutawakkil's demands threatened. "Carta de D. Juan de Silva á S. Md., fecha en Lisboa," June 5, 1578, Estado, leg. 396, Archivo General de

Simancas. Mediterranean historians generally mark 1581 as a year of transition for Ottoman and Spanish empire—each turning away from the Mediterranean as the primary site of offensive military enterprise. See Fernand Braudel, *The Mediterranean and the Mediterranean World in the Age of Philip II*, vol. 1 (Berkeley: University of California Press, 1995; New York: Harper & Row, 1972); Daniel Hershenzon, *The Captive Sea: Slavery, Communication, and Commerce in Early Modern Spain and the Mediterranean* (Philadelphia: University of Pennsylvania Press, 2018), 3.

14. Even in official royal chronicles can be found harsh criticism of Sebastian as immature, for example in the *Chronica d'El-Rei d. Sebastião*, sometimes attributed to Bernardo da Cruz, Bibliotheca de Classicos Portuguezes, vol. 36 (Lisbon, 1903). Juan de Silva noted the king's aversion to women and attributed it to religious fanaticism acquired through his Jesuit education. Juan de Silva to Philip II, 6 March 1576, AGS E, leg. 393. MacKay herself lends credence to these common explanations of Sebastian's behavior. *The Baker*, 6.

15. See, for example, Jerónimo de Mendonça's initial explanation of the reasons for Sebastian's expedition. *Jornada de África* (1607; Porto, 1878), 19.

16. Bailey W. Diffie and George D. Winius, *Foundations of the Portuguese Empire 1415–1850* (Minneapolis: University of Minnesota Press, 1977), 423–27. Malyn Newitt also ascribes to this assessment of the defeat. *A History of Portuguese Overseas Expansion, 1400–1668* (New York: Routledge, 2005), 156. Rafael Valladares disagrees with this critique of Sebastian, and instead argues that the king was primarily interested in instating an absolute monarchy. *La conquista de Lisboa: Violencia militar y comunidad política en Portugal, 1578–1583* (Madrid: Marcial Pons, 2008), 179–94.

17. Henry Kamen, *Philip of Spain* (New Haven, CT: Yale University Press, 1997), 66. MacKay, *The Baker*, 11, 21, especially 24. Mendonça himself suggests this was a motivating factor in the expedition. *Jornada de África*, 41.

18. A factor motivating early modern expansionism, not only during Sebastian's reign, was wheat scarcity. Dias Farinha flags this as one of several factors that may have influenced Sebastian's interest in the expedition to Africa. "Introdução," lxi–lxiii. Vincent Cornell discusses the centrality of wheat to the Atlantic littoral of North Africa. "Socioeconomic Dimensions of Reconquista and Jihād in Morocco: Portuguese Dukkala and Sa'did Sūs, 1450–1557," *International Journal of Middle East Studies* 22 (1990): 383.

19. Dias Farinha, "Introdução," lxi–lxiii.

20. Muḥammad al-Ṣaghīr al-Ifrānī, *Nuzhat al-ḥādī bi akhbār mulūk al-qarn al-ḥādī* (Rabat: Jamī'a al-ḥuqūq maḥfūẓa, 1998), 114–25.

21. Ibid., 130.

22. García-Arenal, *Ahmad Al-Mansur*, 13–14.

23. Cook, *The Hundred Years War*, 247.

24. Robert Brown, ed., in al-Hassan ibn Muhammad al-Wazzaz al-Fasi, *The History and Description of Africa of Leo Africanus*, vol. II, ed. Robert Brown, trans. John Pory (London: The Hakluyt Society, 1896), 681n107.

25. García-Arenal notes: "An Arab chronicler from the court of Ahmad al-Mansur wrote at the time, not without sarcasm, that the bishops of Portugal had been forced to consider the possibility of sanctioning polygamy, so scarce was the number of men left." *Ahmad Al-Mansur*, 7. She refers to al-Mansur's personal secretary Aḥmad ibn Muḥammad ibn al-Qāḍī, whom al-Ifrānī cites: "dhakara ba'uhum anna al-naṣārī damarahum allahu, lammā waqa'at 'alayhim al-kā'inatu al-madhkūratu wa-fanā man fanā minhum, wa-ra'ā asāqifatuhum qillata al-rūmi wa-khalā'a al-bilādi li-kathrati man māta minhum, abāḥū li-l-'āmati fāḥishata al-zanā li-yakthura al-tanāsula wa-yakhlufa mā halaka minhum [some of them remembered that God annihilated the Christians, when the aforementioned state befell them, and those of them who died, and their bishops saw the lack of Europeans and the vacancy of the country because of how many of them had died, and they announced publicly the abomination of adultery in order to augment reproduction and to replace those among them who had perished]." *Nuzhat al-ḥādī*, 143.

26. "Toda la hidalguia de Portugal, dende el hijo del duque de Bargança [*sic*] fasta el escudero, son muertos y cautivos [All of the nobility of Portugal, from the son of the Duke of Braganza to the squire, are dead and captive]." "Lettre d'un médecin juif a son frère," in *Les sources inédites de l'histoire du Maroc*, ed. Henri de Castries, vol. I (Paris: E. Laroux, 1905), 319.

27. Some scholars have speculated that 'Abd al-Malik may have died from the plague, rather than poison. José Maria de Queiroz Velloso examines different stories of his poisoning in *D. Sebastião* (Lisbon: Empresa Nacional de Publicidade, 1935), 246–47. MacKay, *The Baker*, 27.

28. According to Cristobal de Moura, "Pedro de Alcazoba me dijo que S.A. [D. Henrique] me habia de hablar sobre escrebir a V.M. que les dé favor para rescatar el cuerpo del rey, el cual fué hallado en el campo y desnudo dos dias despues de la batalla, con un arcabuzazo en el lado izquierdo, y con cinco heridas en la cara y una gran cuchillada en la cabeza. Permitieron los moros, á ruego de los cristianos, que se le diese sepultura, lo cual se hizo poniendo el cuerpo en unas andas viejas, y echándole un poco de tierra y cal, y desta manera fué puesto debajo de tierra en Alcázar en cas de un alcaide [Pedro de Alcazoba told me that His Highness must speak to me about writing to Your Majesty that you might give them the favor of recovering the body of the king, which was discovered on the battleground and naked two days after the battle, with an arquebus wound in his left side, five wounds on the face, and a great slash on the head. The Moors permitted, on the request of the Christians, that he be buried, which was done putting the body in some old planks and throwing upon him a bit of earth and lime, and in this way, he was put in the ground at al-Qasr in the house of an alcaide]." *Colección de documentos inéditos para la historia de España* (hereafter: *CODOIN*), vol. 40, 145.

29. On August 8, 1578, Antonio Manso, a royal official in Puerto de Santa María, wrote an *aviso* in which he expressed doubt and misgivings about the fate of the Portuguese king. "Avis d'Antonio Manso Puerto de Santa Maria," *Les sources*

inédites de l'histoire du Maroc: Archives et bibliothèques d'Espagne, series IV, vol. III (Paris: E. Laroux, 1905), 452.

30. Sebastianism and its evolution are beyond the scope of this book. For more information on this topic, see Charles Boxer, *The Portuguese Seaborne Empire, 1415–1825* (London: Hutchinson, 1969), 369–78; J. Lúcio de Azevedo, A *evolução do Sebastianismo* (Lisbon: Livraria Clássica Editôra, 1947); Joseph Jacobus van den Besselaar, *O sebastianismo* (Lisbon: Instituto de Cultura e Língua Portuguesa, 1987); and António de Costa Lobo, *Origens do Sebastianismo* (Lisbon: Rolim, 1983).

31. Vitor Amaral de Oliveira, "Introdução," *Sebástica: Bibliografia geral sobre D. Sebastião* (Coimbra: Biblioteca Geral da Universidade, 2002), xxiv.

32. MacKay, *The Baker*, 35.

33. Al-Manṣūr's conquest of parts of the Songhay Empire has been studied by prominent historians of West and North Africa alike. Henri de Castries, "La conquête du Soudan par Moulaye Ahmed el-Mansôur," *Hespéris*, III (1923): 438–88; García-Arenal, *Ahmad al-Mansur*, 91; Marta García Nova, "Ulemas malikíes del Bilad al-Sudan en la bra biográfica de Ahmad Baba al-Tinbukti (963/1556–1036/1627)," in *Estudios onomástico-biográficos de Al-Andalus. Vol. XVII. Biografías magrebíes: identidades y grupos religiosos, sociales y políticos en el Magreb medieval*, ed. Mohamed Méouak (Madrid: CSIC, 2012), 417–51; John O. Hunwick, "Ahmad Baba and the Moroccan invasion of the Sudan (1591)," *Journal of the Historical Society of Nigeria*, 2, no. 3 (1962): 319; Georges Pianel, "Les préliminaires de la conquête du Soudan par Moulaye Ahmed el-Mansôur, d'après trois documents inédits," *Hespéris*, 40 (1953): 185–99.

34. Michelle Hamilton and Núria Silleras-Fernández, *In and of the Mediterranean* (Nashville, TN: Vanderbilt University Press, 2015); Yuen-Gen Liang, Abigail Krasner Balbale, Andrew Devereux, and Camilo Gómez-Rivas argue that even though the "long history of connections between the Iberian Peninsula and North Africa" has garnered occasional attention from scholars, including Braudel's first article on the Mediterranean, Hess's *The Forgotten Frontier*, and García-Arenal's decades of historical work on the Western Mediterranean, it "demands sustained attention today." "Unity and Disunity across the Strait of Gibraltar," *Medieval Encounters* 19 (2013): 3. Braudel, "Les espagnols et l'Afrique du Nord de 1492 à 1577," *Revue Africaine* 69 (1928): 184–233, 315–410.

35. Jean Dangler, *Edging toward Iberia* (Toronto: Toronto University Press, 2017).

36. Américo Castro, *España en su historia: Cristianismo moros y judíos*, 2nd ed. (Barcelona: Crítica, 1983), 200–209. Subsequent scholars—most famously María Rosa Menocal—have romanticized Castro's thesis to focus on the harmonious coexistence of medieval Iberia. *Shards of Love: Exile and the Origins of the Lyric* (Durham, NC: Duke University Press, 1992); *Ornament of the World: How Muslims, Jews, and Christians Created a Culture of Tolerance in Medieval Spain* (New York: Little, Brown and Company, 2002).

37. Claudio Sánchez-Albornoz launched the first and most well-known attack on Castro in *España: Un enigma histórico* (1954; 5th ed. Barcelona: Editora y

Distribuidora Hispanoamericana, 1976). See also J. N. Hillgarth, "Spanish Historiography and Iberian Reality," *History and Theory* 24, no. 1 (1985): 23–43; Reyna Pastor, "Claudio Sánchez-Albornoz y sus claves de la historia medieval de España," *Revista de historia Jerónimo Zurita* 73 (1998): 117–32; and Maya Soifer, "Beyond *convivencia*: Critical Reflections on the Historiography of Interfaith Relations in Christian Spain," *Journal of Medieval Iberian Studies* 1, no. 1 (2009): 19–35.

38. Ryan Szpiech examines the rivalries that undergird the ongoing convivencia debates as a manifestation of a methodological and geographical division of North American hermeneutics and Spanish scientific philology. "The Convivencia Wars: Decoding Historiography's Polemic with Philology," in *A Sea of Languages: Rethinking the Arabic Role in Medieval Literary History*, ed. Suzanne Conklin Akbari and Karla Mallette (Toronto: University of Toronto Press, 2013), 135–61.

39. While scholars in Spain, the United Kingdom, and the United States generally tend to agree that "it was more complicated" than a Manichean clash of civilizations, such scholarly nuance has not stopped public figures like José María Aznar from framing the Muslim "invasion" of the Iberian Peninsula in 711 as a prototerrorist act in the aftermath of the Atocha bombings. Kenneth Wolf Baxter, "Myth, History, and the Origins of al-Andalus: A Historiographical Essay," *Journal of Medieval Iberian Studies* 11, no. 3 (2019): 380–81.

40. Mark Meyerson, *The Muslims of Valencia in the Age of Fernando and Isabel: Between Coexistence and Crusade* (Berkeley: University of California Press, 1991), 271. On *conveniencia*, see Brian A. Catlos, "Cristians, musulmans i jueus a la Corona d'Aragó medieval: un cas de "conveniència"" *L'Avenç* 236 (2001), 8–16, and *The Victors and the Vanquished: Christians and Muslims in Catalonia and Aragon, 1050–1300* (Cambridge: Cambridge University Press, 2004), 407. Menocal, *The Arabic Role in Medieval Literary History: A Forgotten Heritage* (Philadelphia: University of Pennsylvania Press, 1984); David Nirenberg, *Communities of Violence: Persecution of Minorities in the Middle Ages* (Princeton, NJ: Princeton University Press, 1996); Hamilton, *Representing Others in Medieval Iberian Literature* (New York: Palgrave Macmillan, 2007); David A. Wacks, *Framing Iberia:* Maqāmāt *and Frametale Narratives in Medieval Spain* (Leiden: Brill, 2007).

41. Edward D. English and Mark Meyerson, eds., *Christians, Muslims, and Jews in Medieval and Early Modern Spain* (South Bend, IN: University of Notre Dame Press, 2000). Serafín Fanjul contends that the image of al-Andalus as idyllic and cooperative breaks down as soon as one begins to examine the sources. *La quimera de al-Ándalus* (Madrid: Siglo XXI de España Editores, 2004), 22.

42. Where that metropolitan center lay continues to be a source of debate. Anna More, for example, argues that by the late seventeenth century, Mexico City had in some ways supplanted Madrid as the home of Baroque culture and political power, even as the Habsburg dynasty entered irreversible decline. *Baroque Sovereignty: Carlos de Sigüenza y Góngora and the Creole Archive of Colonial Mexico* (Philadelphia: University of Pennsylvania Press, 2013).

43. Hershenzon convincingly argues that the narrow body of water by no means represented a hard barrier between Ottoman Muslim and Spanish Christian blocs, but instead that the body of water represented a medium for connection, trade, negotiation, and, at times, conflict. *The Captive Sea*, 5–7.

44. Braudel was influential in depicting the Mediterranean in oppositional terms. *The Mediterranean*, 23–24. Hess refers to this aqueous divide as "the forgotten frontier." *The Forgotten Frontier.*

45. Leyla Rouhi, "Miguel de Cervantes, Early Modern Spain, and the Challenges to the Meaning of Islam," *Middle East Journal of Culture and Communication* 4 (2011): 11.

46. Barbara Fuchs, *Exotic Nation: Maurophilia and the Construction of Early Modern Spain* (Philadelphia: University of Pennsylvania Press, 2009), 3.

47. Barbara Fuchs, "1492 and the Cleaving of Hispanism," *Journal of Medieval and Early Modern Studies* 37, no. 3 (2007): 493–501.

48. Even as we have begun to acknowledge and study the untidy reality that remained on the Iberian Peninsula for more than a century after the conquest of Granada, Castile continued to be a kingdom with Muslim subjects and Arabic speakers, we continue to mark 1492 as a watershed moment at all levels of the field in undergraduate and graduate seminars, conference papers and panels, book periodization, and even academic appointments.

49. In *The Tropics of Empire: Why Columbus Sailed South to the Indies*, Nicolás Wey Gómez rewrites the geographical history of Columbus's journey to the Americas as taking place on a north–south, rather than east–west, axis, but nonetheless departs from 1492 as the inception point of European expansionism (Cambridge, MA: MIT University Press, 2008). Trade press publications like Charles C. Mann's bestsellers *1491: New Revelations of the Americas* (New York: Vintage, 2006) and *1493: Uncovering the New World Columbus Created* (New York: Vintage, 2012) still see 1492 as the major watershed moment for both sides of the Atlantic.

50. On new theorizations of the Iberian globe, see Ivonne del Valle, More, and Rachel Sarah O'Toole, "Introduction: Iberian Empires and a Theory of Early Modern Globalization," in *Iberian Empires and the Roots of Globalization*, ed. Ivonne del Valle, Anna More, and Rachel Sarah O'Toole (Nashville, TN: Vanderbilt University Press, 2002), 1–22.

51. Robert A. Folger, *Writing as Poaching: Interpellation and Self-Fashioning in Colonial Relaciones de Méritos y Servicios* (Leiden: Brill, 2011), 20–21. Walter D. Mignolo highlights the importance of *cartas relatorias* in bridging the distance between writers on the ground, representatives of the Crown, and the Crown itself, and cites one such regulation that dictated the terms of that mediated exchange of information: "Pues en todas las tierras de las Indias sometidas a la Magestad Imperial *hay orden y mandato* de hacer esto y de dar información fidedigno de lo que se lleva a cabo en las Indias [In all of the lands of the Indies subject to the Imperial Majesty *there is the order and obligation* to do this and to give trustworthy information of what is carried out in the Indies]." "Cartas, crónicas y relaciones

del descubrimiento y la conquista," in *Historia de la literatura hispanoamericana: Época colonial*, ed. Luis Iñigo Madrigal (Madrid: Cátedra, 1982), 59, my emphasis.

52. Enrique Pupo-Walker, *La vocación literaria: Desarrollo de la prosa de ficción—siglos XVI, XVII, XVIII y XIX* (Madrid: Gredos, 1982), 104, 108–11. Folger treats the colonial subject in terms of their communal validation. *Writing as Poaching*, 28–34.

53. See J. H. Elliott on "composite" histories, "A Europe of Composite Monarchies," *Past & Present* 137 (1992): 48–71; on "connected histories," see Sanjay Subrahmanyam, "Connected Histories: Notes toward a Reconfiguration of Modern Eurasia," *Modern Asian Studies* 31, no. 3 (1997): 735–62. See Rachel Stein for the application of these historical frameworks to a material history context, "Re-composing the Global Iberian Monarchy through the Lisbon Press of Pedro Craesbeeck (1597–1632)," (PhD diss., Columbia University, 2017), 13–17.

54. Brian A. Catlos, "Why the Mediterranean?" in *Can We Talk Mediterranean? Conversations on an Emerging Field in Medieval and Early Modern Studies*, ed. Brian A. Catlos and Sharon Kinoshita (New York: Palgrave Macmillan, 2017), 5.

55. Historians have dominated the conversation since Braudel originated the paradigm. Peregrine Horden and Nicholas Purcell's landmark study *The Corrupting Sea* is interdisciplinary in that it considers the Mediterranean from geographical, microecological, economic, and social perspectives, but the thrust of the contribution is still historical. *The Corrupting Sea: A Study of Mediterranean History* (Oxford: Blackwell Publishers, 2000). The classic studies in Mediterranean history also include David Abulafia, *The Great Sea: A Human History of the Mediterranean* (Oxford: Oxford University Press, 2011); S. D. Goitein, *A Mediterranean Society: The Jewish Communities of the Arab World as Portrayed in the Documents of the Cairo Genizah*, 6 vols. (Berkeley and Los Angeles: University of California Press, 1967–93); W. V. Harris, ed., *Rethinking the Mediterranean* (Oxford: Oxford University Press, 2005); Peregrine Horden and Nicholas Purcell, "Mediterranean and 'the New Thalassology,'" in *The American Historical Review* 111, no. 3 (2006): 722–40.

56. Hershenzon explores modes of interaction through captivity networks of the Western Mediterranean during the seventeenth century in *The Captive Sea*. See also Catlos, *The Victors and the Vanquished*; and Joshua White, *Piracy and the Law in the Ottoman Mediterranean* (Stanford, CA: Stanford University Press, 2017). Both push paradigms of coexistence and syncretism to consider cultural exchange as the result of violence.

57. Sharon Kinoshita speaks eloquently to this point in "Medieval Mediterranean Literature," *PMLA* 124, no. 2 (2009): 600–602. See, too, her analysis of the administrative limitations on this burgeoning field in "Negotiating the Corrupting Sea: Literature in and of the Mediterranean," in *Can We Talk Mediterranean?*, 35–38. Suzanne Conklin Akbari notes that the effect of Mediterranean studies has been "less dramatic—or, at least, has been much slower to appear—in the fields of late medieval and early modern history, including cultural and literary history." "The Persistence of Philology," in *A Sea of Languages*, 5. Wacks also addresses the relative paucity of Mediterranean literary studies in his introduction to *Medieval*

Iberian Crusade Fiction and the Mediterranean World (Toronto: University of Toronto Press, 2019), 4–6.

58. Fuchs, "1492 and the Cleaving of Hispanism," 494–95. Hershenzon vividly demonstrates the intensity of the exchange throughout the Mediterranean in *The Captive Sea*. See Wacks on "linguistic polysystem," *Framing Iberia*, and *Double Diaspora in Sephardic Literature: Jewish Cultural Production before and after 1492* (Bloomington: Indiana University Press, 2015).

59. Hamilton's, Gregory Hutcheson's, and Wacks's scholarship, inter alia, elucidates not just the influence of Hebrew and Andalusi literature on the Spanish canon but seeks to create new Sephardic and Andalusi canons by heeding the call to recognize Hebrew and Arabic as coequal Iberian languages along with Castilian, Catalan, Euskara, Gallego, and Portuguese.

60. Margaret Greer articulates a cogent summary of the utility of the terms "Golden Age" and "early modern" in "Thine and Mine: The Spanish 'Golden Age' and Early Modern Studies," *PMLA* 126, no. 1 (2011): 217–24. Fuchs has proposed "imperium studies" as one transnational approach for understanding early modern empire and nation formation in "Imperium Studies: Theorizing Early Modern Expansion," in *Postcolonial Moves: Medieval Through Modern*, ed. Patricia Clare Ingham and Michelle R. Warren (New York: Palgrave Macmillan, 2003), 71–90.

61. Akbari, "The Persistence of Philology," 10.

62. Szpiech outlines the significant divergence of Arabic philology from other branches of philology as a historical artifact dating back to the eighteenth century. "The Convivencia Wars," 148–49.

63. Hamilton and Silleras-Fernández, "Iberia and the Mediterranean," xiii.

64. D. Fairchild Ruggles, "Mothers of a Hybrid Dynasty: Race, Genealogy, and Acculturation in al-Andalus," *Journal of Medieval and Early Modern Studies* 34, no. 1 (2004): 65–94.

65. Bradford Bouley, *Pious Postmortems* (Philadelphia: University of Pennsylvania Press, 2017); Enrique Fernández, *Anxieties of Interiority and Dissection in Early Modern Spain* (Toronto: University of Toronto Press, 2015); Ryan Giles and Steven Wagschal, eds., *Beyond Sight: Engaging the Senses in Iberian Literatures and Cultures 1200–1750* (Toronto: University of Toronto Press, 2017); David Hillman, *Shakespeare's Entrails: Belief, Skepticism and the Interior of the Body* (New York: Palgrave Macmillan, 2007).

66. Nancy Caciola, *Afterlives: The Return of the Dead in the Middle Ages* (Ithaca, NY: Cornell University Press, 2016); Thomas Laqueur, *The Work of the Dead* (Princeton, NJ: Princeton University Press, 2015); Rebecca Schneider, *Performing Remains: Art and War in Times of Theatrical Reenactment* (New York: Routledge, 2011); Margaret Schwartz, *Dead Matter: The Meaning of Iconic Corpse* (Minneapolis: University of Minnesota Press, 2015).

67. Mary Ann Doane, *The Emergence of Cinematic Time: Modernity, Contingency, The Archive* (Cambridge, MA: Harvard University Press, 2002), 16. Tom Gunning has called into question the extent to which a photograph's "truth claim" depends

upon a narrow definition of indexicality in "What is the Point of Indexicality? Or, Faking Photographs," *NORDICOM Review* 5, nos. 1/2 (2004): 39–49.

68. William F. Hanks, "The Evidential Core of Deixis in Yucutan Maya," in *Papers from the Twentieth Regional Meeting of the Chicago Linguistic Society*, ed. J. Drogo et al. (Chicago: Chicago Linguistic Society, 1984), 154–72; "The Indexical Ground of Deictic Reference," in *Rethinking Context: Language as an Interactive Phenomenon*, ed. Alessandro Duranti and Charles Goodwin (Cambridge: Cambridge University Press, 1992), 43–76; "Metalanguage and the Pragmatics of Deixis," in *Reflexive Language: Reported Speech and Metapragmatics*, ed. John A. Lucy (Cambridge: Cambridge University Press, 1993), 127–58.

69. James Collins, "Indexicalities of Language Contact in an Era of Globalization: Engaging with John Gumperz's Legacy," *Text & Talk: An Interdisciplinary Journal of Language, Discourse & Communication Studies* 31 (2011): 409.

70. As Monika Fludernik notes, deixis and reference are among the more controversial notions in linguistics. For the purposes of my argument, I will not enter these controversies here but will follow Fludernik and Hanks in their functional definitions of the term. "Shifters and Deixis: Some Reflections on Jakobson, Jespersen, and Reference," *Semiotica* 86, nos. 3–4 (1991): 193. The classic definition of deixis was given by Emile Benveniste in *Problems in General Linguistics* (Coral Gables, FL: University of Miami Press, 1971). Noam Pines, "Deixis," in *The Princeton Encyclopedia of Poetry & Poetics*, 4th ed., ed. Roland Greene (Princeton, NJ: Princeton University Press, 2012), 344. For the sake of clarity, I retain the strictly linguistic sense of the term *anaphora*, a grammatical system of reference in which the interpretation of an expression depends upon an anteceding expression within context. In rhetoric and poetry, the term refers to the repetition of a word or phrase at the start of successive clauses.

71. Heather Dubrow, *Deixis in Early Modern English Lyric: Unsettling Spatial Anchors Like "Here," "This," "Come"* (New York: Palgrave Macmillan, 2015), 37–39.

72. Deborah Jermyn, "Body Matters: Realism, Spectacle and the Corpse in *CSI*," *Reading CSI: Crime TV Under the Microscope*, ed. Allen Michael (New York: I. B. Tauris, 2007), 81.

73. Jennifer Malkowski argues that the digital turn in new media studies has overly reified the indexicality of the analogue photographic image and argues for a methodological shift in new media studies that focuses on reception rather than production of the digital real. *Dying in Full Detail: Mortality and Digital Documentary* (Durham, NC: Duke University Press, 2017), 3–18. While André Bazin and Amos Vogel insist that it is the iterability of represented death that makes its cinematic rendering obscene, the assumption of a direct, physical correspondence between objects in the world and their representations on the screen has long been debunked as overly simplistic. Bazin, "Death Every Afternoon (1958)," in *Rites of Realism: Essays on Corporeal Cinema*, ed. Ivone Margulies, trans. Mark A. Cohen, 27–31; Vogel, "Grim Death," *Film Comment* 16, no. 2 (1980), 78. Gunning, "Moving away

from the Index: Cinema and the Impression of Reality," *differences* 18, no. 1 (2007): 30–31; Doane, *The Emergence of Cinematic Time*, 25.

74. Schwartz, *Dead Matter*, 5.

75. Ibid., 1–25.

76. Ibid., 2.

77. Dubrow's linguistic approach was particularly useful to my thinking on these points. *Deixis in Early Modern English Lyric*, 12–16.

78. David Herman, *The Basic Elements of Narrative* (Malden, MA: Wiley-Blackwell, 2009), ix.

79. Ibid., 9, 13–22.

80. Brian Massumi, "The Autonomy of Affect," *Cultural Critique* 31 (1995): 83–109; Melissa Gregg and Gregory J. Seigworth, "An Inventory of Shimmers," in *The Affect Theory Reader*, ed. Melissa Gregg and Gregory J. Seigworth (Durham, NC: Duke University Press, 2010), 2–3.

81. Massumi, "The Autonomy of Affect," 90–91.

82. Amaral de Oliveira, *Sebástica*. The sheer volume of literature Amaral de Oliveira lists in his catalogue, even just in Arabic, about al-Qaṣr al-Kabīr directly contradicts Hess's dismissal of the event as historiographically unimportant: "this battle in which three kings perished made only a light mark upon Islamic history. Except for a nineteenth-century North African scholar, Aḥmad ibn Khālid an-Nāṣirī (Es-Salâoui), who saw the Muslim accomplishment as symbolic proof of monotheism's victory over the Trinity, the utter destruction of Iberia's last crusade did not occupy great space in the chronicles of the Islamic community." *The Forgotten Frontier*, 8.

83. Félix Lope de Vega Carpio, "La tragedia del Rey Don Sebastian y el bautismo del Príncipe de Marruecos," in *Onzena parte de las comedias de Lope de Vega Carpio* (Madrid: 1618); Pedro Calderón de la Barca, "A secreto agravio, secreta venganza," *Comedias* (Madrid: 1697); Philip Massinger, *Believe as You List*, ed. T. Crafton Croker (London: The Percy Society, 1849); and George Peele, *The Battell of Alcazar, fought in Barbarie betweene Sebastian King of Portugall, and Abdelmalec King of Marocco. With the death of Captaine Stukeley* (London: 1594).

84. The Portuguese sources have garnered limited attention outside of Portugal. MacKay's *The Baker* engages deeply from a historical perspective with the Spanish archive, especially the documents found in the Archive General de Simancas. Cory and García-Arenal both treat the most significant Moroccan chronicles in historical terms to unpack Saʿdī ideology. Cory, *Reviving the Islamic Caliphate*; García-Arenal, "Mahdī, Murābiṭ, Sharīf: L'avènement de la dynastie saʿdienne," *Studia Islamica* 71 (1990): 77–114; "Sainteté et pouvoir dynastique au Maroc: La résistance de Fès aux Saʿdiens," *Annales* 45 (1990): 1019–42; and *Ahmad al-Mansur*.

85. In a notable example, even Portuguese contemporaries of Jerónimo de Mendonça refer readers to his account of the battle as one of the more reliable sources for information on it, while only cautiously pointing to Girólamo de Conestaggio as a possible source, even warning the reader of the errors the latter

commits. António de Saldanha, a Portuguese captive in al-Manṣūr's court, refers his reader to Mendonça for a thorough account of both the life of ʿAbd al-Malik and of the battle at al-Qaṣr al-Kabīr: "Tudo o mais da vida do Maluco e batalha d'el-rei D. Sebastião está escrito por Jerónimo de Mendonça que cautivou na mesma batalha e Franque que, contando a união de Portugal a Castela, conta esta batalha com alguns erros e atrevimentos a que devem reponder os coronistas do Reino quando chegarem a tratar a corónica do rei D. Sebastião [Everything else about the life of ʿAbd al-Malik and the battle of the King, D. Sebastian, is written by Jerónimo de Mendonça, who was captured at that same battle, and Franchi, who, recounting the union of Portugal to Castile, narrates this battle with some errors and impudence to which the chroniclers of the Kingdom ought to respond when they begin to deal with chronicling the King, D. Sebastian]." António de Saldanha, *Crónica de al-Mançor Sultão de Marrocos (1578–1603)*, ed. António Dias Farinha (Lisbon: Instituto de Investigação Científica Tropical, 1997), 17.

86. Juan de Silva, "Correspondencia de D. Juan de Silva con Felipe II, relativo, en su mayor parte, á la expedición de D. Sebastian a África," in *Colección de documentos inéditos para la historia de España*, ed. Marquis of Pidal, Marquis of Miraflores, and Miguel Salvá, vol. 39, 465–574; vol. 40, 5–131 (Madrid, 1861); "Lettre d'un medecin juif a son frère." In *Dynastie saadienne: Archives et bibliothèques d'Anglaterre*: Les sources inédites de l'histoire du Maroc, 312–21 (Paris, 1920), translated to English as "The copy of a letter written from the camp of the King of Moroccos, Mullie Molloque, by a Jew, physician to the said King; directed to his brother," or "The Battle of Alcazar," Calendar of State Papers Foreign, Elizabeth, 1558–1589, 13: 1578–1579, SP 71/12, The National Archives; Jeronimo de Mendonça, *Jornada de África* (1607; repr. Porto: Imprensa Recreativa do Instituto Escholar de S. Domingos, 1878); Miguel Leitão de Andrade, *Miscellânea do Sitio de N. Senhora Dalzado Pedrogão Grande* (Lisbon, 1629); first edited as *Tārīkh al-dawla al-saʿdiyya*. Edited by George S. Colin. Rabat, 1921; more recently edited as *Tārīkh al-dawla al-saʿdiyya al-Takmadārtiyya* by ʿAbd al-Raḥīm Benḥādda (Marrakesh: Maṭbaʿa Tīnmal, 1994); al-Ifrānī, *Nuzhat al-ḥādī, translated to French as Nozhet-elhâdi: Histoire de la dynastie saadienne au maroc (1511–1670)*, ed. Ernest Laroux, trans. Octave Houdas (Paris, 1889).

87. Benveniste, *Problems in General Linguistics*, 203.

88. Jonathan Sawday, *The Body Emblazoned: Dissection and the Human Body in Renaissance Culture* (New York: Routledge, 1995); Bouley, *Pious Postmortems*. In his study of Alonso de Contreras's autobiography, Miguel Martínez demonstrates that "the authority of [soldiers'] narratives, like their professional, symbolic capital in the society of soldiers, relied largely on killing." *Front Lines: Soldiers' Writing in the Early Modern Hispanic World* (Chicago: University of Chicago Press, 2016), 205–6.

89. Katherine Park, "The Criminal and the Saintly Body: Autopsy and Dissection in Renaissance Italy," *Renaissance Quarterly* 47 (1991): 1–33. Nancy Siraisi, "Signs and Evidence," in *Medicine and the Italian Universities, 1250–1600* (Leiden: Brill, 2001), 356–80. Cara Krmpotich et al., "The Substance of Bones: The Emotive

Materiality and Affective Presence of Human Remains," *Journal of Material Culture* 15, no. 2 (2010): 374.

90. According to Akbari and Jill Ross, "time and space are . . . intimately linked in medieval discourses of the body"—an observation that, on my argument, carries beyond the medieval period. "Introduction: Limits and Teleology: The Many Ends of the Body," in *The Ends of the Body: Identity and Community in Medieval Culture*, ed. Suzanne Conklin Akbari and Jill Ross (Toronto: University of Toronto Press, 2013), 6.

91. Vivian Sobchack, "Inscribing Ethical Space Ten Propositions on Death, Representation, and Documentary," *Quarterly Review of Film Studies* 9, no. 4 (1984): 288; Jane Bennett, *Vibrant Matter: A Political Ecology of Things* (Durham, NC: Duke University Press, 2010), 14.

92. Jason De León, *The Land of Open Graves: Living and Dying on the Migrant Trail* (Berkeley: University of California Press, 2015), 69–72.

93. One example of such lines of communication were the networks for redeeming captives in North Africa, see Hershenzon, *The Captive Sea*, and Lisa Voigt, *Writing Captivity in the Early Modern Atlantic: Circulations of Knowledge and Authority in the Iberian and English Imperial Worlds* (Chapel Hill: University of North Carolina Press, 2009).

1. Presence: Here Are the Dead

1. Barbosa Machado, "Ieronimo de Mendoça," in *Bibliotheca lusitana histórica, critica e cronológica*, vol. 2 (Lisbon, 1747), 508.

2. Barbosa Machado, "Francisco de Sa e Meneses," ibid., 247–50.

3. Stein demonstrates that Craesbeeck, designated the royal printer in 1620 by Philip III, and his workshop operated a truly global press: "Craesbeeck's workshop brings together 'the four parts of the world': Europe, America, Africa, and Asia." Rachel Stein, "Re-composing the Global Iberian Monarchy through the Lisbon Press of Pedro Craesbeeck (1597–1632)," PhD diss., Columbia University, 2017, 3–4.

4. Miguel de Cervantes Saavedra, *Don Quixote de la Mancha*, ed. Francisco Rico (Madrid: Real Academia Española, 2004), 1004–1008.

5. This section of the *Jornada de África* warrants study for the claims Mendonça makes for the saintliness and martyrdom of those killed at al-Qasr al-Kabir and after. He even insists that it was seen at al-Qasr al-Kabir that no Christian corpses were corrupted: "nenhum corpo de christão se corrompeu, antes se mirraram todos sem algum mau cheiro [no Christian body rotted, instead they all wrinkled without any foul odor]." Jeronimo de Mendonça, *Jornada de África* (Porto: Imprensa Recreativa do Instituto Escholar de S. Domingos, 1878), 232.

6. For Margaret Schwartz's illuminating discussion of corpses as communicative objects, see her introduction to *Dead Matter: The Meaning of Iconic Corpse* (Minneapolis: University of Minnesota Press, 2015), 1–25.

7. Elaine Scarry, *The Body in Pain: The Making and Unmaking of the World* (New York: Oxford University Press, 1985), 14.

8. Andrea Frisch rightly argues that the testimonial turn Anthony Pagden and other scholars point to as an early modern innovation evolves from a longer, established acceptance of the figure as witness, particularly in medieval juridical systems. "The Ethics of Testimony: A Genealogical Perspective," *Discourse* 25 (2003): 38. She extends this idea in her monograph *The Invention of the Eyewitness: Witnessing and Testimony in Early Modern France* (Chapel Hill: University of North Carolina Press, 2004). For the colonial Latin American context, see Rolena Adorno, "Discourses of Colonialism: Bernal Díaz, Las Casas, and the Twentieth-Century Reader," *MLN* 103, no. 2 (1988): 239–58; Anthony Pagden, *European Encounters with the New World: From Renaissance to Romanticism* (New Haven, CT: Yale University Press, 1992), 51.

9. Frisch, "The Ethics of Testimony," 40.

10. Thomas W. Laqueur, *The Work of the Dead: A Cultural History of Mortal Remains* (Princeton, NJ: Princeton University Press, 2015), 11–12. See also Vincent Brown, *The Reaper's Garden: Death and Power in the World of Atlantic Slavery* (Cambridge, MA: Harvard University Press, 2008), 4–5; Robert Pogue Harrison, *The Dominion of the Dead* (Chicago: University of Chicago Press, 2003), x–xi; Katherine Verdery, *The Political Lives of Dead Bodies: Reburial and Postsocialist Change* (New York: Columbia University Press, 1999), 31; Laura Wittman, *The Tomb of the Unknown Soldier, Modern Mourning, and the Reinvention of the Mystical Body* (Toronto: University of Toronto Press, 2011).

11. Heather Dubrow, *Deixis in the Early Modern English Lyric: Unsettling Spatial Anchors Like "Here," "This," "Come"* (New York: Palgrave Macmillan, 2015).

12. See Folger's chapter on "Strategic Interpellation and Tactical Writing in Colonial Historiography," especially, for an insightful consideration of this issue. Robert A. Folger, *Writing as Poaching Interpellation and Self-Fashioning in Colonial Relaciones de Méritos y Servicios* (Leiden: Brill, 2011), 13–66. In a Latin American context, Rolena Adorno has studied these scriptural economies extensively: "Discourses of Colonialism," 239–58. Walter Mignolo highlights the importance of *cartas relatorias* in bridging the distance between writers on the ground, representatives of the Crown, and the Crown itself in "Cartas, crónicas y relaciones del descubrimiento y la conquista," in *Historia de la literatura hispanoamericana: Época colonial*, ed. Luis Iñigo Madrigal (Madrid: Cátedra, 1982), 57–116, at 59. Anthony Pagden argues that colonial eyewitnesses sought to cope with the incommensurability of the "new" world with the "old" by reducing the distance between colony and metropole in "*Ius et Factum*: Text and Experience in the Writings of Bartolomé de Las Casas," *Representations* 33 (1991): 147–48.

13. The book is divided in three parts: Livro I, comprising seven chapters, recounts the events leading up to al-Qaṣr al-Kabīr; Livro II, comprising seventeen chapters, traces the experience of surviving Portuguese soldiers from the surrender of the battle through their captivity in Morocco, including several accounts of escape attempts; finally, Livro III, comprising fifteen chapters, turns from the material sacrifice Portuguese soldiers made to the spiritual one, describing the

martyrs that "padeceram pela fé de Christo n'esta jornada [suffered for their faith in Christ on this expedition]" (231).

14. Mendonça, *Jornada de África*, 61.

15. "com frente serena e levantada se viam muito promptos a qualquer assalto [with a serene and raised countenance they saw themselves ready for any assault]." Ibid.

16. Ibid.

17. Ibid., 66–67.

18. Laqueur, *The Work of the Dead*, 8.

19. Rebecca Schneider considers the concept of a "flesh memory" within the context of performance and reenactment, but the capacity of the body to "keep the past alive" is richly suggestive for bodies in textual or representative contexts, too. *Performing Remains: Art and War in Times of Theatrical Reenactment* (London: Routledge, 2011), 1–31.

20. Leitão de Andrade, another veteran of al-Qasr al-Kabir, cites Mendonça's account of the battle as accurate, an assessment that seems to have been widely accepted in Portugal in the subsequent centuries. The *Jornada de África* has been reedited at least once a century since its original publication, first in 1785, again in 1878, and most recently was included in the collection *Bibliotheca de Clássicos Portugueses*, ed. Mello de Azevedo, vols. 1 and 2 (Lisbon: Livraria Clássica Editora, 1904).

21. Conestaggio was a commercial representative of the Genoese government in the Lisbon customs house and is thought to have been in Lisbon at the time of the battle. The book was quickly translated into several European languages—Spanish (1587), French (1596), German (1599), English (1600), and Latin (1602)—revealing a widespread international interest in the event. António Sérgio, *O Desejado: Depoimentos de Contemporaneos de D. Sebastião sôbre êste mesmo rei e sua jornada de Africa* (Paris and Lisbon: Aillaud and Bertrand, 1924), 352. Sérgio also suggests that Mendonça wrote his *Jornada* to call to account both the Jesuits and the nobles close to the monarch who were seen as complicit in permitting the disastrous enterprise to take place (114). Bailey W. Diffie and George D. Winius suggest that the Jesuits were "the only sane men who had much influence over him [Sebastião] . . . and these only when they purported to go along with him." *Foundations of the Portuguese Empire 1415–1850* (Minneapolis: University of Minnesota Press, 1977), 423.

22. Richard Kagan, *Clio and the Crown: The Politics of History in Medieval and Early Modern Spain* (Baltimore: Johns Hopkins University Press, 2009), 131–32.

23. Stein shows that the same bookseller financed at least five other books printed by Craesbeeck between 1603 and 1620. Interestingly, Mendonça's is the only somewhat secular text that we know of to come from this collaboration, though its latter focus on soldiers of the battle as martyrs somewhat blurs the line between secular and spiritual. Stein observes, "As the state of research stands, it is impossible to say why the former soldier Jerónimo de Mendonça took his account of the

infamous Portuguese expedition to Morocco to this bookseller to ask for financial help. For all we know, Mendonça could have met Artur at a bookstore on Rue Nova dos Mercadores and negotiated the project on that commercial thoroughfare." What we do know, however, is that "the capital that Artur invested to arm Mendonça in a historiographical battle against a Genoese adversary would have come, in large part, from his sales of Catholic rituals." "Re-composing the Global Monarchy," 116–17.

24. "a sombra de la misma verdad ha querido menoscabar tan de proposito el valor de los Portugueses, como si por averles sucedido aquella desgracia, perdiessen por esso en un punto el credito y reputacion que han adquirido en tantos años con tanta satisfacion de la mayor parte del mundo [under the shadow of the same truth he has wished to deprecate purposefully the valor of the Portuguese, as though because this misfortune befell them, because of it they lost in a moment the credit and reputation they had acquired over so many years with such satisfaction from most of the world]." Antonio de San Román de Rivadeneyra, *Jornada y muerte del rey Don Sebastián de Portugal* (Valladolid, 1603), 2.

25. Mendonça, *Jornada de África*, vi.

26. Folger, *Writing as Poaching*, 13–66. The key studies on the growing prestige of experiential witnessing in the Americas are Mary B. Campbell, *The Witness and the Other World* (Ithaca, NY: Cornell University Press, 1988); Stephen Greenblatt, *Marvelous Possessions: The Wonder of the New World* (Chicago: University of Chicago Press, 1992); and Pagden, *European Encounters with the New World*. Richard Helgerson considers the problems of writing empire from a poetic stance in his masterful reading of Garcilaso's sonnet "A Boscán desde la Goleta." His chapter on how Boscán uses the word "Aquí" to grapple with the placelessness of empire is particularly insightful. *A Sonnet from Carthage: Garcilaso de la Vega and the New Poetry of Sixteenth-Century Europe* (Philadelphia: University of Pennsylvania Press, 2007), 40–48.

27. Folger argues that the power dynamic that governed colonial writing was governed by the relationship between the writing colonial subject operating tactically under the constraints imposed by the bureaucratic hierarchy. *Writing as Poaching*, 15.

28. Frisch, "The Ethics of Testimony," 38. Consider, too, Adorno's analysis of Bernal Díaz del Castillo's eyewitness account of the Spanish conquest of the Americas that he presents in opposition to accounts by figures like court chronicler Francisco López de Gómara in "Discourses on Colonialism," especially 245–46.

29. Pagden, *European Encounters with the New World*, 55.

30. Frisch, "Ethics of Testimony," 43.

31. The analogy between legal and historiographical evidence is not coincidental. As Roberto González Echevarría demonstrates, "the forms and constraints of legal writing . . . permeated the writing of history." *Myth and Archive: A Theory of Latin American Literature* (Durham, NC: Duke University Press, 1990), 45.

32. Frisch, "Ethics of Testimony," 39–43.

33. Enrique Pupo-Walker, *La vocación literaria del pensamiento histórico en América: Desarrollo de la prosa de ficción—siglos XVI, XVII, XVIII y XIX* (Madrid: Gredos, 1982), 104, 108–11. Folger, too, treats the colonial subject in terms of their communal validation. *Writing as Poaching*, 28–34. On the epistemic status of compurgatory witnessing, see Frisch, "The Ethics of Testimony," 40–45, especially 43.

34. Miguel Martínez, *Front Lines: Soldiers' Writing in the Early Modern Hispanic World* (Chicago: University of Chicago Press, 2016), 94–95.

35. Kathleen Ross, "Historians of the Conquest and Colonization of the New World: 1550–1620," in *The Cambridge History of Latin American Literature*, ed. Roberto González Echevarría and Enrique Pupo-Walker (Cambridge: Cambridge University Press, 1996), 111–14.

36. Charles V. Ganelin, "Bodies of Discovery: Vesalian Anatomy and Luis de Barahona de Soto's Las lágrimas de Angélica," *Calíope* 6, no. 1–2 (2000): 295; Enrique Fernández, "Fragmentación corporal y exégesis política en Quevedo," *La perinola* 14 (2010): 315. Fernández points out that this interest extended beyond a mere cataloguing of the interior parts of the physical body but extended to the embodied manifestations of human psychology and intentionality. Fernández, *Anxieties of Interiority and Dissection in Early Modern Spain* (Toronto: University of Toronto Press, 2015), 3. Although Elizabeth A. R. Brown argues that dissection and dismemberment was by no means universally taboo in medieval Europe, Juan de Valverde de Hamusco laments that lack of expertise on the subject "por ser cosa fea entre españoles, despedazar los cuerpos muertos [it being an ugly thing among Spaniards to tear apart dead bodies]." *Historia de la composición del cuerpo humano* (Rome, 1556), ii. Sergio Bertelli also describes the practice of partitioning the royal body as an act of generosity to the populace: "By distributing their bodies, kings anticipated requests from below; they gave rather than asked." *The King's Body: Sacred Rituals of Power in Medieval and Early Modern Europe*, trans. R. Burr Litchfield (University Park: Pennsylvania State University Press, 2001), 32–34.

37. Jonathan Sawday, *The Body Emblazoned: Dissection and the Human Body in Renaissance Culture* (New York: Routledge, 1995), ix.

38. Jonathan Sawday, "The Fate of Marsyas: Dissecting the Renaissance Body," in *Renaissance Bodies: The Human Figure in English Culture c. 1540–1660*, ed. Lucy Gent and Nigel Llewellyn (London: Reaktion Books, 1990), 118.

39. Ibid., 126.

40. For example, in the dedication to his plague manual, *Remedios preservativos y curativos, para en tiempo de la peste y otras curiosas experiencias* (1599), Miguel Martínez de Levya supports his claim to expertise by claiming, "Yo propio los podré mostrar con el dedo [I myself can show it with my finger]." In medical settings, too, then, firsthand experiences of the body supplant and correct previously accepted authoritative information disseminated in written form. In doing so, Levya not only shares the firsthand knowledge he has acquired by interacting with sick, dying, and dead bodies but actually introduces his own body into this indexical chain of knowledge transmission that mediates between the corpse as object of knowledge and the reader as recipient. José María López Piñero, "Las *Controversiae medicae et*

philosophical (1556), de Francisco Vallés y el galenismo del siglo XVI," in *Los temas polémicos de la medicina renacentista: Las* controversias (1556), *de Francisco Vallés*, ed. José María López Piñero and Francisco Calero (Madrid: Consejo Superior de Investigaciones Científicas, 1988), 7–8.

41. Elizabeth L. Spragins, "Embodied Authority: The Virgin, Audience, and the Body of the Devotee in Marian Miracles," *La corónica* 45, no. 2 (2017): 9–36.

42. Mendonça, *Jornada de África*, 67, my emphasis. The turn of phrase is strange since a crosier is, of course, not a writing instrument at all, but a symbolic object carried to point to a bishop's pastoral role. In this rather forced analogy, Mendonça alludes to the popular Renaissance debate between arms and letters. Don Quixote participates in this debate in part I, chapter thirty-eight of *Don Quixote*. Cervantes, *Don Quijote de la Mancha*, 394–98. This passage can also be read as an oblique reference to Mendonça's earlier valorization of witnessing over writing—like Mendonça himself, the bishop of Coimbra is valued primarily for his presence at and participation in the battle.

43. Conestaggio's account claims that the Portuguese soldiers were such cowards they began the battle already cowering on the ground. Mendonça refutes this and points to this moment as evidence, instead, of their devotion to Christ, since they knelt to pray to an image of Christ, not out of fear. *Jornada de África*, 61.

44. Mendonça, Jornada de África, 67–69.

45. Vivian Sobchack, "Inscribing Ethical Space: Ten Propositions on Death, Representation, and Documentary," *Quarterly Review of Film Studies* 9, no. 4 (1984): 283–300, at 282.

46. Jennifer Malkowski, *Dying in Full Detail: Mortality and Digital Documentary* (Durham, NC: Duke University Press, 2017); Laqueur, *The Work of the Dead*, 365–66, 413–46.

47. Monika Fludernik discusses the narratological implications for shifters and deixis at length in "Shifters and Deixis: Some Reflections on Jakobson, Jespersen, and Reference," *Semiotica* 86, nos. 3–4 (1991): 193–230.

48. Dubrow proposes the concept of "deictic chains" and "convergers" in *Deixis in Early Modern English Lyric*, 37–38.

49. The term was first introduced by Otto Jespersen in 1923, was taken up by Roman Jakobson, and has since been widely used among linguists and literary scholars alike. While in classical Peircian semiotics, signs can be classified as symbols, indexes, and icons, shifters combine two of these functions—symbol and index—the conventional association between sign and object and the existential relation between sign and object. Jespersen, *The Philosophy of Grammar* (London: Allen and Unwin, 1924); Jakobson, "Shifters, Verbal Categories, and the Russian Verb," in *Selected Writings*, vol. 2 (The Hague: Mouton, 1971), 130–47. See also Fludernik, "Shifters and Deixis."

50. Peter Auer, "Spatial Indexicalities and Spatial Pragmatics," in *Pragmaticizing Understanding*, ed. Jan-Ola Östman and Michael Meeuwis (Philadelphia: John Benjamins, 2012), 53.

51. William F. Hanks, "Explorations in the Deictic Field," *Current Anthropology* 46 (2005): 192.

52. Hanks works specifically on demonstrative reference like spatial and temporal adverbs in his landmark study, but other linguists and narratologists include verbs with indexical function within the category. "The Indexical Ground of Deictic Reference," in *Rethinking Context: Language as an Interactive Phenomenon*, ed. Alessandro Duranti and Charles Goodwin, 43–76 (Cambridge: Cambridge University Press, 1992), 43–76.

53. Auer, "Spatial Indexicalities," 57.

54. Hanks, "The Indexical Ground of Deictic Reference," 56–57.

55. Schwartz, *Dead Matter*, 4.

56. Scott Newstok, *Quoting Death in Early Modern England: The Poetics of Epitaphs beyond the Tomb* (New York: Palgrave Macmillan, 2009), 56.

57. Dubrow proposes that deictics and related referential elements act as *convergers*, which tend to aggregate together and converge toward someone or something, "generally with the aim of gathering in and gathering together." Dubrow, *Deixis in the Early Modern English Lyric*, 37.

58. Fludernik, "Shifters," 212.

59. David Herman, *The Basic Elements of Narrative* (Malden, MA: Wiley-Blackwell, 2009), 115–16, 123–24.

60. Dubrow, *Deixis in the Early Modern English Lyric*, 6.

61. Mary Galbraith, "Deictic Shift Theory and the Poetics of Involvement in Narrative," in *Deixis in Narrative: A Cognitive Science Perspective*, ed. Judith F. Duchan, Gail A. Bruder, and Lynne E. Hewitt (Hillsdale, NJ: Lawrence Erlbaum, 1995), 46.

62. Susan Stewart, *Poetry and the Fate of the Senses* (Chicago: University of Chicago Press, 2002), 156.

63. Dubrow, *Deixis in the Early Modern English Lyric*, 37.

64. Mendonça, *Jornada de África*, vi.

65. Helgerson explores Garcilaso de la Vega's similarly creative use of the single word "Aquí" in his magisterial reading of the sonnet "A Boscán desde la Goleta." Helgerson reads the naming of Carthage as the deictic "here" as an anti-imperial gesture. *A Sonnet from Carthage*, 40–47.

66. Collins, "Indexicalities of Language," 409.

67. Helgerson, *A Sonnet from Carthage*, 40–45.

68. Scarry, *The Body in Pain*, 71.

69. Mendonça, *Jornada de África*, 67.

70. Newstok, *Quoting Death in Early Modern England*, 56.

71. Fludernik, "Shifters and deixis," 216–217.

72. See Stewart on the generative power of deixis in poetry. *Poetry and the Fate of the Senses*, 156.

73. Mendonça, *Jornada de África*, 74–75, my emphasis.

74. Laqueur, *The Work of the Dead*, 366.

75. Laura Wittman explores how the Tomb of the Unknown Soldier experimented with tropes of necronominalism in the face of changing European concepts of mortality during and after World War I. The burial of an anonymous

soldier represents an innovation in our perceptions of death, mass destruction and tragedy in the face of the unprecedented number of dead and missing soldiers produced by that war. *The Tomb of the Unknown Soldier, Modern Mourning, and the Reinvention of the Mystical Body* (Toronto: Toronto University Press, 2011).

76. Laqueur, *The Work of the Dead*, 417.

77. Here I rely upon Hanks's language of pragmatics to situate our understanding of what is happening in an indexical sense. See his "The indexical ground of deictic reference," 62. He, in turn, draws upon Stephen Wallace's definitions of paradigmatic opposition in "Figure and Ground: The Interrelationships of Linguistic Categories," in *Tense-Aspect: Between Semantics and Pragmatics*, ed. P. J. Hopper (Philadelphia: John Benjamins, 1982), 201–26.

78. My conversation with Isidro Rivera at the Western Michigan University Medieval Congress (2016) about the importance of the material object for Leitão's readership was particularly illuminating for my thinking about this point. See Spragins, "Embodied Authority," 26–30.

79. Spragins, "Embodied Authority," 9–36.

2. Absence: Disappearing the Royal Dead

1. Narrators on both sides of the conflict speculate about alternative outcomes of the battle had the doctor been less successful in the cover-up of ʿAbd al-Malik's death: Mendonça suggests that the Moroccan forces might have lost hope sooner and retreated back to Fez if they knew their king was dead, which would have left the Portuguese and their allies victorious on the field; the anonymous chronicler of the Saʿdīs credits God himself for endowing the chamberlain with the foresight to conceal that information and thus secure a Muslim victory.

2. Jeronimo de Mendonça, *Jornada de África* (Porto: Imprensa Recreativa do Instituto Escholar de S. Domingos, 1878), 65.

3. Subsequent film and new media theorists like Amos Vogel, Matthew Noble-Olson, Laura Mulvey, Jennifer Malkowski, and Vivian Sobchack have explored the mimetic representation of death as a central ethical problem that exposes the very limits of representation. These theorists expand upon Bazin's central concept in their work, using it to shed light on documentary film, realism, and digital media. I suggest that the insights of Bazin and other cinema and new media scholars apply beyond the originally intended visual objects of study, in particular because of film theorists' long-standing interest in the index as a central

4. André Bazin, "Death Every Afternoon," trans. Mark A. Cohen, in *Rites of Realism: Essays on Corporeal Cinema*, ed. Ivone Margulies (Durham, NC: Duke University Press, 2003), 27–31, at 31.

5. The classic reference for the development of the concepts of the body politic and body natural of the monarchy is Ernst Kantorowicz, *The King's Two Bodies A Study in Mediaeval Political Theology*, 7th ed. (Princeton, NJ: Princeton University Press, 1997).

6. Elizabeth Freeman, "Packing History, Count(er)ing Generations," *New Literary History* 31 (2000): 727–44.

7. Carolyn Dinshaw, *How Soon Is Now? Medieval Texts, Amateur Readers, and the Queerness of Time* (Durham, NC: Duke University Press, 2012), 3.

8. Vivian Sobchack, "Inscribing Ethical Space: Ten Propositions on Death, Representation, and Documentary." *Quarterly Review of Film Studies* 9, no. 4 (1984): 283–300, at 294–97.

9. Mendonça, *Jornada de África*, 79.

10. Margaret Schwartz, *Dead Matter: The Meaning of Iconic Corpse* (Minneapolis: University of Minnesota Press, 2015), 4.

11. Laura Mulvey, *Death 24x a Second: Stillness and the Moving Image* (London: Reaktion Books, 2006), 9–10.

12. Noëleen Murray and Louise Green, "Notes for a Guide to the Ossuary," *African Studies* 68, no. 3 (2009): 371.

13. Cara Krmpotich, Joost Fontein, and John Harries, "The Substance of Bones: The Emotive Materiality and Affective Presence of Human Remains," *Journal of Material Culture* 15, no. 2 (2010): 371–84, at 377.

14. Dinshaw begins her theorization of the complexity of the *now* by emphasizing the shiftiness of the common deictics *soon* and *now* (linguistic puns intended). *How Soon Is Now?*, 2.

15. Bazin, "Death Every Afternoon," 27–31. Mary Ann Doane argues that cinema is a technology invested in first embalming and then reproducing at a rate of twenty-four times per second a "world of actuality." *The Emergence of Cinematic Time: Modernity, Contingency, the Archive* (Cambridge, MA: Harvard University Press, 2002), 2. Film theorists are interested in the technological achievement that the successful representation of the moment of death would represent. Doane argues that film's mimetic achievement can be measured by its successful reproduction of that moment. *The Emergence of Cinematic Time*, 140–71. Matthew Noble-Olson suggests that "the figuration of death in cinema signifies a limit of representability and meaning; it represents the contingency of the real in a medium that orders time into meaningful and unmeaningful, investing time's very passage with meaning." "Reviving the Elephant; or, Cinema Plays Dead," *Cultural Critique* 97 (2017): 88.

16. Ursula Coope argues that "there is time *when* there is change and *only when* there is change." *Time For Aristotle: Physics IV. 10–14* (Oxford: Oxford University Press, 2005), 31. Dinshaw builds on this concept to argue that the Western philosophical tradition has long suspected and undermined the notion that time is strictly linear. Even Aristotle, Dinshaw suggests, recognized that the *now* is multitemporal. *How Soon Is Now?*, 8–10.

17. Jennifer Malkowski, *Dying in Full Detail: Mortality and Digital Documentary* (Durham, NC: Duke University Press, 2017), 3.

18. Bazin, "Death Every Afternoon," 30.

19. Juan Eulogio Pérez Fadrique, *Modo practico de embalsamar cuerpos defunctos para preservarlos incorruptos y eternizarlos en lo posible* (Seville: Thomé Miranda, 1666), 46.

20. Paul Ricouer, *Oneself as Another*, trans. Kathleen Blamey (Chicago: University of Chicago Press, 1992), 147.

21. David Herman, *Basic Elements of Narrative* (Malden, MA: Wiley-Blackwell, 2009), 19.

22. Peter Brooks, *Reading for the Plot: Design and Intention in Narrative* (New York: Knopf, 1984), xii.

23. Ricoeur further argues: "what is ultimately at stake in the case of the structural identity of the narrative function as well as that in that of the truth claim of every narrative work, is the temporal character of human experience." *Time and Narrative*, vol. 1, trans. Kathleen McLaughlin and David Pellauer (Chicago: University of Chicago Press, 1984), 3.

24. Sobchack, "Inscribing Ethical Space," 293.

25. Sobchack delineates the characteristics of a documentary filmmaker's gaze that would render their indexical representation of death ethically excusable: the accidental, helpless, endangered, interventional, or human gaze. Suspect, in contrast, is the professional gaze, because it implies that the filmmaker is gaining professional or personal benefit from breaching this taboo. "Inscribing Ethical Space," 296–97.

26. Sergio Bertelli, *The King's Body: Sacred Rituals of Power in Medieval and Early Modern Europe*, trans. R. Burr Litchfield (University Park: Pennsylvania State University Press, 2001), 38.

27. Kantorowicz, *The King's Two Bodies*, 314.

28. On syncopation, see Rebecca Schneider, *Performing Remains: Art and War in Times of Theatrical Reenactment* (London: Routledge, 2011), 2.

29. Adeline Rucquoi, for example, contends that the Castilian monarchy always presupposed a collapse of spiritual and temporal interests because of its perpetual position as defender of the faith and patria. "De los reyes que no son taumaturgos: Los fundamentos de la realeza en España," *Relaciones: Estudios de Historia y Sociedad* 13, no. 51 (1992): 66–68. Teofilo F. Ruiz points to the absence of sacred rituals such as unction, coronation, and consecration as indications that medieval Castilian kings did not consider their office sacred. "Unsacred Monarchy: The Kings of Castile in the Late Middle Ages," in *Rites of Power: Symbolism, Ritual and Politics since the Late Middle Ages*, ed. Sean Wilentz (Philadelphia: University of Pennsylvania Press, 1985), 109–10.

30. Barbara F. Weissberger, *Isabel Rules: Constructing Queenship, Wielding Power* (Minneapolis: University of Minnesota Press, 2003), 100–103.

31. Bernardo da Cruz [*sic*], *Chronica d'El-Rei D. Sebastião, Bibliotheca de Classicos Portuguezes*, vol. 36, (Lisbon, 1903), 2: 19. E. V. Bovill and H. V. Livermore both argue that the Portuguese monarchy achieved a version of absolute monarchy *avant la lettre* during the late fifteenth and early seventeenth centuries. E. V. Bovill, *The*

Battle of Alcazar: An Account of the Defeat of Don Sebastian of Portugal at El-Ksar el-Kebir (London: Batchworth, 1952), 10; H. V. Livermore, A *New History of Portugal* (Cambridge: Cambridge University Press, 1966), 123–25. Edward McMurdo points to Louis XI of France as a model for João II's centralization of monarchical power, arguing: "João II imitated Louis IX, not only in his especial conceits, but even in his dissimulation and cruelty" in *The History of Portugal from the Reign of D. João II to the Reign of D. João V* (London, 1889), 6.

32. Dinshaw, *How Soon Is Now?*, 5; Kantorowicz, *The King's Two Bodies.*

33. Sobchack, "Inscribing Ethical Space," 294–99.

34. Ibid., 296–97.

35. Schneider, *Performing Remains*, 37.

36. Freeman, "Packing History," 728. Dinshaw describes "now" as constituted by purposes and attachments that link it indissolubly to pasts and futures, rendering the present "complex and vascular." *How Soon Is Now?*, 4. Schneider, *Performing Remains*, 15. Freeman refers to these processes as *chrononormativity*, "the use of time to organize individual human bodies toward maximum productivity. . . . People are bound to one another, en-grouped, made to feel coherently collective, through particular orchestrations of time." *Time Binds: Queer Temporalities, Queer Histories* (Durham, NC: Duke University Press, 2010), 3. Lee Edelman discusses the temporal significance of queerness for the future-oriented *promissory* identity conferred by reproduction. By this standard, since queerness signifies no reproduction, and children embody the future, then queerness truncates the possibility of a future. "The Future Is Kid Stuff: Queer Theory, Disidentification, and the Death Drive," *Narrative* 6, no. 1 (1998): 18–30.

37. Rolena Adorno, *The Polemics of Possession in Spanish America* (New Haven, CT: Yale University Press, 2007) 176–77; Robert A. Folger, *Writing as Poaching: Interpellation and Self-Fashioning in Colonial Relaciones de Méritos y Servicios* (Leiden: Brill, 2011); Roland Greene, *Unrequited Conquests: Love and Empire in the Colonial Americas* (Chicago: University of Chicago Press, 1999).

38. Kathleen Ross, "Historians of the Conquest and Colonization of the New World: 1550–1620," in *The Cambridge History of Latin American Literature*, ed. Roberto González Echevarría and Enrique Pupo-Walker (Cambridge: Cambridge University Press, 1996), 107.

39. Andrea Frisch, "Ethics of Testimony: A Genealogical Perspective," *Discourse* 25, no. 1 (2003): 36–54, 42–43.

40. Adorno, "Discourses on Colonialism," 241–42; Ross, "Historians of the Conquest," 107–8.

41. Adorno, "Discourses on Colonialism," 242; D. A. Brading, "The Incas and the Renaissance: *The Royal Commentaries* of Inca Garcilaso de la Vega," *Journal of Latin American Studies* 18, no. 1 (1986): 8.

42. Mendonça, *Jornada de África*, vi, my emphasis.

43. Ernst R. Curtius, *European Literature and the Latin Middle Ages*, trans. Willard R. Trask (London: Routledge and Kegan Paul, 1953), 83–85. This rhetorical

technique was particularly useful as an instrument within the colonial textual economy "as a device for deflecting the suspicion that verbal arts distort 'the truth' and similitudes . . . veil it." Mary B. Campbell, *The Witness and the Other World: Exotic European Travel Writing 400–1600* (Ithaca, NY: Cornell University Press, 1988), 230–31.

44. Jonathan P. A. Sell, *Rhetoric and Wonder in English Travel Writing, 1560–1613* (Burlington, VT: Ashgate, 2006), 66.

45. Mendonça, *Jornada de África*, 66–67.

46. Sobchack, "Inscribing Ethical Space." The quotations in this paragraph are at 294–95.

47. Ibid.

48. Mendonça, *Jornada de África*, 79.

49. Ibid., my emphasis.

50. Ibid.

51. On "flesh archive," see Melissa Kagen, *Wandering Games* (Cambridge, MA: MIT Press, 2022). On the archive as a repository of dead materials waiting to be reanimated, see Michel Foucault, *The Archaeology of Knowledge and the Discourse on Language*, trans. A. M. Sheridan Smith (New York: Pantheon Books, 1972); Jacques Derrida, *Archive Fever: A Freudian Impression*, trans. E. Prenowitz (Chicago: University of Chicago Press, 1995); Carolyn Steedman, "Something She Called a Fever: Michelet, Derrida, and Dust," *American Historical Review* 106, no. 4 (2001): 1159–80; Marlene Manoff, "Theories of the Archive from across the Disciplines," *Portal: Libraries and the Academy* (2004) 4, no. 1: 9–25.

52. "The Battle of Alcazar," Calendar of State Papers Foreign, Elizabeth, 1558–1589. The National Archives, 1578, ed. Arthur John Butler, 164 (London, 1903).

53. "Lettre d'un médecin juif," in *Dynastie saadienne: Archives et bibliothèques d'Angleterre* (Paris, 1920), 320–21. García-Arenal, Gerard A. Wiegers, and Martin Beagles, *A Man of Three Worlds: Samuel Pallache, a Moroccan Jew in Catholic and Protestant Europe* (Baltimore, MD: Johns Hopkins University Press, 2010), 22. This number comes from Luis del Mármol's account of his visit to Fez during the early sixteenth century. *Descripción general de África* (Málaga, 1599), f. 91v–r.

54. "The Battle of Alcazar," 164.

55. Mercedes García-Arenal remarks: "The letter is kept in the Public Record Office in London [whose collection has subsequently been incorporated into the National Archive] together with a contemporary English translation, suggesting the interest the battle aroused throughout Europe, and the difficulty of finding reliable information about it." *Ahmad al-Mansur: Beginnings of Modern Morocco* (Oxford: OneWorld Press, 2009), 19.

56. García-Arenal, *Ahmad al-Mansur*, 20.

57. "Me mandou logo hum judeu seu Medico, que traz sempre consigo, de quem confia sua pessoa, & saude: chamase Ioseph Valença, por averẽ sido seus mayores naturais daquella Cidade de Hespanha: he homem velho, & foy ja Medico de Moley Hamet pay de Moley Zidam, e de Moley Boferes seu irmaõ, de boa pessoa &

presença, gentilmente Hespanholado, douto na disciplina dos Arabes, particularmente em Aviçena que traz consigo, tresladado em Hebraico, porem ignorante da scholla Grega, & Latina totalmente, se bem algũa vez allega Galeno: & com tudo pella longa experiencia, & larga idade, pratico de nam desprezar entre outros medicos dos nossos [he later sent me a Jewish doctor of his, that he always brought with him, and in whom he entrusted his person and health: his name is Joseph Valencia, because his forebears were natives of that city in Spain: he is an old man, and he was already doctor to Mulay Aḥmad, father to Mulay Zidān, and to Mulay Abū Fāris his brother, he is of good bearing and presence, genteelly Hispanized, learned in the discipline of the Arabs, especially in Avicenna, which he brings with him, translated into Hebrew, but nevertheless totally ignorant of the Greek and Latin school, although sometimes he commands Galen, and all in all, because of his long experience and great age, his practice would not be disparaged by other doctors of ours]." Gonçalo Coutinho, *Discurso da Jornada de D. Gonçalo Coutinho a villa de Mazagam, e seu governo nella* (Lisbon: 1629), f. 143v. My thanks to Mercedes García-Arenal and Rachel Stein for their help in tracking down this reference.

58. Jonathan Ray points to an acceleration in the migration of Iberian Jews to Muslim territory as the result of the persecution of Jewish minorities throughout the Peninsula in the final decade of the fourteenth century. This stream of migration persisted over the course of the fifteenth century tended to aim toward already established diaspora communities in urban centers in North Africa and the Levant. Jonathan Ray, "Iberian Jewry between West and East: Jewish Settlement in the Sixteenth-Century Mediterranean," *Mediterranean Studies* 18 (2009): 45. Following the Portuguese defeat at al-Qaṣr al-Kabīr, the Jewish communities of Fez and Tétouan attested to their identification with the Islamic side by establishing "a purim, or ritual expression of gratitude at the dispersal of a destructive threat, a ceremony still celebrated to this day." García-Arenal, Wiegers, and Beagles, *A Man of Three Worlds*, 23. See also Abraham I. Larédo, "Les 'purim' de Tánger," in *Hésperis* 35 (1948): 193–203; and Francisco Cantera Burgos, "El 'Purim' del Rey Don Sebastián," *Sefarad* 5 (1945): 219–25. See David Nirenberg, *Communities of Violence: Persecution of Minorities in the Middle Ages* (Princeton, NJ: Princeton University Press, 1996), 18–40, on the pogroms of the late fourteenth century.

59. Jonathan Ray, *The Sephardic Frontier: The Reconquista and the Jewish Community in Medieval Iberia* (Ithaca, NY: Cornell University Press, 2006), 84; Maud Kozodoy, "The Jewish Physician," in *Jews in Space and Time: The Jews in Medieval Iberia 1100–1500*, ed. Jonathan Ray (Boston: Academic Studies Press, 2011), 126.

60. Kozodoy, "The Jewish Physician," 118.

61. "Lettre d'un médecin juif," 314.

62. Dinshaw, *How Soon Is Now?*, 4.

63. "Lettre d'un médecin juif," 315, my emphasis.

64. Mendonça, *Jornada de África*, vi; Miguel Leitão de Andrade, *Miscellânea do Sitio de N. Senhora Dalzado Pedrogão Grande* (Lisbon, 1629), http://purl.pt/14193, 175.

65. Anonymous, "Lettre d'un medecin juif," 317, my emphasis.

66. Sobchack, "Inscribing Ethical Space," 296.
67. Dinshaw, *How Soon Is Now?*, 4.
68. Anonymous, "Lettre d'un médecin juif," 314.
69. Kagen follows Steedman in defining the archive principally in terms of the gaps and silences left in a network of possible understandings. "Archival Adventuring," *Convergence: The International Journal of New Media Technologies* 20, no. 10 (2019): 5–6; Carolyn Steedman "Something She Called a Fever: Michelet, Derrida, and Dust," *American Historical Review* 106, no. 4 (2001): 1159–80, at 1117.
70. Steedman reads Derrida's "Archive Fever" as a contemplation of the relationship between memory and writing. "Something She Called a Fever," 1161–62.
71. Sobchack, "Inscribing Ethical Space," 296.
72. Anonymous, "Lettre d'un medecin juif," 318.
73. Ibid., 319. The following quotation is at 320.
74. Ibid., 320.

3. Vitality: Wounded Narrators and the Living Dead

1. Diogo de Andrade, also born in Pedrogão Grande, belonged to a group of forty Jesuits who were martyred by Calvinist corsairs near the Canary Islands en route to their mission in Brazil. The leader of this mission, Ignacio de Azevedo, also martyred, was known for having brought the cult of the Madonna of San Luca to Portugal with the gift of an image of the Madonna to Sebastian's grandmother, D. Catherine. Maria Cristina Osswald suggests that Leitão must have seen an image of his godfather in the Igreja de São Roque, which would have inspired the image on the frontispiece of his text. "O martírio de Inácio de Azevedo e dos seus trinta e nove companheiros (1570) na hagiografia da Companhia de Jesus entre os séculos XVI e XIX," *Cultura: Revista de História e Teoria das Ideias* 27 (2010): 163–86.
2. A. Allaria, "St. Peter of Verona," in *The Catholic Encyclopedia* (New York: Robert Appleton Company, 1911). My thanks to Katharina Piechocki for her suggested readings of these images.
3. The name of the Portuguese shipwreck from whose wood the coffin for the first successor to that reign, Philip I of Portugal, was built was also called the *Cinco Chagas*. Carlos M. N. Eire, *From Madrid to Purgatory: The Art and Craft of Dying in Sixteenth-Century Spain* (Cambridge: Cambridge University Press, 1995), 277.
4. Bruno Latour, "How to Talk about the Body? The Normative Dimension of Science Studies," *Body and Society* 2, no. 3 (2004): 205. Gregory Seigworth and Melissa Gregg argue that agency exists as a potential: "Affect as promise: increases in capacities to act (expansions in affectability: both to affect and be affected), the start of 'being-capable' . . . resonant affinities of body and world being open to more life and more to life." Gregory J. Seigworth and Melissa Gregg, "An Inventory of Shimmers," in *The Affect Theory Reader*, ed. Melissa Gregg and Gregory J. Seigworth (Durham, NC: Duke University Press, 2010), 1–25, at 12.

5. For instance, Thomas W. Laqueur provocatively affirms, "The dead are just dead," but then acknowledges that "they are at the same time something: witnesses to lost causes, lost genius, lost pasts of which they might be made to speak." *The Work of the Dead: A Cultural History of Mortal Remains* (Princeton, NJ: Princeton University Press, 2015), 341.

6. Georg Bossong, "Differential Object Marking in Romance and Beyond," in *New Analyses in Romance Linguistics: Selected Papers from the XVIII Linguistic Symposium on Romance Languages 1988*, ed. D. Wanner and D. Kibbee (Amsterdam: John Benjamins, 1991), 159–62.

7. My definition of agency, as I will show going forward, also relies on actor-network notions of agency as advanced by Latour and others who draw on Latour's work on this point. "How to Talk about the Body?" 205.

8. Throughout this chapter I distinguish between *nominative* and *accusative* categories but depart somewhat from the strict linguistic sense of the terms. Although Romance languages are not considered strongly inflectional languages, I use these categories metaphorically to address the relative agency or objecticity of actants in a literary context. Georg Bossong's system of differential object markings is particularly illuminating on this point for how it recognizes direct objects with differing degrees of *prominence*, or the extent to which an object is animate and definite. "Differential Object Marking," 143–70. See also Bossong, "Animacy and Markedness in Universal Grammar," *Glossologia* 2–3 (1982–1983): 7–20.

9. Leitão de Andrade, "Prologo aos leitores benévolos," *Miscellânea do Sitio de N. Senhora Dalzado Pedrogão Grande* (Lisbon, 1629), http://purl.pt/14193.

10. Ibid., f. 1v. Pagination of the book is inconsistent: it switches from foliation at the beginning to sequential pagination at page/folio 9.

11. Innocêncio Francisco da Silva praised the 1867 edition of the *Miscellânea* as a patriotic act, as well as for making more widely available a book whose original edition was rife with "faltas e erros" (gaps and errors) and that was available only for an "avultado preço" (vast price). The *Miscellânea* was printed as the first in a series of new editions of rare books by Portuguese writers. "Miguel Leitão de Andrade," *Diccionario bibliográfico português*, vol. 6, *Letras Ma–Pe* (Lisbon: Imprensa Nacional, 1862), 240–41.

12. "Miguel Leitão de Andrade," 239.

13. The Order of Christ was a military order originating from the Knights Templar that traditionally was governed in early modern Portugal by a prince and headquartered at Tomar. During the sixteenth and early seventeenth centuries, the order underwent a series of reforms instituted by João III, Sebastian, Philip I, and finally Philip II (Philip III of Spain, r. 1598–1621). These reforms endeavored to reestablish its monastic discipline and impose vows of celibacy on its members. The order may have initially supported D. António's claim to the throne but reconciled itself to Philippine rule following António's defeat at Alcântara and welcomed the Spanish king to Tomar in March 1581. José Vieira Guimarães, A *Ordem de Christo* (Lisbon: 1901), 231.

14. Leitão de Andrade, *Miscellânea*, 592.

15. António Cirurgião, "Camões e Miguel Leitão de Andrade," *Revista Colóquio/Letras* 108 (1989): 18. According to Jorge Fonseca, Pinheiro was both a printer and bookseller who resided and worked from the Poço da Fótea, in the *juderia velha* (Jewish Quarter) of Lisbon. *Os livreiros de Lisboa los séculos XVI e XVII: Estratégias económicas, sociais e familiares* (Lisbon: Edições Colibri, 2019), 197. The location of his shop seems to have been atypical for the publishing industry in Lisbon of the time, which was primarily centered on the Rua Nova dos Mercaderes.

16. Maria Cristina Osswald, "O martírio de Inácio de Azevedo e dos seus trinta e nove companheiros (1570) na hagiografia da Companhia de Jesus entre os séculos XVI e XIX," *Cultura: Revista de História e Teoria das Ideias* 27 (2010): 163–86, https://journals.openedition.org/cultura/354.

17. Details about the foundation of the convent itself are available in Luis de Cácegas *Primeira parte da Historia de S. Domingos*, ed. Luis de Sousa (Lisbon, 1866), 388.

18. The poetry comprises sonnets, *romances*, and *canções*, many of which are not original compositions by Leitão himself, but rather verse by Luis de Camões, António Ribeiro dos Sanctos, and others. The lyrics and music to the song about the battle come at the end of the seventh dialogue. Leitão de Andrade, *Miscellânea*, 228–31.

19. Leitão embeds his account of the Battle of al-Qaṣr al-Kabīr within the *Miscellânea* as an episode in an ongoing dialogue between Devoto and Galacio. In a sense, the *Miscellânea* itself can be seen as an assemblage, but this is not the central point of this chapter. Ibid., 1–2.

20. While the significance of the name "Devoto" is apparent, that of his companion, Galacio, is less clear. An overreading of Galacio's introduction in the text, "entre os quaes foi hũ Cavaleiro por nome Galacio, o qual assim, porque nacera naquella Villa [among those was one Gentleman by name Galacio, he in this manner, because he was born in that Village]," in which the causative "o qual assim, porque" could describe the character's onomastic origins rather than explain why Galacio may be found among those in Pedrogão Grande for the festival. Given the central location of Pedrogão Grande within Portugal, equidistant between Porto and Lisbon, translating it as a misspelled toponym referring to Galicia is a stretch. There seem to be no clear parallels between the character's name and the very few figures named Galacio in classical or sacred sources, nor indeed in Iberian hagiographies. One such figure appears in a secular and ecclesiastical history of Palencia, which tells of the transfer of power during an interregnum period from Thedorico, duke of Aquitaine and king of Tolosa, to "Furco Galacio." Pedro Fernãndez de Pulgar, *Libro segundo de la historia secular y eclesiástica de la ciudad de Palencia: Contiene la restauración de la ciudad, reedificación de el templo de San Antonino* (Madrid, 1697?), 237–40. Nevertheless, given that this seventh-century Galacio is represented as a tyrannical, infidel ruler, a connection between him and our seventeenth-century Portuguese pilgrim is tenuous at best.

21. In the first dialogue, the reader learns that Galacio is a native of Pedrogão Grande, "hũ Cavaleiro" [a knight], and is visiting his hometown to participate in the celebrations of the Senhora de Pedrogão Grande on September 8, 1612. Devoto is identified as a childhood friend of Galacio's, and "o devoto que fazia as festas" (the devotee who organized the festivals). Leitão de Andrade, *Miscellânea*, 1.

22. Miguel Martínez, *Front Lines: Soldiers' Writing in the Early Modern Hispanic World* (Chicago: University of Chicago Press, 2016), 19–21. In another context, I have also considered how soldiers in a social fraternity establish their textual authority by demarcating violence within a gendered frame of embodied activity. Elizabeth L. Spragins, "Cuerpos, cuernos, and espadas ceñidas: Sedimenting Gender through Violence in La monja alférez," *ConSecuencias* 1, no. 1 (2019), https://ejournals.bc.edu/index.php/consecuencias/article/view/11769.

23. Leitão, *Miscellânea*, 175; my emphasis.

24. Andrea Frisch, "The Ethics of Testimony: A Genealogical Perspective," *Discourse* 25, no. 1 (2003): 36–54, 40–43; Martínez, *Front Lines*, 5–6.

25. Martínez, *Front Lines*, 21.

26. Leitão de Andrade, *Miscellânea*, 223.

27. Martínez, *Front Lines*, 173.

28. Frisch, "Ethics of Testimony," 40.

29. Leitão de Andrade, *Miscellânea*, 191. My emphasis.

30. Elizabeth L. Spragins, "Embodied Authority: The Virgin, Audience, and the Body of the Devotee in Marian Miracles," *La corónica* 45, no. 2 (2017): 9–36.

31. Martínez, *Front Lines*, 178.

32. Rebecca Schneider, *Performing Remains: Art and War in Times of Theatrical Reenactment* (London: Routledge, 2011), 41.

33. Melissa Kagen, *Wandering Games* (Cambridge, MA: MIT Press, 2022); Schneider, *Performing Remains*, 99–102, and "Judith Butler is My Hands," in *Bodily Citations: Religion and Judith Butler*, ed. Ellen Armour and Susan St. Ville (New York: Columbia University Press, 2006), 225–51.

34. Elizabeth A. R. Brown, "Death and the Human Body in the Later Middle Ages: The Legislation of Boniface VIII on the Division of the Corpse," *Viator* 12 (1981): 221–70, at 267.

35. On Philip's commitment to enforcing the reforms of the Council of Trent, see Henry Kamen, *Philip of Spain* (New Haven, CT: Yale University Press, 1997), 101–4; Timothy J. Schmitz, "The Spanish Hieronymites and the Reformed Texts of the Council of Trent," *The Sixteenth Century Journal* 37 (2006): 375–78.

36. Katrina B. Olds, "The Ambiguities of the Holy: Authenticating Relics in Sixteenth-Century Spain," *Renaissance Quarterly* 65 (2012): 139–40; Bradford Bouley, *Pious Postmortems: Anatomy, Sanctity, and the Catholic Church in Early Modern Europe* (Philadelphia: University of Pennsylvania Press, 2017), 13–15; Peter Brown, *The Cult of the Saints: Its Rise and Function in Latin Christianity*, rev. ed. (1981; repr. Chicago: University of Chicago Press, 2015), 86–105.

37. Carlos M. N. Eire, *From Madrid to Purgatory: The Art and Craft of Dying in Sixteenth-Century Spain* (Cambridge: Cambridge University Press, 1995), 298.

38. One is tempted to speculate that Philip II, having witnessed the upheaval caused by the disorderly interregnum following Sebastian's death, may have altered his heir's accession to the crown to ensure the smoothest possible transition of power.

39. Eire, *From Madrid to Purgatory*, 299.

40. Ibid.

41. Jane Bennett, *Vibrant Matter: A Political Ecology of Things* (Durham, NC : Duke University Press, 2010), 14.

42. Ibid., xvi, 9.

43. Ibid., ix, 21–24. Bruno Latour defines an *actant* as "something that acts or to which activity is granted by others. It implies no special motivation of human individual actors, nor of humans in general." "On Actor-Network Theory: A Few Clarifications," *Soziale Welt* 47 (1996): 373.

44. Vivian Sobchack, remarking on the paradoxical semiotic force of the corpse, observes that "the dreadfulness of the corpse lies in its claim to be the body of the person, while it is wholly unrevealing of the person. What was once so expressive of the human soul has suddenly become a mask." "Inscribing Ethical Space: Ten Propositions on Death, Representation, and Documentary," *Quarterly Review of Film Studies* 9, no. 4 (1984): 283–300, at 288.

45. Bennett, *Vibrant Matter*, 6.

46. Margaret Schwartz, *Dead Matter: The Meaning of Iconic Corpse* (Minneapolis: University of Minnesota Press, 2015), 2.

47. Katherine Verdery, *The Political Lives of Dead Bodies: Reburial and Postsocialist Change* (New York: Columbia University Press, 1999), 108. Loren D. Lybarger argues that dead bodies' effectiveness "lies in how they connect with the transcendent claims of imagined collective identities." "The Demise of Adam in the 'Qisas al-Anbiya': The Symbolic Politics of Death and Re-Burial in Islamic 'Stories of the Prophets," *Numen* 5 (2008): 499. Erin Finnegan, Timothy Hart, and David Halkett argue that in eighteenth-century Cape Town, South Africa, burial practices reinforced social and political divisions: "the colonial burial landscape enforced class and religious segregation in the form of 'official' and 'unofficial' burial grounds." "The 'Informal' Burial Ground at Prestwich Street, Cape Town: Cultural and Chronological Indicators for the Historical Cape Underclass," *The South African Archaeological Bulletin* 66 (2011): 137.

48. The significance of corpses is often discussed in terms of how the living relate to the dead and use them to map the boundaries of society, both geographically and symbolically. The bibliography that describes this process is too large to cite in full, but the following are for notable examples in a range of contexts. Miruna Achim has shown that colonial and transatlantic authors influenced imperial networks through the latent power of socially and politically significant corpses in "The

Autopsy of Fray García Guerra: Corporal Meanings in Seventeenth-Century Mexico," in *Death and Dying in Colonial Spanish America*, ed. Martina Will de Chaparro and Miruna Achim (Tucson: University of Arizona Press, 2011), 78–99. Peter Brown discusses the power of a saint's *praesentia* in a particular place in *The Cult of the Saints*. Vincent Brown asserts that the dead form part of the world of the living through their recontextualization within these predetermined boundaries "by aligning individual experiences of loss and memory with the interests of the community, church, or state. *The Reaper's Garden: Death and Burial in the World of Atlantic Slavery* (Cambridge, MA: Harvard University Press, 2008). Sara T. Nalle observes the significance of location to the evolution of a community rooted in a cult of a saint. "A Saint for All Seasons: The Cult of St. Julián," in *Culture and Control in Counter-Reformation Spain* (Minneapolis: University of Minnesota Press, 1992), 28. Zeb Tortorici examines suicide cases from the Mexican Inquisition and argues that they signified "a sacred geography of postmortem inclusion and exclusion." "Reading the (Dead) Body: Histories of Suicide in New Spain," in Will de Chaparo and Achim, *Death and Dying in Colonial Spanish America*, 64.

49. Bossong, "Differential Object Marking," 159–62.

50. On inherence, see Michael Silverstein, "Hierarchy of Features and Ergativity," in *Grammatical Categories in Australian Languages*, ed. Richard Dixon, 112–71 (Canberra: Australian Institute of Aboriginal Studies, 1976).

51. For example, Fred Astren compares rabbinic texts from the first millennium BCE that regulated Jewish mourning practices with similar regulations of mortuary practices that are outlined in hadith. He finds that these two sets of death rituals both sought to distance their faith communities from the excesses of grief emblematic of pagan cult activity at the grave. "Depaganizing Death: Aspects of Mourning in Rabbinic Judaism and Early Islam," in *Bible and Qur'ān: Essays in Scriptural Intertextuality*, ed. J. C. Reeves (Leiden: Brill, 2003), 183–99.

52. Sobchack, "Inscribing Ethical Space," 288, emphasis in original.

53. Ibid., 287–88.

54. Latour, "On Actor-Network Theory," 373.

55. Bossong, "Animacy and Markedness," 151–53; Silverstein, "Hierarchy of Features and Ergativity," 112–71.

56. Bennett, *Vibrant Matter*, 21.

57. The classic example of this syntactically marked gradient of animacy comes when the speaker refers animals: a favorite pet will warrant use of the preposition *a*, but a general animal will not. Bossong's research on differential object marking emphasizes that "positive object marking inside a DOM [differential object marking] system marks subject-like objects." "Differential Object Marking," 162.

58. Cara Krmpotich, Joost Fontein, and John Harries, "The Substance of Bones: The Emotive Materiality and Affective Presence of Human Remains," *Journal of Material Culture* 15, no. 2 (2010): 371–84, at 372. Here, they expand what Carl Knappett and Lambros Malafouris say about the property of agency not being exclusive to humans. "Material and Nonhuman Agency: An Introduction," in

Material Agency: Towards a Non-Anthropocentric Approach, ed. Carl Knappett and Lambros Malafouris (New York: Springer, 2008), ix–xix.

59. Deborah Posel and Pamela Gupta, "The Life of the Corpse: Framing Reflections and Questions," *African Studies* 68, no. 3 (2009): 299–301.

60. Krmpotich, Fontein, and Harries, "The Substance of Bones," 373.

61. Ibid., 375.

62. Bossong's preferred term for *prominence*, or position in the hierarchy of animacy, is *inherence*. "Differential Object Marking," 159.

63. Leitão de Andrade, *Miscellânea*, 192.

64. John Frow argues that the differences between people and objects should be "flattened, read horizontally as a juxtaposition rather than vertically as a hierarchy of being. It's a feature of our world that we can and do distinguish . . . things from persons. But the sort of world we live in makes it constantly possible for these two sets of kinds to exchange properties." "A Pebble, a Camera, a Man," *Critical Inquiry* 28, no. 1 (2001): 283.

65. Seigworth and Gregg, "An Inventory of Shimmers," 2.

66. Bennett, *Vibrant Matter*, xvi.

67. Seigworth and Gregg, "An Inventory of Shimmers," 1.

68. Recall Bennett's definition of Thing-Power, *Vibrant Matter*, especially 4–13.

69. Leitão de Andrade, *Miscellânea*, 195–96.

70. Certainly, Leitão's loss of agency could in part be attributed to his captivity, but the strong identification with the corpses of both the friar and Sebastian in quick succession, and contemplation of his own threatened and threatening mortality warrant considering other angles.

71. Bennett, *Vibrant Matter*, 32.

72. Sergio Bertelli describes the symbolic significance of the movement of the king through the public space, arguing that this kind of movement makes that space into "a physical extension of their own bodies." *The King's Body: Sacred Rituals of Power in Medieval and Early Modern Europe*, trans. R. Burr Litchfield (University Park: Pennsylvania State University Press, 2001), 77. In this way, the movement of Sebastian's corpse through space is almost an inversion of this image, marking his diminished territorial claims.

73. The stripping of this king's body in some ways replicates medieval and early modern European funeral ceremonies, which sometimes included the circumscribed violence of a custom of robbing the lord's clothing upon their death. Bertelli, *The King's Body*, 60. Obviously, the stripping of Sebastian's corpse would have been more disturbing to the contemporary reader, since there was no promise of the restoration of order after a limited interregnum.

74. The simple clothing in which Sebastian is dressed in this scene is not necessarily a show of disrespect to the defeated king. Indeed, his uncle and eventual successor, Philip II, would also be buried dressed in a simple tunic, though probably not that taken from the back of his aide. Eire, *From Madrid to Purgatory*, 285.

75. Schneider, *Performing Remains*, 8–14.

4. Assemblage: Recovering Diplomatic Power with Corpses

1. See, for example, E. V. Bovill, *The Battle of Alcazar: An Account of the Defeat of Don Sebastian of Portugal at El-Ksar el-Kebir* (London: Batchworth, 1952); Weston F. Cook Jr., *The Hundred Years War for Morocco: Gunpowder and the Military Revolution in the Early Modern Muslim World* (Boulder, CO: Westview Press, 1994); Bailey W. Diffie and George D. Winius, *Foundations of the Portuguese Empire 1415–1850* (Minneapolis: University of Minnesota Press, 1977); Ruth MacKay, *The Baker Who Pretended to Be King of Portugal* (Chicago: University of Chicago Press, 2012); and Dahiru Yahya, *Morocco in the Sixteenth Century: Problems and Patterns in African Foreign Policy* (Atlantic Highlands, NJ: Humanities Press, 1981).

2. Andrea Gasparo Corzo (spelled "Corso" in some French scholarship and occasionally so in primary sources) and his brother, Francisco, even met 'Abd al-Malik and his brother when they were in exile in Algiers in the 1560s. Despite Silva's snobbery toward the agent, the archival evidence demonstrates that the entire Gasparo Corzo family played a key role in Mediterranean diplomacy on behalf of the Spanish crown beginning in the 1560s. Claire M. Gilbert, *In Good Faith: Arabic Translation and Translators in Early Modern Spain* (Philadelphia: University of Pennsylvania Press, 2020), 114; Chantal de La Véronne, "Les frères Gasparo Corso et le Chérif Moulay 'Abd El-Malek (1569–1574)," in *Archives et bibliothèques d'Espagne*, Les sources inédites de l'histoire du Maroc (Paris: Paul Geuthner, 1974), 157–65.

3. The original manuscript letters are held in the collection of the Consejo de Estado, among other state documents at the Archivo General de Simancas and were edited in the nineteenth century as volumes 39 and 40 of the *Colección de documentos inéditos para la historia de España* (hereafter *CODOIN*). This collection was a nationalistic undertaking begun during the nineteenth century by the Marquises de Pidal and Miraflores and the Academia de la Historia to collect, organize, and conserve documents held in various private and public collections throughout Spain. Some of the diplomatic correspondence in question was held by the family of Medinasidonia in their private library in Sanlúcar de Barrameda, Cadiz, as well much material now held in Simancas. As compiled in *CODOIN*, Silva's correspondence appears in chronological fashion, spanning just over a year between January 6, 1578, and February 16, 1579.

4. Privileged courtiers and ambassadors served as surrogates for their royal masters in the most intimate circumstances, as in Philip II's marriage to his third wife, Elizabeth of Valois, in which the Duke of Alba not only stood as his proxy in the wedding ceremony at Notre Dame but is also said to have also stood in for him in the official consummation ceremony. This ceremony consisted of the Duke of Alba placing one arm and one leg on the marriage bed, the "posesión del tálamo" (possession of the marriage bed), which would be a stopgap measure until the marriage was physically consummated with Philip II when Isabel reached maturity at the age of fifteen. Chris Skidmore, *Death and the Virgin: Elizabeth, Dudley, and*

the Mysterious Fate of Amy Robsart (London: Phoenix, 2011), 122; Henry Kamen, *Philip of Spain* (New Haven, CT: Yale University Press, 1997), 74.

5. Michael J. Levin, *Agents of Empire: Spanish Ambassadors in Sixteenth-Century Italy* (Ithaca, NY: Cornell University Press, 2005), 6, 10. See also Michael Mallett, "Ambassadors and their Audiences in Renaissance Italy," *Renaissance Studies* 8 (1994): 232.

6. Jane Bennett, *Vibrant Matter: A Political Ecology of Things* (Durham, NC: Duke University Press, 2010), 22.

7. Gilles Deleuze and Félix Guattari first propose this term in *A Thousand Plateaus: Capitalism and Schizophrenia*, trans. Brian Massumi (Minneapolis: University of Minnesota Press, 1987). Foucault proposes the term *dispositif* or *apparatus* in "Confessions of the Flesh," published posthumously as *Confessions of the Flesh: The History of Sexuality*, vol. 4, ed. Frederic Gros, trans. Robert Hurley (New York: Pantheon, 2021), 35–36.

8. Lone Bertelson and Andrew Murphie, "An Ethics of Everyday Infinities and Powers: Félix Guattari on Affect and the Refrain," in *The Affect Theory Reader*, ed. Gregory J. Seigworth and Melissa Gregg (Durham, NC: Duke University Press, 2010), 138–57, at 155. Guattari's analogous term for the assemblage is "collective." *Chaosmosis: An Ethico-Aesthetic Paradigm*, trans. paul bains and Julian Pefanis (Sydney: Power, 1995), 9.

9. Bennett, *Vibrant Matter*, 32.

10. Heather Dubrow, *Deixis in the Early Modern Lyric: Unsettling Spatial Anchors Like "Here," "This," "Come"* (New York: Palgrave Macmillan, 2015), 12.

11. Robert A. Folger, *Writing as Poaching: Interpellation and Self-Fashioning in Colonial Relaciones de Méritos y Servicios* (Leiden: Brill, 2011), 5.

12. Sebastián de Covarrubias Orozco, *Tesoro de la lengua castellana o española* (Madrid: 1611), 1753.

13. Folger, *Writing as Poaching*, 3–7.

14. In chapter 2, I first discussed the most famous theorization of the organological metaphor of kingship in Ernst H. Kantorowicz, *The King's Two Bodies: A Study in Mediaeval Political Theology*, 7th ed. (Princeton, NJ: Princeton University Press, 1997). More recent work on the corporeal understanding of Iberian monarchy includes Adeline Rucquoi, "De los reyes que no son taumaturgos: Los fundamentos de la realeza en España," *Relaciones: Estudios de Historia y Sociedad* 13, no. 51 (1992): 55–100; Teofilo F. Ruiz, "Unsacred Monarchy: The Kings of Castile in the Late Middle Ages," in *Rites of Power: Symbolism, Ritual and Politics since the Late Middle Ages*, ed. Sean Wilentz (Philadelphia: University of Pennsylvania Press, 1985), 109–44; and Javier Varela, *La muerte del rey: El ceremonial funerario de la monarquía española (1500–1885)* (Madrid: Turner, 1990).

15. Folger, *Writing as Poaching*, 10.

16. J. H. Elliott, "The Court of the Spanish Habsburgs: A Peculiar Institution?" in *Spain and Its World 1500–1700* (New Haven: Yale University Press, 1989); Jeremy Black, *A History of Diplomacy* (London: Reaktion Books, 2010), 46.

17. Margaret Schwartz, *Dead Matter: The Meaning of Iconic Corpse* (Minneapolis: University of Minnesota Press, 2015), 4.

18. Dubrow, *Deixis in Early Modern English Lyric*, 6.

19. Juan de Borja cautions Silva: "Uno de los mayores travaxos que a de tener El-Enbajador de Portugal a de ser la desconfianza con que tratan los negocios El-Rey y sus ministros pareciéndoles que qualquier descuido que aya, o qualquier cumplimento que a ellos se dexe de hazer es por tenerles en poco no considerando las muchas ocupaciones ni otras cosas graves que impiden. Hacerse esto como ellos querrian, asi combiene andar siempre muy sobre aviso en todos los negocios que se trataren con el-rrey y sus ministros [One of the primary concerns that the Ambassador of Portugal must consider is the suspicion with which the King and his ministers treat issues, it seeming to them that any oversight that there might be, or whatever task is left to them to complete is to undervalue them, not considering the many preoccupations or other grave things that hinder them. Do this as they wish, it is convenient to always be very much up to date on the issues with which the king and his ministers are currently dealing]." "Advertimientos de don Juan de Borja para don Juan de Silva quando le embió su Majestad por embaxador a Portugal," Consejo de Estado, leg. 392, f. 217, Archivo General de Simancas.

20. Levin relates the ongoing debate at the papal court over whether, as representative of the Catholic monarch, the Spanish ambassador deserved precedence over the French ambassador. Levin notes, "Ceremonies [in the early modern period] involving ambassadors transformed into political theater: where envoys stood or sat in relation to each other served as a barometer for relationships between states and rulers." *Agents of Empire*, 6, 81. See also William Roosen, "Early Modern Diplomatic Ceremonial: A Systems Approach," *Journal of Modern History* 52 (1980): 455.

21. Elliott and Fernando Bouza Álvarez both comment on the reorganization of Charles V's court. Bouza Álvarez suggests that the reorganization of Philip II's court while he was still the crown prince affected Silva's early career, preventing him from traveling with the prince's court to the Low Countries from 1548 to 1551. "Corte es decepción: Don Juan de Silva, Conde De Portalegre," in *La corte de Felipe II*, ed. José Martínez Millán (Madrid: Alianza, 1994), 457. For example, at the court of Portugal, Sebastian's courtiers wondered at the young king's utter lack of interest in women and expressed concern that he was impotent and therefore incapable of producing an heir. This was not only salacious interest in the king's sex life but also a political concern whose consequences would be borne out between August 1578 and 1580, when Sebastian's death without an heir left Portugal in a tenuous geopolitical position. By the time Silva was named ambassador to Portugal, questions of the king's impotence and his marriage had become such a sensitive subject at the Portuguese court that Juan de Borja, Silva's predecessor, warns him to not discuss the subject with either the king or his ministers: "A se de evitar lo possible no venir a tratar de cosas Pasadas en materia de casamientos del rrey con el ni con sus ministros [One must avoid as much as possible to not come to discuss past things on the matter

of the marriage of the king with him nor with his ministers]." "Advertimientos," f. 217r. Similar speculation was common in the English court. *Calendar of State Papers, Foreign, Mary, 1553–1558*, 174. Catherine Loomis notes that, upon Elizabeth's death, she left orders that her body not be opened, possibly because it would show she had not truly been a virgin. "Elizabeth Southwell's Manuscript Account of the Death of Queen Elizabeth," *English Literary Renaissance* 26 (1996): 494.

22. Annemarie Jordan, "Queen of the Seas and Overseas: Dining at the Table of Catherine of Austria, Queen of Portugal," in *Mesas reais europeias: Encomendas e ofertas*, ed. Leonor d'Orey (Lisbon: Instituto Português de Museus, 1999), 17.

23. "Lesser dignitaries were received in one or other of the outer rooms, and the right of entry to the holy of holies, the king's study or *aposento*, was restricted to the papal nuncio, the President of the Council of Castile, cardinals, viceroys, and those fortunate individuals who had been accorded special royal permission." Elliott, "The Court of the Spanish Habsburgs," 149.

24. Leitão de Andrade, *Miscellânea*, 402. Leitão's description of the court is reminiscent of the account of the emerging notion of *The King's Two Bodies* that Kantorowicz gives, particularly considering the explanation the latter offers regarding the emergence of the state model from that of the church. See chapter 5, especially 202.

25. Hillay Zmora, *Monarchy, Aristocracy, and the State in Europe, 1300–1800* (New York: Routledge, 2000), 81.

26. Carlos M. N. Eire, *From Madrid to Purgatory: The Art and Craft of Dying in Sixteenth-Century Spain* (Cambridge: Cambridge University Press, 1995), 215.

27. Schwartz, *Dead Matter*; Eire, *From Madrid to Purgatory*, 258.

28. Eire takes Philip II's death and burial as his case study in the second section of *From Madrid to Purgatory* but suggests that many of the rites he identifies from this transition represent values held by Charles V and his successors. Eire, *From Madrid to Purgatory*, 288. See also Steven N. Orso, *Art and Death at the Spanish Court: The Royal Exequies for Philip IV* (Columbia: University of Missouri Press, 1989), 6–26.

29. An indication of what a small circle was entrusted with access to Habsburg royal corpses can be found in the figure of Cristóval de Moura. Silva's substitute at the Portuguese court while the latter was captured and convalescing from his injury was thus not only responsible for arranging Sebastian's funerals *in absentia*, but two decades later was also asked personally by Philip II to "bury him in a simple gown, to wrap him in a winding sheet, and to hang a plain wooden cross around his neck. Eire, *From Madrid to Purgatory*, 277.

30. Eire, *From Madrid to Purgatory*, 299.

31. Schwartz, *Dead Matter*, 4.

32. Katherine Verdery, *The Political Lives of Dead Bodies: Reburial and Postsocialist Change* (New York: Columbia University Press, 1999), 27. Here I allude again to Bennett's mobilization of Spinoza's sense of the conative "as a stubborn or inertial tendency to persist." *Vibrant Matter*, 22.

33. Schwartz, *Dead Matter*, 4.
34. Bennett, *Vibrant Matter*, 22–23.
35. Schwartz, *Dead Matter*, 4.
36. Bouza Álvarez, "Corte es decepción," 457.
37. M. Rodríguez-Salgado observes that "there were constant conflicts over finance between the monarch and his regents and governors. Almost every letter they exchanged contained either a request for money or a complaint about the level of financial contributions being demanded. These officials sent frequent and pitiful cries of exhaustion as well as complaints about the misuse of funds." *The Changing Face of Empire: Charles V, Philip II, and Habsburg Authority, 1551–1559* (Cambridge: Cambridge University Press, 1988), 22. See Bouza Álvarez on Silva's correspondence. "Corte es decepción," 468–69.
38. MacKay, *The Baker*, 4.
39. So restricted was access to the women of the royal family that only women were allowed to serve Sebastian's grandmother Catherine at meals. Annemarie Jordan, "Queen of the Seas and Overseas: Dining at the Table of Catherine of Austria, Queen of Portugal," in *Mesas Reais Europeias. Encomendas e Ofertas/ Royal and Princely Tables of Europe. Commissions and Gifts/Tables Royales en Europe. Commandes et Cadeaux*, ed. Leonor d' Orey (Lisbon: Instituto Português de Museus, 1999), 16–17.
40. *CODOIN* 39:465–66.
41. Covarrubias, *Tesoro de la lengua castellana*, 1753.
42. Both quotations *CODOIN* 39:497–98.
43. Both quotations ibid., 489–500.
44. Ibid., 501–2.
45. Ibid., 502.
46. Ibid.
47. For example, *CODOIN* 39:465–66.
48. Documents in the Consejo de Estado at the Archivo General de Simancas make it possible to follow the discussion about Silva's captivity and recovery that took place between Philip, Spanish officials, Portuguese ambassadors, and other parties in the months following al-Qaṣr al-Kabīr. For example, a letter from Philip October 5, 1578, mentions that he received a letter from Moura, Silva's substitute in Portugal, reporting that Silva was alive and captive in Larache. Philip II to Christoval de Mora [*sic*], letter, 5 October, 1578, Consejo de Estado, leg. 395, f. 187, Archivo General de Simancas.
49. We read Philip's response to this news in a letter to Moura from 20 October, 1578, in which he asks to be kept abreast of Silva's healing "del Arcabuzaso del braço" (from harquebus wound in the arm). Philip II to Christóval de Mora [*sic*], letter, 20 October 1578, Consejo de Estado, leg. 395, f. 274, Archivo General de Simancas.
50. *CODOIN* 40:89.
51. Covarrubias, *Tesoro de la lengua castellana o española*, 1753.
52. *CODOIN* 39:74.
53. Ibid., 40:89.

54. Ibid., 92, my emphasis.

55. For examples of this usage of the verb as "it occurred to [object]," see ibid. 39: 514–15; 536–37; 539.

56. *CODOIN* 39, quotations at 496, 536, 537, 541.

57. Ibid., 40: 87. Silva's snobbery in discussing Corzo is evident when compared with a number of other agents with whom he collaborates or interacts before the battle. He refers to other men of similar status with more complimentary language that assumes the king's familiarity with them: "Estéban Lercaro . . . es hombre de bien" (*CODOIN* 39:485); "en recomendación de Lorenzo Ribero" (485); or "el buen Francisco Cano" (487).

58. *CODOIN* 40:91–92, my emphasis.

59. Both quotations ibid.

60. This redundancy contrasts with earlier efforts to not duplicate communicated information. For example, on July 25, 1578, Silva comments: "El despacho fué por vía del duque de Medinasidonia ó del asistente de Sevilla; no dubdo que habrá llegado por uno destos dos caminos, y así *no duplicaré de lo que entónces escrebí* [the dispatch went either by way of the Duke of Medina-Sidonia or the aide in Seville; I do not doubt that it will have arrived for one of these two routes, and so *I shall not duplicate what I then wrote*]." *CODOIN* 40:71.

61. La Véronne, "Les frères Gasparo Corso," 158, 160. It is ironic that someone like Silva, whose status at court depended on his ability to render service to the king and on his familial connections failed to recognize the value of Corzo's connections on the other side of the Mediterranean. While Silva's treatment of Corzo might make us overlook his importance in this matter, the networks he had at his disposal allowed him to render a wide range of service to the Spanish Crown. See Gilbert on the importance of fiduciary agents who mediated Spanish interests across the Mediterranean, especially those who acted as translators. *In Good Faith*, 114–15.

62. Corzo was one of those mediating figures who flourished in the "espacio fronterizo" (frontier space) that Mercedes García-Arenal, Fernando Rodríguez Mediano, and Rachid el Hour describe as fundamental to understanding Moroccan society of the late sixteenth and early seventeenth century. *Cartas marruecas: Documentos de Marruecos en archivos españoles (siglos XVI–XVII)* (Madrid: Consejo Superior de Investigaciones Científicas, 2002), 17–19. While Andrea operated mostly out of Algiers, where he met ʿAbd al-Malik and al-Manṣūr, his elder brother, Francisco, managed the clearing house for dispatching and translating messages to and from the Court in Valencia. La Véronne notes their importance as intermediaries surrounding al-Qasr al-Kabir. "Les frères Gasparo Corso," 159.

63. *CODOIN* 40:87.

64. Silva endeavors to obscure the extent to which Corzo's agency was responsible for his release, and instead plays to Philip's vanity and his own by framing his debt as accruing only to the Spanish king: "los pagó el Corzo para servir á V.M.d; y habiendo de ir el dicho Corzo con negocios á esa corte, pienso que dentro en quince dias podrémos atravesar á Castilla [Corzo paid them (those

responsible for Silva's care) in order to serve Your Majesty; and the said Corzo having to go on business to that court, I think that within fifteen days, we will be able to travel to Castile].” Ibid., 89.

65. According to a document signed by Corzo himself, other agents in the recovery of Sebastian's corpse to Ceuta were D. Lionis Pereira, D. Rodrigo Meneses, and Fr. Roque do Spirito Sancho. Ibid., 93–94.

66. Ibid., 91–92, my emphasis.

67. Ibid., 55.

68. Ibid., 92, my emphasis.

69. Ibid., my emphasis.

70. Ricardo Padrón reminds us that for early modern Spaniards, space and time were intimately linked concepts, as travel was primarily calculated by the duration a trip took, which then informed the travelers' understanding of the distance traversed. *The Spacious Word: Cartography, Literature, and Empire in Early Modern Spain* (Chicago: University of Chicago Press, 2004), 47–49.

71. *CODOIN* 40, both quotations 91–92.

72. This process would have involved a series of coordinated operations “more complex than securing funds and obtaining the necessary permits from the Spanish crown. An official from one of the Spanish garrisons in the Maghrib or a friar sent for the purposes had to travel to the city where the orders planned to ransom captives and purchase a safe conduct from its governor.” Daniel Hershenzon, *The Captive Sea: Slavery, Communication, and Commerce in Early Modern Spain and the Mediterranean* (Philadelphia: University of Pennsylvania Press, 2018), 63. Hershenzon is not describing the recovery of Sebastian's corpse and Silva from captivity, but the order of operations that governed the economy of captivity and redemption in the Mediterranean during the sixteenth and seventeenth centuries.

5. Erasure: Corpse Desecration for Narrative Control

1. Francisco Rodríguez Mediano briefly mentions the case as a prime example of the dehumanization of the body of the victim in “Justice, Crime and Punishment in 10th/16th-Century Morocco,” in *Public Violence in Islamic Societies: Power, Discipline, and the Construction of the Public Sphere, 7th–19th Centuries CE*, ed. Christian Lange and Maribel Fierro (Edinburgh: Edinburgh University Press, 2009), 187.

2. Although it is a set of practices identified with relative frequency in death studies, Jason De León is responsible for labeling them with this term. Necroviolence has been widely identified and commented with other labels and other criteria elsewhere. *The Land of Open Graves: Living and Dying on the Migrant Trail* (Berkeley: University of California Press, 2015), 68–72. For a sampling of scholarship on this phenomenon, see Michel Foucault, *Discipline and Punish: The Birth of the Prison*, 2nd ed., trans. Alan Sheridan (New York: Vintage Books, 1977), 34; Thomas W. Laqueur, *The Work of the Dead: A Cultural History of Mortal Remains* (Princeton, NJ: Princeton

University Press, 2015), 4–8; Franny Nudelman, *John Brown's Body: Slavery, Violence, and the Culture of War* (Chapel Hill: University of North Carolina Press, 2004).

3. Linda Jones discusses this at length in an Islamic context in "Bodily Performances and Body Talk," in *The Ends of the Body: Identity and Community in Medieval Culture*, ed. Suzanne Conklin Akbari and Jill Ross (Toronto: University of Toronto Press, 2013), 211–35.

4. Ibid., 218–19; Christian Lange, "Where on Earth Is Hell? State Punishment and Eschatology in the Islamic Middle Period," in *Public Violence in Islamic Societies: Power, Discipline, and the Construction of the Public Sphere, 7th–19th Centuries CE*, ed. Christian Lange and Maribel Fierro (Edinburgh: Edinburgh University Press, 2009), 160–62; Mediano, "Justice, Crime and Punishment," 180.

5. Brian Massumi, "The Future Birth of the Affective Fact: The Political Ontology of Threat," in *The Affect Theory Reader*, ed. Melissa Gregg and Gregory J. Seigworth (Durham, NC: Duke University Press, 2010), 52–70.

6. Michel Foucault, *The History of Sexuality: An Introduction, Vol. 1*, trans. Robert Hurley (New York: Vintage Books, 1978), 139–41.

7. Because the known manuscripts are unsigned and acephalous, scholars since Fagnan and Colin have struggled to date it with precision. Edmond Fagnan, *Extraits inédits relatifs au Mahgreb (Géographie et histoire): Traduits de l'arabe et annotés* (Algiers: Jules Carbonel, 1924), 360–61.

8. Julie Scott Meisami argues that scholars of Arabic and Persian historiography have continued to be invested in positivist agendas, parsing "truth" from "fiction," rather than recognize the "'literary' devices—narrative structure, discourse, rhetorical embellishment, and so on" that were hardwired into historians' work." "History as Literature," *Iranian Studies* 33, nos. 1–2 (2000): 15.

9. Stephen Cory, *Reviving the Islamic Caliphate in Early Modern Morocco* (New York: Routledge, 2013), 65–84, 225–28. Evariste Lévi-Provençal refers to the text as a "virulent diatribe" in *Les historiens des chorfa: Essai sur la litterature historique et biographique au Maroc du XVIe au XXe siècle* (Paris: Larose, 1922), 132; *Tārīkh al-dawla al-saʿdiyya al-Takmadārtiyya*, ed. ʿAbd al-Raḥīm Benḥādda (Marrakesh: Maṭbaʿa Tīnmal, 1994), 98. The chronicler claims that the Spanish negotiated this at the beginning of al-Manṣūr's reign, sweetening the deal with a generous gift. This is a particularly interesting line of critique from the anonymous scholar, considering the origins of the Saʿdī regime in promoting jihad. Vincent J. Cornell and Stephen Cory specify that this jihad emerged in response to the abuses of Portuguese presidios on the Atlantic coast. Cornell, "Socioeconomic Dimensions of Reconquista and Jihād in Morocco: Portuguese Dukkala and Saʿdid Sūs, 1450–1557," *International Journal of Middle East Studies* 22 (1990): 379–418; Cory, *Reviving the Islamic Caliphate*, 4–5. Mercedes García-Arenal suggests instead that more material interests were responsible for mobilizing jihadi discourse and that the rhetoric of jihad acted in service of those interests. "Mahdī, Murābiṭ, Sharīf: L'avènement de la dynastie saʿdienne," *Studia Islamica* 71 (1990): 77–114, at 87, 104.

10. Cory, *Reviving the Islamic Caliphate*, 226. For an in-depth study of the circulation and evolution of jihadi discourse during the Saʿdī and ʿAlawī periods,

see Amira K. Bennison, *Jihad and Its Interpretations in Pre-Colonial Morocco: State-Society Relations during the French Conquest of Algiers* (London: Routledge, 2002), 15–41. See also Bennison, "'Abd al-Qādir's *Jihād* in the Light of the Western Islamic Jihād Tradition," *Studia Islamica* 106, no. 2 (2011), especially 201–3.

11. Cory, *Reviving the Islamic Caliphate*, 227. *Pace* Cory, I have found occasional reference in the *Tārīkh* to the Saʿdī regime as a *khilāfa*, but on balance I agree with Cory that use of such terminology is sparse and does not establish a sustained defense of a Saʿdī caliphate. See, for example, *Tārīkh al-dawla*, 98.

12. Lévi-Provençal, *Les historiens des chorfa*, 132. Scholars generally agree that the Saʿdīs succeeded in marshaling their sharīfi status to support their claim to religious as well as political authority beginning in the first quarter of the sixteenth century. The 'Alawīs, the dynasty that succeeded the Saʿdīs and remains in power in Morocco today, relied and continue to rely heavily on sharīfi claims as a source of their legitimacy. Henry Munson Jr., *Religion and Power* (New Haven, CT: Yale University Press, 1993), 39–43; Jamil M. Abun Nasr, *A History of the Maghrib in the Islamic Period* (Cambridge: Cambridge University Press, 1987), 206–19; Vincent J. Cornell, *Realm of the Saint: Power and Authority in Moroccan Sufism* (Austin: University of Texas Press, 1998), 155–95; Stephen Cory, "Sharīfian Rule in Morocco (Tenth–Twelfth/Sixteenth–Eighteenth Centuries," in *The Western Islamic World, Eleventh to Eighteenth Centuries*, ed. Maribel Fierro (Cambridge: Cambridge University Press, 2010), 453–79; Natalie Zemon Davis, *Trickster Travels: A Sixteenth-Century Muslim Between Worlds* (New York: Hill and Wang, 2006), 26–27; Mercedes García-Arenal, "Sainteté et pouvoir dynastique au Maroc: La résistance de Fès aux Saʿdiens," *Annales* 45 (1990): 1019–42; Dahiru Yahya, *Morocco in the Sixteenth Century: Problems and Patterns in African Foreign Policy* (Atlantic Highlands, NJ: Humanities Press, 1981), 2–7. Fernando Rodríguez Mediano highlights the emergence of sharīfism as political ideology during the time of the Marīnids. Mediano, "The Post-Almohad Dynasties in Al-Andalus and the Maghrib (Seventh–Ninth/Thirteenth–Fifteenth Centuries)," in Fierro, *The Western Islamic World*, 125–26.

13. Cory, *Reviving the Islamic Caliphate*, 225–28; Lévi-Provençal, *Les historiens des Chorfa*, 131–40. Benḥādda mentions that Abū al-Qāsim al-Ziyānī believed the anonymous historian was from Meknes rather than Fez, but on balance agrees with Lévi-Provençal and suggests that al-Ziyani may have been referring to the manuscript's copyist rather the historian. Benḥādda, ed., *Tārīkh al-dawla*, 7.

14. He retracts this praise almost as quickly as he gives it by questioning the ways in which this wealth was used. See Cory, *Reviving the Islamic Caliphate*, 226.

15. Edmond Fagnan, *Extraits inédits relatifs au Maghreb (Géographie et histoire): Traduits de l'arabe et annotés* (Algiers: Jules Carbonel, 1924), 360–457; Georges S. Colin, ed., *Tārīkh al-dawla al-saʿdiyya al-takmadārtiyya* (Rabat, 1934), and Benḥādda, *Tārīkh al-dawla*.

16. Though this variance between editions is, of course, noteworthy, the overall meaning of the passages I analyze does not differ greatly between them, and

therefore I feel comfortable presenting this argument based on textual analysis of the editions rather than the original manuscripts.

17. John O. Hunwick, "Source Materials for the History of Songhay, Borneo, and Hausaland in the Sixteenth Century," *Journal of the Historical Society of Nigeria* 7, no. 3 (1974): 581–82.

18. Hunwick tracks primary sources about Maghrebi portrayals of sub-Saharan Africans through al-Ifrānī's account of the invasion of the Songhay empire in 1591. "Askia al-Ḥājj Muḥammad and His Successors: The Account of al-Imām al-Takrūrī," *Sudanic Africa* 1 (1990): 85–89; "Secular Power and Religious Authority in Muslim Society: The Case of Songhay," *The Journal of African History*, 37, no. 2 (1996): 183–84. John Ralph Willis refers to the chronicle as a useful introduction to Sadī history and treats it as a source for reconstructing a factual history of Moroccan presence in Western Sudan in "The Western Sudan from the Moroccan Invasion (1591) to the Death of al-Mukhtar al-Kunti (1811)," in *The History of West Africa*, vol. 1, ed. J. F. A. A. Ajayi and Michael Crowder (Bristol, UK: Longman Group Ltd., 1971): 441–84. Patricia Mercer focuses more centrally on the Maghreb as such and examines *Nuzhat al-ḥādī* for what it can tell us about the early ʿAlawī dynasty as a tributary state. "Palace and Jihād in the Early ʿAlawī State in Morocco," *The Journal of African History* 18, no. 4 (1977): 537.

19. García-Arenal, "*Mahdī, murābiṭ, sharīf*," 80.

20. Nadia al-Bagdadi, "Registers of Arabic Literary History," *New Literary History* 39, no. 3 (2008): 439.

21. Consider, in contrast, Houari Touati's observations about Yaʿqūbī's geographical prose when compared with his writing on historical subjects. *Islam and Travel* (Chicago: University of Chicago Press, 2010), 131.

22. De León, *The Land of Open Graves*, 69–72. See also Laqueur, *The Work of the Dead*, 4–8.

23. Saul W. Olyan, "The Instrumental Dimensions of Ritual Violence against Corpses in Biblical Texts," in *Ritual Violence in the Hebrew Bible: New Perspectives*, ed. Saul W. Olyan (Oxford: Oxford University Press, 2015), 125–36; Foucault, *Discipline and Punish*; Caroline Ford, "Violence and the Sacred in Nineteenth-Century France," *Historical Studies* 21, no. 1 (1998): 101–12; De León, *The Land of Open Graves*, 69–72.

24. Nicholas Morton argues that public displays of torture of captives and corpse mutilation in the Near East between the First and Second Crusades "would have seemed alien to a local religious leader." The near ubiquitous practice of torture and corpse desecration throughout the premodern Mediterranean contradicts the idea that these practices were foreign imports into the Mediterranean from the central Asian steppe; on the contrary, Mediterranean peoples demonstrate their willingness and capability of similar levels of corpse-directed violence. *The Field of Blood: The Battle for Aleppo and the Remaking of the Medieval Middle East* (New York: Basic Books, 2018), 117.

25. Homer, *Iliad* 23, ll. 390–476.

26. Olyan, "Ritual Violence against Corpses," 126.

27. Foucault, *The History of Sexuality*, 139–41.

28. Achille Mbembe, "Necropolitics," *Public Culture* 15, no. 1 (2003): 11–12. He expanded on his ideas in a full monograph of the same title, *Necropolitics* (Durham, NC: Duke University Press, 2019).

29. A sampling of recent bibliography beyond those already cited includes Robert Bartlett, *Why Can the Dead Do Such Great Things? Saints and Worshippers from the Martyrs to the Reformation* (Princeton, NJ: Princeton University Press, 2013); Patrick Geary, *Living with the Dead in the Middle Ages* (Ithaca, NY: Cornell University Press, 1994); Katrina B. Olds, "The Ambiguities of the Holy: Authenticating Relics in Sixteenth-Century Spain." *Renaissance Quarterly* 65 (2012): 135–84; Kaara L. Peterson, "Elizabeth I's Virginity and the Body of Evidence: Jonson's Notorious Crux," *Renaissance Quarterly* 68 (2015): 840–71; Zeb Tortorici, "Reading the (Dead) Body: Histories of Suicide in New Spain," in *Death and Dying in Colonial Spanish America*, ed. Martina Will de Chaparro and Miruna Achim (Tucson: University of Arizona Press, 2011), 53–77; Craig Young and Duncan Light, "Corpses, Dead Body Politics and Agency in Human Geography: Following the Corpse of Dr. Petru Groza," *Transactions of the Institute of British Geographers* 38, no. 1 (2012): 135–48.

30. Deborah Posel and Pamela Gupta, "The Life of the Corpse: Framing Reflections and Questions," *African Studies* 68, no. 3 (2009): 300.

31. For example, Vincent Brown, *The Reaper's Garden: Death and Burial in the World of Atlantic Slavery* (Cambridge, MA: Harvard University Press, 2008); Erin Finnegan, Timothy Hart, and David Halkett, "The 'Informal' Burial Ground at Prestwich Street, Cape Town: Cultural and Chronological Indicators for the Historical Cape Underclass," *The South African Archaeological Bulletin* 66 (2011): 136–48; Joost Fontein, "Between Tortured Bodies and Resurfacing Bones: The Politics of the Dead in Zimbabwe," *Journal of Material Culture* 15, no. 4 (2010): 423–48; Cara Krmpotich, Joost Fontein, and John Harries, "The Substance of Bones: The Emotive Materiality and Affective Presence of Human Remains," *Journal of Material Culture* 15, no. 2 (2010): 371–84.

32. Thomas Laqueur argues that "there seems to be a universally shared feeling not only that there is something deeply wrong about not caring for the dead body in some fashion, but that the uncared-for body, no matter the cultural norms, is unbearable." *The Work of the Dead*, 8.

33. Leor Halevi, *Muhammad's Grave: Death Rites and the Making of Islamic Society* (New York: Columbia University Press, 2007), 158–59; Laqueur, *The Work of the Dead*, 4–8.

34. It is this kind of necroviolence that most interests De León, who sees the "taphonomic" postmortem processes of the Southwestern desert as an operationalized agent of US government policy. *The Land of Open Graves*, 68.

35. Ibid., 71. In 2018, Almudena Carracedo's film *El silencio de otros* spoke to the lasting damage caused to survivors when the Spanish state denied justice for

perpetrators of crimes against humanity under the Franco regime and impeded the exhuming of the bodies of their victims.

36. De León, *Land of Open Graves*, 71; Pauline Boss, "Ambiguous Loss Research, Theory, and Practice: Reflections after 9/11," *Journal of Marriage and Family* 66 (2004): 551–66.

37. Mbembe, "Necropolitics."

38. Olyan speaks to the "fundamental strategic and contextual quality of ritual action," and notes the potential of ritual violence against corpses to achieve sociopolitical ends, establish new relationships, or end existing ones. "Ritual Violence Against Corpses," 126–27, 130–31; Foucault, *Discipline and Punish*, 34.

39. For instance, after the second Battle of Tell Danith (August 14, 1119), Tughtakin of Damascus decapitated his former friend Robert Fitz-Fulk, carried his head around Aleppo, and then finally turned the skull into a drinking vessel—an unmistakably public display of dominance and rupture of an alliance after an ambiguous victory at an important battle. Morton, *The Field of Blood*, 96, 114. My thanks to Brian Catlos for drawing my attention to both spectacular forms of necroviolence during the Mediterranean Seminar at Toronto (October 2019).

40. Carolyn Korsmeyer, *Savoring Disgust: The Foul and the Fair in Aesthetics* (New York: Oxford University Press, 2011), 4.

41. Massumi, "The Future Birth of the Affective Fact," 64; Charles S. Peirce, "What Is a Sign?" in *The Essential Peirce*, Vol. 2, *Selected Philosophical Writings, 1893–1913*, ed. Peirce Edition Project, 4–10 (Bloomington: Indiana University Press, 1998).

42. The apt example Massumi uses to explain this phenomenon was the Bush administration's justification of the invasion of Iraq to prevent Saddam Hussein from developing weapons of mass destruction. Although ultimately it was discovered that no such program existed, the administration stuck by the original justification and argued that had it not invaded, Hussein *would have* or *could have* posed a threat by eventually developing such weapons.

43. De León, *The Land of Open Graves*, 72–79.

44. Massumi, "The Future Birth of the Affective Fact," 62.

45. Benḥādda, *Tārikh al-dawla*, 64. Colin's edition recounts: "wa lammā wajada al-ʿawwāmūna bi-1 -ghawṣi fī-1 -māʾi mawlā muḥammadan wa-1 -sulṭāna al-naṣāriyyi bi-1 -mawḍʿi alladhī bi-izāʾi al-qanṭarati baʿda al-baḥthi ʿalayhim wa-akhrajūhumā [When the divers found, in diving in the water, Mulay Muḥammad and the king of the Christians, in the place that faced the bridge, after looking for them, they took them both out]." *Tarīkh al-dawla al-sa ʿdiyya*, 65.

46. All sources agree that al-Mutawakkil died when he tried to flee by fording the river.

47. For example, such distinguishing characteristics in burial have been used to challenge the timeline of eighth-century Muslim military expeditions and may suggest more permanent Muslim settlements in the south of France than previously thought. Yves Gleize et al., "Early Medieval Muslim Graves in France: First

Archaeological, Anthropological and Palaeogenomic Evidence," *PLoS One* 11 (2016). See also Finnegan, Hart, and Halkett, "The 'Informal' Burial Ground at Prestwich Street, Cape Town," 136–48.

48. See Imam Malik ibn Anas, *Al-Muwatta of Imam Malik ibn Anas: The First Formulation of Islamic Law*, trans. Aisha Abdurrahman Bewley (New York: Kegan Paul International, 1989), 184; and Ibn Rushd, *The Distinguished Jurist's Primer: A Translation of Bidāyat al-Mujtahid*, trans. Imran Ahsan Khan Nyazee (Reading, UK: Garnet Publishing, 1994), 1:259. See also John Eduardo Campo, "Between the Prescribed and Performed: Muslim Ways of Death," in *Death and Religion in a Changing World*, ed. Kathleen Garcés-Foley (Armonk, NY: M. E. Sharpe, 2005), 159–60; Halevi, *Muhammad's Grave*, 51, 233; Lila Abu Lughod, "Islam and the Gendered Discourses of Death," *International Journal of Middle East Studies* 25 (1993): 223–36; A. S. Tritton, "Djanāza," in *Encyclopedia of Islam, Second Edition*, ed. P. Bearman, Thomas Bianquis, Clifford E. Bosworth, E. van Donzel, and W. P. Heinrichs (Brill Online, 2012), http://dx.doi.org/10.1163/1573-3912_islam_SIM_1985.

49. Tritton, "Djanāza." Halevi remarks, "If [the dead man] is one of God's friends, he entreats the pallbearers to rush toward the grave. If he is one of God's enemies, he begs them to tarry, as if hoping to postpone the inevitable encounter with the angels in the grave." *Muhammad's Grave*, 209.

50. Maribel Fierro notes that with the passage of time, belief in the trial of the grave became more pronounced in the Muslim West. Fierro, "El espacio de los muertos: Fetuas andalusíes sobre tumbas y cementerios," in *L'urbanisme dans l'occident musulman au moyen âge: Aspects juridiques*, ed. Maribel Fierro, Patrice Cressier, and Jean-Pierre van Staëvel (Madrid: Casa Velázquez: Consejo Superior de Investigaciones Científicas CSIC, 2000), 159, 161. See Halevi, *Muhammad's Grave*, 197–233. We also see this interrogation represented in the hadith of ʿAissa with the skull discussed in the preface. "El diálogo de Jesucristo con la calavera," in *Desde la penumbra de la fosa: La concepción de la muerte en la literatura aljamiada morisca*, ed. Miguel Ángel Vázquez (Madrid: Editorial Trotta, 2007), 158–64.

51. Scott Kugle, *Sufis and Saints Bodies: Mysticism, Corporeality, and Sacred Power in Islam* (Chapel Hill: University of Carolina Press, 2007), 46–47.

52. Halevi, *Muhammad's Grave*, 27–31.

53. Ibn Rushd, *The Distinguished Jurist's Primer: A Translation of Bidāyat al-Mujtahid*, trans. Imran Ahsan Khan Nyazee (Reading, UK: Garnet, 1994), 1:259–60.

54. "On retrouva également parmi les morts Abou Abdallah Mohammed ben Asker, l'auteur du Dauhat ennâchir; il avait accompagnait l'Écorcher dans sa fuite et s'état rendu avec lui au pays des chrétiens en qualité de courtisan: son cadavre gisait au milieu de ceux des infidèles. A ce propos on a raconté diverses choses, entr'autres que son corps avait été trouvé couché sur le côté gauche et tournament le dos à la kibla." Muḥammad al-Ṣaghīr al-Ifrānī, *Nozhat al-ḥādī bi-akhbār mulūk al-qarn al-ḥādī*, ed. Ernest Leroux and Octave Houdas (Paris: Libraire de la Société Asiatique de l'École des Langues Orientales, 1888), 135. This passage was also

translated to French by H. Dastugue in "La bataille d'al-Kazar el-Kebir: D'après deux historiens musulmans," *Revue Africaine* 11 (1867): 130–45.

55. Al-Ifrānī cites a poetic reflection on the significance of that position to make clear that this embodied disposition would have been interpreted as evidence of Ibn Asker's apostasy: "Mohammed Asker qui eut un sort funeste / S'il avait commis une faute manifeste, son couer cependant était our de tout scepticisme." Al-Ifrānī, *Nozhat al-hadi*, 136. Halevi discusses the significance of a body's position after death as analogous to the position of the living body in prayer. *Muhammad's Grave*, 187–91.

56. Al-Ifrānī's poetic source protests that one should not interpret "fatal fate" to indicate that he was not a true Muslim, a protestation that itself suggests that this would have been the most common interpretation of such an embodied text.

57. *Tārīkh al-dawla al-sa 'diyya*, edited by 'Abd al-Raḥīm Benḥādda (Marrakesh: Maṭba'a Tīnmal, 1994), 64, my emphasis.

58. Al-Ifrānī also emphasizes the importance of the bridge in his account. *Nozhat al-ḥādī*, 74–77.

59. Benḥadda, ed., *Tārīkh al-dawla al-sa'diyya*, 65. In this translation, I have deliberately chosen to translate the masculine pronoun, *hu*, which refers to the masculine gendered noun, *jild* skin, with the gender neutral pronoun, "it."

60. Mediano argues that this is a clear case in which corpse desecration "animalizes" al-Mutawakkil's corpse. "Justice, Crime and Punishment," 187.

61. David Riches contends that violent actors' behavior is grounded in strategy and meaning. "The Phenomenon of Violence," in *The Anthropology of Violence*, ed. David Riches (New York: Blackwell, 1986), 5.

62. Sara Ahmed, *Queer Phenomenology: Orientations, Objects, Others* (Durham, NC: Duke University Press, 2006), 32–33.

63. W. Wright, *Arabic Grammar*, ed. W. Robertson Smith and M. J. de Goege (Mineola, NY: Dover Publications, 2005), 1:50.

64. Residents in contact zones with these Christian strongholds regularly appealed to local and regional legal scholars to seek guidance on how to interact with them. For example, Jocelyn Hendrickson highlights one document in which an anonymous individual asks a mufti, Ibn Barṭāl (d. ca. 1495), about the status of Muslims living in Christian-occupied territory who pay tribute to their Christian overlords. The jurist's response explicitly excludes Muslims who have compromised their religious integrity from those who may reliably witness and testify but does attest to their right to life and property. Jocelyn Hendrickson, "Muslim Responses to Portuguese Occupation in Late Fifteenth-Century North Africa," *Journal of Spanish Cultural Studies* 12, no. 2 (2012): 315.

65. Cornell gives a thorough overview of the economic effects of the Portuguese presence on the Atlantic littoral of Morocco in the fifteenth and sixteenth centuries and how this contributed to the success of the Sa'dīs in rallying support against the Waṭṭasids. "Reconquista and Jihad in Morocco," especially 395–407. See also Cory, *Reviving the Islamic Caliphate*, 4–5; García Arenal, *Ahmad al-Mansur*, 3–4; and Hendrickson, "Muslim Responses," 311–12.

66. The Oran fatwa of 1504, which outlined the ways in which Muslims under Christian rule could satisfy their religious obligations while living under political and religious persecution, is seen as one disputation of this perspective. Whereas Wansharīsī and his followers dismissed as apostates those Muslims who, for example, chose to remain in lands under Portuguese control on the Moroccan Atlantic coast, the anonymous scholar who wrote the Oran fatwa argued for greater lenience about who might still be considered a true Muslim and the ways in which they could pray, ritually bathe, eat forbidden foods, and otherwise deviate from normative Muslim practice. L. P. Harvey, *Muslims in Spain 1500–1615* (Chicago: University of Chicago Press, 2005), 60–64; Jocelyn Hendrickson, "The Islamic Obligation to Emigrate: Al-Wansharīsī's *Asnā Al-Matājir* Reconsidered" (PhD diss., Emory University, 2009). For the Arabic text of the fatwa, see Muḥammad 'Abd Allāh 'Inān, *Dawlat al-Islām fī al-Andalus. al-'Aṣr al-awwal, al-qism al-awwal* (Cairo: Maktabat al-Khānjī, 1896), 342–44.

67. Two groups whose status Ibn Barṭāl discusses are those Muslims who work against the interests of the Muslim community or fight for the Christians against Muslims and prayer leaders and callers who are exempted from paying tribute to Christians. These two groups the jurist judges more harshly than those less powerful Muslims who simply pay tribute. Hendrickson, "Muslim Responses," 315–16.

68. Mediano describes the reluctance to use torture under Muslim law as in line with a general "repugnance against mutilation." "Justice, Crime and Punishment," 184.

69. Ibn Rushd, *The Distinguished Jurist's Primer*, 1:261. Al-Shāfi'ī's more moderate position would place al-Manṣūr's actions even farther beyond the pale juridically.

70. "The proscription of mutilating the bodies (muthla) of the enemy is fully established [within the legal tradition]." Ibid., 1:460.

71. Uriel Heyd, *Studies in Old Ottoman Criminal Law* (Oxford: Clarendon Press, 1973), 268. Mármol is particularly detailed in his descriptions of penal customs in Fez during the second half of the sixteenth century: common practices included public crucifixion, throat-slitting, disembowelment, and public exposure. *Descripción General de África*, 2:32, 95–96.

72. On *tashhīr*, see Lange, "Where on Earth Is Hell?," 166–67. On the role of *tashhīr* specifically in Fez and Marrakesh, see Mediano, "Justice, Crime and Punishment," 183–84.

73. Mediano, "Justice, Crime and Punishment," 180; Pierre Clastres, *La société contre l'État: Recherches d'anthropologie politique* (Paris: Éditions de Minuit, 1974), in particular the chapter "De la torture dans les sociétés primitives," 152–60.

74. As a member of the educated elite in Fez, the author of this text had access to this Quranic reference, so the intertextual resonances between the chronicle and this sura are certainly present and palpable. Whether the average observer on the streets of Marrakesh would have read al-Maslūkh as a Quranic reference is perhaps a different story, but also beside the point of my argument here.

75. Lange, "Where on Earth Is Hell?," 160–62. The quotations are at 160 and 161.

76. Benḥadda, ed., *Tārīkh al-dawla al-saʿdiyya*, 65.

77. Ibid., 65–66.

78. Korsmeyer argues, "Disgust is an affective response that can be mustered to patrol social boundaries and norms." She cautions that such slippage between material and moral disgust becomes morally questionable. It is precisely the sort of boundary policing that arises from that slippage at work here. *Savoring Disgust*, 5.

79. Sara Ahmed and Jackie Stacey argue that "the substance of the skin itself is dependent on regimes of writing that mark the skin in different ways or that produce the skin as marked." "Introduction: Dermographics," in *Thinking through the Skin*, ed. Sara Ahmed and Jackie Stacey (New York: Routledge, 2001), 15.

80. Sarah Kay eloquently explicates how the materiality of parchment, as the product of flayed skin, retains references to and play with the semiotics of their own writing on flayed skin. On her reading, "the parchment itself becomes included among the layers of potential meaning that constitute medieval textuality." "Original Skin: Flaying, Reading, and Thinking in the Legend of Saint Bartholomew and Other Works," *Journal of Medieval and Early Modern Studies* 36, no. 1 (2006): 47.

81. Ahmed and Stacey, "Dermographics," 15.

82. Benḥadda, ed., *Tārīkh al-dawla al-sa 'diyya*, 65.

Epilogue

1. Seymour Hersh, "The Killing of Osama bin Laden," *London Review of Books*, May 21, 2015, 3.

2. Seymour Hersh explored this more than a decade earlier in "Who Lied to Whom? Why Did the Administration Endorse a Forgery about Iraq's Nuclear Program?" *The New Yorker*, March 31, 2003, http://www.newyorker.com/magazine/2003/03/31/who-lied-to-whom.

3. "Covid in the U.S.: Latest Map and Case Count," *The New York Times*, September 24, 2020, https://www.nytimes.com/interactive/2020/us/coronavirus-us-cases.html.

4. Jada Yuan, "Burials on Harts Island, Where New York's Unclaimed Dead Lie in Mass Graves, Have Risen Fivefold," *Washington Post*, April 16, 2020, https://www.washingtonpost.com/national/hart-island-mass-graves-coronavirus-new-york/2020/04/16/a0c413ee-7f5f-11ea-a3ee-13e1ae0a3571_story.html.

5. Chloé Cooper Jones, "Fearing for His Life," *The Verge*, March 13, 2019, https://www.theverge.com/2019/3/13/18253848/eric-garner-footage-ramsey-orta-police-brutality-killing-safety.

6. Louise Matsakis, "Body Cameras Haven't Stopped Police Brutality. Here's Why," *Wired*, June 17, 2020, https://www.wired.com/story/body-cameras-stopped-police-brutality-george-floyd/. Similar efforts by public officials to impede public access to representations of the corpse also affected the ability of photojournalists to

document the return of soldiers' corpses to the United States from 2007 to 2016. Sarah Sentilles, "When We See Photographs of Some Dead Bodies and Not Others," *New York Times Magazine*, August 14, 2018, https://www.nytimes.com/2018/08/14/magazine/media-bodies-censorship.html.

7. Subhabrata Bobby Banerjee refers to this as *necrocapitalism*. "Live and Let Die: Colonial Sovereignties and the Death Worlds of Necrocapitalism," *Borderlands* 5, no. 1 (2006), http://www.borderlands.net.au/vol5no1_2006/banerjee_live.htm.

8. John Beusterien, "Necrocapitalism and the Early Modern African Black Diaspora as Academic Field," in *Early Modern Black Diaspora Studies*, ed. Cassander L. Smith, Nicholas R. Jones, and Miles P. Grier (New York: Palgrave Macmillan, 2018), 200.

Bibliography

Abu Lughod, Lila. "Islam and the Gendered Discourses of Death." *International Journal of Middle East Studies* 25 (1993): 223–36.

Abulafia, David. *The Great Sea: A Human History of the Mediterranean*. Oxford: Oxford University Press, 2011.

Abun Nasr, Jamil M. *A History of the Maghrib in the Islamic Period*. Cambridge: Cambridge University Press, 1987.

Achim, Miruna. "The Autopsy of Fray García Guerra: Corporal Meanings in Seventeenth-Century Mexico." In *Death and Dying in Colonial Spanish America*, edited by Martina Will de Chaparro and Miruna Achim, 78–99. Tucson: University of Arizona Press, 2011.

Adorno, Rolena. "Discourses on Colonialism: Bernal Díaz, Las Casas, and the Twentieth-Century Reader." *MLN* 103, no. 2 (1988): 239–58.

———. *The Polemics of Possession in Spanish America*. New Haven, CT: Yale University Press, 2007.

Agamben, Giorgio. *Nudities*. Translated by David Kishik and Stefan Pedatella. Stanford, CA: Stanford University Press, 2010.

Ahmed, Sara. *Queer Phenomenology: Orientations, Objects, Others*. Durham, NC: Duke University Press, 2006.

Ahmed, Sara, and Jackie Stacey. "Introduction: Demographics." In *Thinking through the Skin*, edited by Sara Ahmed and Jackie Stacey, 1–17. New York: Routledge, 2001.

Akbari, Suzanne Conklin. "The Persistence of Philology: Language and Connectivity in the Mediterranean." In *A Sea of Languages: Rethinking the Arabic Role in Medieval Literary History*, edited by Suzanne Conklin Akbari and Karla Mallette, 3–22. Toronto: University of Toronto Press, 2013.

Akbari, Suzanne Conklin, and Jill Ross. "Introduction: Limits and Teleology: The Many Ends of the Body." In *The Ends of the Body: Identity and Community in*

Medieval Culture, edited by Suzanne Conklin Akbari and Jill Ross, 3–21. Toronto: University of Toronto Press, 2013.

Allaria, A. "St. Peter of Verona." In *The Catholic Encyclopedia*. New York: Robert Appleton Company, 1911.

Amaral de Oliveira, Vítor, ed. *Sebástica: Bibliografia geral sobre D. Sebastião*. Coimbra: Biblioteca Geral da Universidade, 2002.

Astren, Fred. "Depaganizing Death: Aspects of Mourning in Rabbinic Judaism and Early Islam." In *Bible and Qur'an: Essays in Scriptural Intertextuality*, edited by John C. Reeves, 183–99. Atlanta: American Academy of Religion, 2003.

Auer, Peter. "Spatial Indexicalities and Spatial Pragmatics." In *Pragmaticizing Understanding*, edited by Jan-Ola Östman and Michael Meeuwis, 53–76. Philadelphia: John Benjamins, 2012.

Bagdadi, Nadia al-. "Registers of Arabic Literary History." *New Literary History* 39, no. 3 (2008): 437–61.

Banerjee, Subhabrata Bobby. "Live and Let Die: Colonial Sovereignties and the Death Worlds of Necrocapitalism." *Borderlands* 5, no. 1 (2006). http://www.borderlands.net.au/vo15no1_2006/banerjee_live.htm.

Barbosa Machado, Diogo. *Bibliotheca Lusitana historica, critica, e cronologica*. 4 vols. Lisbon: A. I. da Fonseca, 1741–59.

Bartlett, Robert. *Why Can the Dead Do Such Great Things? Saints and Worshippers from the Martyrs to the Reformation*. Princeton, NJ: Princeton University Press, 2013.

Baxter, Kenneth Wolf. "Myth, History, and the Origins of al-Andalus: A Historiographical Essay." *Journal of Medieval Iberian Studies* 11, no. 3 (2019): 378–401.

Bazin, André. "Death Every Afternoon (1958)." Translated by Mark A. Cohen. In *Rites of Realism: Essays on Corporeal Cinema*, edited by Ivone Margulies, 27–31. Durham, NC: Duke University Press, 2003.

Bennett, Jane. *Vibrant Matter: A Political Ecology of Things*. Durham, NC : Duke University Press, 2010.

Bennison, Amira K. "ʿAbd al-Qādir's Jihād in the Light of the Western Islamic Jihād Tradition." *Studia Islamica* 106, no. 2 (2011): 196–213.

——. *Jihad and Its Interpretations in Pre-Colonial Morocco: State-Society Relations during the French Conquest of Algiers*. London: Routledge, 2002.

Benveniste, Emile. *Problems in General Linguistics*. Translated by M. E. Meek. Coral Gables, FL: University of Miami Press, 1971.

Bertelli, Sergio. *The King's Body: Sacred Rituals of Power in Medieval and Early Modern Europe*. Translated by R. Burr Litchfield. University Park: Pennsylvania State University Press, 2001.

Bertelson, Lone, and Andrew Murphie. "An Ethics of Everyday Infinities and Powers: Félix Guattari on Affect and the Refrain." In *The Affect Theory Reader*, edited by Gregory J. Seigworth and Melissa Gregg, 138–57. Durham, NC: Duke University Press, 2010.

Besselaar, Joseph Jacobus van den. *O sebastianismo*. Lisbon: Instituto de Cultura e Língua Portuguesa, 1987.
Beusterien, John. "Necrocapitalism and the Early Modern African Black Diaspora as Academic Field." In *Early Modern Black Diaspora Studies*, edited by Cassander L. Smith, Nicholas R. Jones, and Miles P. Grier, 199–221. New York: Palgrave Macmillan, 2018.
Black, Jeremy. *A History of Diplomacy*. London: Reaktion Books, 2010.
Blackmore, Josiah. "Imaging the Moor in Medieval Portugal." *diacritics* 36, nos. 3–4 (2006): 27–43.
Borja, Juan de. Advertimientos de don Juan de Borja para don Juan de Silva quando le embió su Majestad por embaxador a Portugal. Archivo General de Simancas.
Boss, Pauline. "Ambiguous Loss Research, Theory, and Practice: Reflections after 9/11." *Journal of Marriage and Family* 66, no. 3 (2004): 551–66.
Bossong, Georg. "Animacy and Markedness in Universal Grammar." *Glossologia* 2–3 (1982–1983): 7–20.
———. "Differential Object Marking in Romance and Beyond." In *New Analyses in Romance Linguistics: Selected Papers from the XVIII Linguistic Symposium on Romance Languages 1988*, edited by D. Wanner and D. Kibbee, 143–70. Amsterdam: John Benjamins, 1991.
Bouley, Bradford. *Pious Postmortems: Anatomy, Sanctity, and the Catholic Church in Early Modern Europe*. Philadelphia: University of Pennsylvania Press, 2017.
Bouza Álvarez, Fernando. "Corte es decepción: Don Juan de Silva, conde de Portalegre." In *La corte de Felipe II*, edited by José Martínez Millán, 451–502. Madrid: Alianza, 1994.
Bovill, E. V. *The Battle of Alcazar: An Account of the Defeat of Don Sebastian of Portugal at El-Ksar el-Kebir*. London: Batchworth, 1952.
Boxer, Charles R. *The Portuguese Seaborne Empire, 1415–1825*. London: Hutchinson, 1969.
Boyer, H. Patsy. "The War Between the Sexes and the Ritualization of Violence in Zayas's Disenchantments." In *Sex and Love in Golden Age Spain*, edited by Alain Saint-Saëns and with a foreword by Mary Elizabeth Perry, 123–45. New Orleans: University Press of the South, 1999.
Brading, D. A. "The Incas and the Renaissance: The Royal Commentaries of Inca Garcilaso de la Vega." *Journal of Latin American Studies* 18, no. 1 (1986): 1–23.
Braudel, Fernand. "Les espagnols et l'Afrique du Nord de 1492 à 1577." *Revue Africaine* 69 (1928): 184–233, 351–410.
———. *The Mediterranean and the Mediterranean World in the Age of Philip II*, vol. 1. Berkeley: University of California Press, 1995. New York: Harper & Row, 1972.
Brooks, Peter. *Reading for the Plot: Design and Intention in Narrative*. New York: Knopf, 1984.
Brown, Elizabeth A. R. "Death and the Human Body in the Later Middle Ages: The Legislation of Boniface VIII on the Division of the Corpse." *Viator* 12 (1981): 221–70.

Brown, Peter. *The Cult of the Saints: Its Rise and Function in Late Christianity.* 1981; repr. Chicago: University of Chicago Press, 2015.

Brown, Vincent. *The Reaper's Garden: Death and Burial in the World of Atlantic Slavery.* Cambridge, MA: Harvard University Press, 2008.

Cácegas, Luis de. *Primeira parte da Historia de S. Domingos.* Edited by Luis de Sousa. Lisbon, 1866.

Caciola, Nancy. *Afterlives: The Return of the Dead in the Middle Ages.* Ithaca, NY: Cornell University Press, 2016.

Calderón de la Barca, Pedro. *Comedias.* Madrid, 1697.

Campbell, Mary B. *The Witness and the Other World: Exotic European Travel Writing 400–1600.* Ithaca, NY: Cornell University Press, 1988.

Campo, John Eduardo. "Between the Prescribed and Performed: Muslim Ways of Death." In *Death and Religion in a Changing World*, edited by Kathleen Garcés-Foley, 147–77. Armonk, NY: M. E. Sharpe, 2005.

Cantera Burgos, Francisco. "El 'Purim' del Rey Don Sebastián." *Sefarad* 5 (1945): 219–25.

Carrecedo, Almudena. *El silencio de otros* (The Silence of Others). 96 min. Spain: Netflix, 2018.

Castries, Henri de. "La conquête du Soudan par Moulaye Ahmed el-Mansôur." *Hespéris* 3 (1923): 438–88.

Castro, Américo. *España en su historia: Cristianos, moros y judíos.* Buenos Aires: Editorial Losada, 1948.

Catlos, Brian A. "Cristians, musulmans i jueus a la Corona d'Aragó medieval: Un cas de 'conveniència.'" *L'Avenç* 236 (2001): 8–16.

——. *The Victors and the Vanquished: Christians and Muslims of Catalonia and Aragon, 1050–1300.* Cambridge: Cambridge University Press, 2004.

——. "Why the Mediterranean?" In *Can We Talk Mediterranean? Conversations on an Emerging Field in Medieval and Early Modern Studies*, edited by Brian A. Catlos and Sharon Kinoshita, 1–17. New York: Palgrave Macmillan, 2017.

Cervantes Saavedra, Miguel de. *Don Quijote de la Mancha.* Edited by Francisco Rico. Madrid: Real Academia Española, 2004.

Cirurgião, António. "Camões e Miguel Leitão de Andrade." *Revista Colóquio/Letras* 108 (1989): 18–26.

Clastres, Pierre. *La société contre l'État: Recherches d'anthropologie politique.* Paris: Éditions de Minuit, 1974.

Collins, James. "Indexicalities of Language Contact in an Era of Globalization: Engaging with John Gumperz's Legacy." *Text & Talk: An Interdisciplinary Journal of Language, Discourse & Communication Studies* 31 (2011): 407–28.

Conestaggio Franchi, Girólamo de. *Dell'unione del Regno di Portugallo alla corona di Castiglia.* Geneva, 1585.

Cook, Weston F., Jr. *The Hundred Years War for Morocco: Gunpowder and the Military Revolution in the Early Modern Muslim World.* Boulder, CO: Westview Press, 1994.

Coope, Ursula. *Time for Aristotle: Physics IV. 10–14*. Oxford: Oxford University Press, 2005.

Cornell, Vincent J. *Realm of the Saint: Power and Authority in Moroccan Sufism*. Austin: University of Texas Press, 1998.

——. "Socioeconomic Dimensions of Reconquista and Jihād in Morocco: Portuguese Dukkala and Sa'did Sūs, 1450–1557." *International Journal of Middle East Studies* 22 (1990): 379–418.

Cory, Stephen. *Reviving the Islamic Caliphate in Early Modern Morocco*. New York: Routledge, 2013.

——. "Sharīfian Rule in Morocco (Tenth–Twelfth/Sixteenth–Eighteenth Centuries)." In *The Western Islamic World, Eleventh to Eighteenth Centuries*, edited by Maribel Fierro, 453–79. Cambridge: Cambridge University Press, 2010.

Costa Lobo, António de. *Origens do Sebastianismo*. Lisbon: Rolim, 1983.

Coutinho, Gonçalo. *Discurso da Jornada de D. Gonçalo Coutinho a villa de Mazagam, e seu governo nella*. Lisbon, 1629.

Covarrubias Orozco, Sebastián de. *Tesoro de la lengua castellana o española*. Madrid, 1611.

"Covid in the U.S.: Latest Map and Case Count." *New York Times*, September 24, 2020. https://www.nytimes.com/interactive/2020/us/coronavirus-us-cases.html.

Cruz, Bernardo da. *Chronica d'El-Rei D. Sebastião*. 2 vols. Bibliotheca de Classicos Portuguezes. Lisbon, 1903.

Curtius, Ernst R. *European Literature and the Latin Middle Ages*. Translated by Willard R. Trask. London: Routledge and Kegan Paul, 1953.

Dangler, Jean. *Edging toward Iberia*. Toronto: Toronto University Press, 2017.

Dastugue, H. "La bataille d'al-Kazar el-Kebir: D'après deux historiens musulmans." *Revue Africaine* 11 (1867): 130–45.

Davis, Natalie Zemon. *Trickster Travels: A Sixteenth-Century Muslim between Worlds*. New York: Hill and Wang, 2006.

De León, Jason. *The Land of Open Graves: Living and Dying on the Migrant Trail*. Berkeley: University of California Press, 2015.

del Valle, Ivonne, Anna More, and Rachel Sarah O'Toole. "Introduction: Iberian Empires and a Theory of Early Modern Globalization." In *Iberian Empires and the Roots of Globalization*, edited by Ivonne del Valle, Anna More, and Rachel Sarah O'Toole, 1–22. Nashville, TN: Vanderbilt University Press, 2002.

Deleuze, Gilles, and Félix Guattari. *A Thousand Plateaus: Capitalism and Schizophrenia*. Translated by Brian Massumi. Minneapolis: University of Minnesota Press, 1987.

Derrida, Jacques. *Archive Fever: A Freudian Impression*. Translated by E. Prenowitz. Chicago: University of Chicago Press, 1995.

Dias Farinha, António. "Introdução." In *Crónica de Almançor Sultão de Marrocos (1578–1603)*, edited by António Dias Farinha, xxi–cxv. Lisbon: Instituto de Investigação Científica Tropical, 1997.

Diffie, Bailey W., and George D. Winius. *Foundations of the Portuguese Empire 1415–1850*. Minneapolis: University of Minnesota Press, 1977.

Dinshaw, Carolyn. *How Soon Is Now? Medieval Texts, Amateur Readers, and the Queerness of Time*. Durham, NC: Duke University Press, 2012.

Doane, Mary Ann. *The Emergence of Cinematic Time: Modernity, Contingency, the Archive*. Cambridge, MA: Harvard University Press, 2002.

Dubrow, Heather. *Deixis in Early Modern English Lyric: Unsettling Spatial Anchors Like "Here," "This," "Come."* New York: Palgrave Macmillan, 2015.

Edelman, Lee. "The Future Is Kid Stuff: Queer Theory, Disidentification, and the Death Drive." *Narrative* 6, no. 1 (1998): 18–30.

Eire, Carlos M. N. *From Madrid to Purgatory: The Art and Craft of Dying in Sixteenth-Century Spain*. Cambridge: Cambridge University Press, 1995.

"El diálogo de Jesucristo con la calavera." In *Desde la penumbra de la fosa: La concepción de la muerte en la literatura aljamiada morisca*, edited by Miguel Ángel Vázquez, 158–64. Madrid: Editorial Trotta, 2007.

Elliott, J. H. "The Court of the Spanish Habsburgs: A Peculiar Institution?" In *Spain and Its World 1500–1700*, 142–61. New Haven, CT: Yale University Press, 1989.

——. "A Europe of Composite Monarchies." *Past & Present* 137 (1992): 48–71.

English, Edward D., and Mark Meyerson, eds. *Christians, Muslims, and Jews in Medieval and Early Modern Spain*. South Bend, IN: University of Notre Dame Press, 2000.

Fagnan, Edmond. *Extraits inédits relatifs au Mahgreb (Géographie et histoire): Traduits de l'arabe et annotés*. Algiers: Jules Carbonel, 1924.

Fanjul, Serafín. *La quimera de al-Andàlus*. Madrid: Siglo XXI de España Editores, 2004.

Fernández, Enrique. *Anxieties of Interiority and Dissection in Early Modern Spain*. Toronto: University of Toronto Press, 2015.

——. "Fragmentación corporal y exégesis política en Quevedo." *La perinola* 14 (2010): 305–19.

Fernãndez de Pulgar, Pedro. *Libro segundo de la historia secular y eclesiástica de la ciudad de Palencia: Contiene la restauración de la ciudad, reedificación de el templo de San Antonino . . .* Madrid: Viuda de Francisco Nieto, 1679(?).

Fierro, Maribel. "El espacio de los muertos: Fetuas andalusíes sobre tumbas y cementerios." In *L'urbanisme dans l'occident musulman au moyen âge: Aspects juridiques*, edited by Maribel Fierro, Patrice Cressier, and Jean-Pierre van Staëvel, 153–90. Madrid: Casa Velázquez: Consejo Superior de Investigaciones Científicas CSIC, 2000.

Finkel, Caroline. *Osman's Dream: The History of the Ottoman Empire*. New York: Basic Books, 2007.

Finnegan, Erin, Timothy Hart, and David Halkett. "The 'Informal' Burial Ground at Prestwich Street, Cape Town: Cultural and Chronological Indicators for the

Historical Cape Underclass." *The South African Archaeological Bulletin* 66 (2011): 136–48.
Fishtālī, Abū Fāris ʿAbd al-ʿAzīz al-. *Manāhil al-ṣafā fī maʾ āthir mawālīnā al-shurafāʾ*. Edited by ʿAbd al-Karīm Kurayyīm. Rabat: Maṭbūʿāt Wizārat al-Awqāf, 1972.
Fludernik, Monika. "Shifters and Deixis: Some Reflections on Jakobson, Jespersen, and Reference." *Semiotica* 86, nos. 3–4 (1991): 193–230.
Folger, Robert A. *Writing as Poaching: Interpellation and Self-Fashioning in Colonial Relaciones de Méritos y Servicios*. Leiden: Brill, 2011.
Fonseca, Jorge. *Os Livreiros de Lisboa los séculos XVI e XVII: Estratégias económicas, sociais e familiares*. Lisbon: Edições Colibri, 2019.
Fontein, Joost. "Between Tortured Bodies and Resurfacing Bones: The Politics of the Dead in Zimbabwe." *Journal of Material Culture* 15, no. 4 (2010): 423–48.
Ford, Caroline. "Violence and the Sacred in Nineteenth-Century France." *Historical Studies* 21, no. 1 (1998): 101–12.
Foucault, Michel. *The Archaeology of Knowledge and the Discourse on Language*. Translated by A. M. Sheridan Smith. New York: Pantheon Books, 1972.
——. *Confessions of the Flesh: The History of Sexuality, Vol. 4*. Translated by Robert Hurley. Edited by Frederic Gros. New York: Pantheon, 2021.
——. *Discipline and Punish: The Birth of the Prison*. 2nd ed. Translated by Alan Sheridan. New York: Vintage Books, 1977.
——. *The History of Sexuality: An Introduction, Vol. 1*. Translated by Robert Hurley. New York: Vintage Books, 1990. New York, Random House: 1978.
Freeman, Elizabeth. "Packing History, Count(er)ing Generations." *New Literary History* 31 (2000): 727–44.
——. *Time Binds: Queer Temporalities, Queer Histories*. Durham, NC: Duke University Press, 2010.
Frisch, Andrea. "The Ethics of Testimony: A Genealogical Perspective." *Discourse* 25, no. 1 (2003): 36–54.
——. *The Invention of the Eyewitness: Witnessing and Testimony in Early Modern France*. Chapel Hill: University of North Carolina Press, 2004.
Frow, John. "A Pebble, a Camera, a Man." *Critical Inquiry* 28, no. 1 (2001): 270–85.
Fuchs, Barbara. "1492 and the Cleaving of Hispanism." *Journal of Medieval and Early Modern Studies* 37, no. 3 (2007): 493–510.
——. *Exotic Nation: Maurophilia and the Construction of Early Modern Spain*. Philadelphia: University of Pennsylvania Press, 2009.
——. "Imperium Studies: Theorizing Early Modern Expansion." In *Postcolonial Moves: Medieval through Modern*, edited by Patricia Clare Ingham and Michelle R. Warren, 71–90. New York: Palgrave Macmillan, 2003.
Galbraith, Mary. "Deictic Shift Theory and the Poetics of Involvement in Narrative." In *Deixis in Narrative: A Cognitive Science Perspective*, edited by Judith F. Duchan, Gail A. Bruder, and Lynne E. Hewitt, 19–59. Hillsdale, NJ: Lawrence Erlbaum, 1995.

Ganelin, Charles V. "Bodies of Discovery: Vesalian Anatomy and Luis de Barahona de Soto's Las lágrimas de Angélica." *Calíope* 6, no. 1–2 (2000): 295–308.

García Nova, Marta. "Ulemas malikíes del Bilad al-Sudan en la obra biográfica de Ahmad Baba al-Tinbukti (963/1556–1036/1627)." In *Estudios onomástico-biográficos de Al-Andalus. Vol. XVII. Biografías magrebíes: Identidades y grupos religiosos, sociales y políticos en el Magreb medieval*, edited by Mohamed Méouak, 417–51. Madrid: CSIC, 2012.

García-Arenal, Mercedes. *Ahmad al-Mansur: Beginnings of Modern Morocco.* Oxford: OneWorld Press, 2009.

———. "Los andalusíes en el ejército saʿdī: Un intento de golpe de estado contra Aḥmad al-Manṣūr al-Dahabī (1578)." *Al-Qanṭara* 2 (1981): 169–202.

———. "Mahdī, Murābiṭ, Sharīf: L'avènement de la dynastie saʿdienne." *Studia Islamica* 71 (1990): 77–114.

———. "Sainteté et pouvoir dynastique au MarocLa résistance de Fès aux Saʿdiens." *Annales* 45 (1990): 1019–42.

García-Arenal, Mercedes, Gerard A. Wiegers, and Martin Beagles. *A Man of Three Worlds: Samuel Pallache, a Moroccan Jew in Catholic and Protestant Europe.* Baltimore, MD: Johns Hopkins University Press, 2010.

García-Arenal, Mercedes, Fernando Rodríguez Mediano, and Rachid el Hour, eds. *Cartas marruecas: Documentos de Marruecos en archivos españoles (siglos XVI–XVII).* Madrid: Consejo Superior de Investigaciones Científicas, 2002.

Geary, Patrick. *Living with the Dead in the Middle Ages.* Ithaca, NY: Cornell University Press, 1994.

Gilbert, Claire M. *In Good Faith: Arabic Translation and Translators in Early Modern Spain.* Philadelphia: University of Pennsylvania Press, 2020.

Giles, Ryan, and Steven Wagschal, eds. *Beyond Sight: Engaging the Senses in Iberian Literatures and Cultures 1200–1750.* Toronto: University of Toronto Press, 2017.

Gleize, Y., F. Mendisco, M. H. Pemonge, C. Hubert, A. Groppi, B. Houix, M. F. Deguilloux, and J. Y. Breuil. "Early Medieval Muslim Graves in France: First Archaeological, Anthropological and Palaeogenomic Evidence." *PLoS One* 11, no. 2 (2016): e0148583. https://doi.org/10.1371/journal.pone.0148583. http://www.ncbi.nlm.nih.gov/pubmed/26910855.

Goitein, S. D. *A Mediterranean Society: The Jewish Communities of the Arab World as Portrayed in the Documents of the Cairo Genizah.* 6 vols. Berkeley: University of California Press, 1967–93.

González Echevarría, Roberto. *Myth and Archive: A Theory of Latin American Literature.* Durham, NC: Duke University Press, 1990.

Greenblatt, Stephen. *Marvelous Possessions: The Wonder of the New World.* Chicago: University of Chicago Press, 1992.

Greene, Roland. *Unrequited Conquests: Love and Empire in the Colonial Americas.* Chicago: University of Chicago Press, 1999.

Greer, Margaret. "Thine and Mine: The Spanish 'Golden Age' and Early Modern Studies." *PMLA* 126, no. 1 (2011): 217–24.

Guattari, Félix. *Chaosmosis: An Ethico-Aesthetic Paradigm*. Translated by paul bains and Julian Pefanis. Sydney: Power, 1995.

Gunning, Tom. "Moving away from the Index: Cinema and the Impression of Reality." *differences* 18, no. 1 (2007): 29–52.

———. "What Is the Point of Indexicality? Or, Faking Photographs." *NORDICOM Review* 5, no. 1/2 (2004): 39–49.

Halevi, Leor. *Muhammad's Grave: Death Rites and the Making of Islamic Society*. New York: Columbia University Press, 2007.

Hamilton, Michelle M. *Representing Others in Medieval Iberian Literature*. New York: Palgrave MacMillan, 2007.

Hamilton, Michelle M., and Núria Silleras-Fernández, eds. *In and of the Mediterranean: Medieval and Early Modern Iberian Studies*. Nashville, TN: Vanderbilt University Press, 2015.

Hanks, William F. "The Evidential Core of Deixis in Yucutan Maya." In *Papers from the Twentieth Regional Meeting of the Chicago Linguistic Society*, edited by J. Drogo et al., 154–72. Chicago: Chicago Linguistic Society, 1984.

———. "Explorations in the Deictic Field." *Current Anthropology* 46 (2005): 191–220.

———. "The Indexical Ground of Deictic Reference." In *Rethinking Context: Language as an Interactive Phenomenon*, edited by Alessandro Duranti and Charles Goodwin, 43–76. Cambridge: Cambridge University Press, 1992.

———. "Metalanguage and the Pragmatics of Deixis." In *Reflexive Language: Reported Speech and Metapragmatics*, edited by John A. Lucy, 127–58. Cambridge: Cambridge University Press, 1993.

Harris, W. V., ed. *Rethinking the Mediterranean*. Oxford: Oxford University Press, 2005.

Harrison, Robert Pogue. *The Dominion of the Dead*. Chicago: University of Chicago Press, 2003.

Harvey, L. P. *Muslims in Spain 1500–1615*. Chicago: University of Chicago Press, 2005.

Helgerson, Richard. *A Sonnet from Carthage: Garcilaso de la Vega and the New Poetry of Sixteenth-Century Europe*. Philadelphia: University of Pennsylvania Press, 2007.

Hendrickson, Jocelyn. "The Islamic Obligation to Emigrate: Al-Wansharīsī's Asnā al-matājir Reconsidered." PhD dissertation, Emory University, 2009.

———. "Muslim Responses to Portuguese Occupation in Late Fifteenth-Century North Africa." *Journal of Spanish Cultural Studies* 12, no. 2 (2012): 309–25.

Herman, David. *The Basic Elements of Narrative*. Malden, MA: Wiley-Blackwell, 2009.

Hersh, Seymour. "The Killing of Osama bin Laden." *London Review of Books*, May 21, 2015, 3–12.

———. "Who Lied to Whom? Why Did the Administration Endorse a Forgery about Iraq's Nuclear Program?" *The New Yorker*, March 31, 2003. http://www.newyorker.com/magazine/2003/03/31/who-lied-to-whom.

Hershenzon, Daniel. *The Captive Sea: Slavery, Communication, and Commerce in Early Modern Spain and the Mediterranean*. Philadelphia: University of Pennsylvania Press, 2018.

Hess, Andrew C. *The Forgotten Frontier: A History of the Sixteenth Century Ibero-African Frontier*. Chicago: University of Chicago Press, 1978.

Heyd, Uriel. *Studies in Old Ottoman Criminal Law*. Edited by V. L. Ménage. Oxford: Clarendon Press, 1973.

Hillgarth, J. N. "Spanish Historiography and Iberian Reality." *History and Theory* 24, no. 1 (1985): 23–43.

Hillman, David. *Shakespeare's Entrails: Belief, Skepticism and the Interior of the Body*. New York: Palgrave Macmillan, 2007.

Homer. *The Iliad*. Edited by Bernard Knox. Translated by Robert Fagles. New York: Penguin, 1990.

Horden, Peregrine, and Nicholas Purcell. *The Corrupting Sea: A Study of Mediterranean History*. Oxford: Blackwell Publishers, 2000.

———. "Mediterranean and 'the New Thalassology.'" *The American Historical Review* 111, no. 3 (2006): 722–40.

Hunwick, John O. "Ahmad Baba and the Moroccan Invasion of the Sudan (1591)." *Journal of the Historical Society of Nigeria* 2, no. 3 (1962): 311–28.

———. "Askia al-Ḥājj Muḥammad and His Successors: The Account of al-Imām al-Takrūrī." *Sudanic Africa* 1 (1990): 85–89.

———. "Secular Power and Religious Authority in Muslim Society: The Case of Songhay." *The Journal of African History* 37, no. 2 (1996): 175–94.

———. "Source Materials for the History of Songhay, Borneo, and Hausaland in the Sixteenth Century." *Journal of the Historical Society of Nigeria* 7, no. 3 (1974): 579–86.

Ibn Abī Dunyā, Abū Bakr ʿAbd Allāh ibn Muḥammad ibn ʿAmr. *Kitāb al-mawt wa kitāb al-qubūr*. Edited by Leah Kinberg. Haifa: Qism al-Lughah al-ʿArabīyah wa-Ādābihā, Jāmiʿat Ḥayfā, 1983.

Ibn al-Qāḍī, Aḥmad ibn Muḥammad. *Al-Muntaqā al-maqṣūr ʿalā māthir al-khalīfat Abī al-ʿAbbās*. 2 volumes. Edited by Muḥammad Razzuf. Rabat: Maktabat al-muʿārif, 1986.

ibn Anas, Malik. *Al-Muwatta of Imam Malik ibn Anas: The First Formulation of Islamic Law*. Translated by Aisha Abdurrahman Bewley. New York: Kegan Paul International, 1989.

Ibn Rushd. *The Distinguished Jurist's Primer: A Translation of Bidāyat al-Mujtahid*. Translated by Imran Ahsan Khan Nyazee. Reading, UK: Garnet, 1994.

Ifrānī, Muḥammad al-Ṣaghīr al-. *Nozhet-elhâdi: Histoire de la dynastie saadienne au maroc* (1511–1670). Edited by Ernest Laroux. Translated by Octave Houdas. Paris: Libraire de la Société Asiatique de l'École des Langues Orientales, 1889.

——. *Nuzhat al-ḥādī bi-akhbār mulūk al-qarn al-ḥādī*. Rabat: Jamīʿa al-ḥuqūq maḥfūẓa, 1998.

——. *Nuzhat al-ḥādī bi-akhbār mulūk al-qarn al-ḥādī*. Edited by Ernest Leroux and Octave Houdas. Paris: Libraire de la Société Asiatique de l'École des Langues Orientales, 1888.

ʿInān, Muḥammad ʿAbd Allāh. *Dawlat al-Islām fī al-Andalus. Al-ʿaṣr al-awwal, al-qism al-awwal*. Cairo: Maktabat al-Khānjī, 1896.

Jakobson, Roman. "Shifters, Verbal Categories, and the Russian Verb." In *Selected Writings*, 130–47. The Hague: Mouton, 1971.

Jermyn, Deborah. "Body Matters: Realism, Spectacle and the Corpse in CSI." In *Reading CSI: Crime TV under the Microscope*, edited by Allen Michael, 79–89. New York: I. B. Tauris, 2007.

Jespersen, Otto. *The Philosophy of Grammar*. London: Allen and Unwin, 1924.

Jones, Chloé Cooper. "Fearing for His Life." *The Verge*, March 13, 2019. https://www.theverge.com/2019/3/13/18253848/eric-garner-footage-ramsey-orta-police-brutality-killing-safety.

Jones, Linda G. "Bodily Performances and Body Talk in Medieval Islamic Preaching." In *The Ends of the Body: Identity and Community in Medieval Culture*, edited by Suzanne Conklin Akbari and Jill Ross, 211–35. Toronto: University of Toronto Press, 2013.

Jordan, Annemarie. "Queen of the Seas and Overseas: Dining at the Table of Catherine of Austria, Queen of Portugal." In *Mesas Reais Europeias. Encomendas e Ofertas/Royal and Princely Tables of Europe. Commissions and Gifts/Tables Royales en Europe. Commandes et Cadeaux*, edited by Leonor d' Orey, 14–43. Lisbon: Instituto Português de Museus, 1999.

Kagan, Richard. *Clio and the Crown: The Politics of History in Medieval and Early Modern Spain*. Baltimore, MD: Johns Hopkins University Press, 2009.

Kagen, Melissa. "Archival Adventuring." *Convergence: The International Journal of New Media Technologies* 20, no. 10 (2019): 1–14.

——. *Wandering Games*. Cambridge, MA: MIT Press, 2022.

Kamen, Henry. *Philip of Spain*. New Haven, CT: Yale University Press, 1997.

Kantorowicz, Ernst H. *The King's Two Bodies: A Study in Mediaeval Political Theology*. 7th ed. Princeton, NJ: Princeton University Press, 1997.

Kay, Sarah. "Original Skin: Flaying, Reading, and Thinking in the Legend of Saint Bartholomew and Other Works." *Journal of Medieval and Early Modern Studies* 36, no. 1 (2006): 35–73.

Kinoshita, Sharon. "Medieval Mediterranean Literature." *PMLA* 124, no. 2 (2009): 600–8.

——. "Negotiating the Corrupting Sea: Literature in and of the Mediterranean." In *Can We Talk Mediterranean?*, edited by Brian A. Catlos and Sharon Kinoshita, 33–47. New York: Palgrave Macmillan, 2017.

Knappett, Carl, and Lambros Malafouris. "Material and Nonhuman Agency: An Introduction." In *Material Agency: Towards a Non-Anthropocentric Approach*, edited by Carl Knappett and Lambros Malafouris, ix–xix. New York: Springer, 2008.

Korsmeyer, Carolyn. *Savoring Disgust: The Foul and the Fair in Aesthetics.* Oxford: Oxford University Press, 2011.

Kozodoy, Maud. "The Jewish Physician in Medieval Iberia." In *Jews in Space and Time: The Jews in Medieval Iberia 1100–1500*, edited by Jonathan Ray, 102–37. Boston: Academic Studies Press, 2011.

Krmpotich, Cara, Joost Fontein, and John Harries. "The Substance of Bones: The Emotive Materiality and Affective Presence of Human Remains." *Journal of Material Culture* 15, no. 2 (2010): 371–84.

Kugle, Scott. *Sufis and Saints' Bodies: Mysticism, Corporeality, and Sacred Power in Islam.* Chapel Hill: University of Carolina Press, 2007.

La Véronne, Chantal de. "Les frères Gasparo Corso et le Chérif Moulay 'Abd El-Malek (1569–1574)." In *Archives et bibliothèques d'Espagne.* Les sources inédites de l'histoire du Maroc. Paris: Paul Geuthner, 1974.

Lange, Christian. "Where on Earth Is Hell? State Punishment and Eschatology in the Islamic Middle Period." In *Public Violence in Islamic Societies: Power, Discipline, and the Construction of the Public Sphere, 7th–19th Centuries CE*, edited by Christian Lange and Maribel Fierro, 156–78. Edinburgh: Edinburgh University Press, 2009.

Laqueur, Thomas W. *The Work of the Dead: A Cultural History of Mortal Remains.* Princeton, NJ: Princeton University Press, 2015.

Larédo, Abraham I. "Les 'purim' de Tánger." *Hésperis* 35 (1948): 193–203.

Latour, Bruno. "How to Talk about the Body? The Normative Dimension of Science Studies." *Body and Society* 2, no. 3 (2004): 205–29.

———. "On Actor-Network Theory: A Few Clarifications." *Soziale Welt* 47 (1996): 369–81.

Leitão de Andrade, Miguel. *Miscellânea do Sitio de N. Senhora Dalzado Pedrogão Grande.* Lisbon, 1629. http://purl.pt/14193.

"Lettre d'un medecin juif a son frère." In *Dynastie saadienne: Archives et bibliothèques d'Anglaterre.* Les sources inédites de l'histoire du Maroc, 312–21. Paris, 1920.

Lévi-Provençal, Evariste. *Les historiens des chorfa: Essai sur la litterature historique et biographique au Maroc du XVIe au XXe siècle.* Paris: Larose, 1922.

Levin, Michael J. *Agents of Empire: Spanish Ambassadors in Sixteenth-Century Italy.* Ithaca, NY: Cornell University Press, 2005.

Liang, Yuen-Gen, Abigail Krasner Balbale, Andrew Devereux, and Camilo Gómez-Rivas. "Unity and Disunity across the Strait of Gibraltar." *Medieval Encounters* 19 (2013): 1–40.

Livermore, H. V. *A New History of Portugal.* Cambridge: Cambridge University Press, 1966.

Loomis, Catherine. "Elizabeth Southwell's Manuscript Account of the Death of Queen Elizabeth." *English Literary Renaissance* (1996): 482–509.

Lope de Vega Carpio, Félix. “La tragedia del Rey Don Sebastian y el bautismo del Príncipe de Marruecos.” In *Onzena parte de las comedias de Lope de Vega Carpio*. Madrid, 1618.

López Piñero, José María. “Las Controversiae medicae et philosophical (1556), de Francisco Vallés y el galenismo del siglo XVI.” In *Los temas polémicos de la medicina renacentista: Las controversias* (1556), *de Francisco Vallés*, edited by José María López Piñero and Francisco Calero, 3–67. Madrid: Consejo Superior de Investigaciones Científicas, 1988.

Lúcio de Azevedo, J. *A evolução do Sebastianismo*. Lisbon: Livraria Clássica Editôra, 1947.

Lybarger, Loren D. “The Demise of Adam in the ‘Qisas al-Anbiya’: The Symbolic Politics of Death and Re-Burial in Islamic ‘Stories of the Prophets.’” *Numen* 5 (2008): 497–535.

MacKay, Ruth. *The Baker Who Pretended to Be King of Portugal*. Chicago: University of Chicago Press, 2012.

Malkowski, Jennifer. *Dying in Full Detail: Mortality and Digital Documentary*. Durham, NC: Duke University Press, 2017.

Mallett, Michael. “Ambassadors and Their Audiences in Renaissance Italy.” *Renaissance Studies* 8 (1994): 229–43.

Mann, Charles C. *1491: New Revelations of the Americas*. New York: Vintage, 2006.

———. *1493: Uncovering the New World Columbus Created*. New York: Vintage, 2012.

Manoff, Marlene. “Theories of the Archive from across the Disciplines.” *Portal: Libraries and the Academy* 4, no. 1 (2004): 9–25.

Manso, Antonio. “Avis d’Antonio Manso Puerto de Santa Maria.” In *Archives et bibliothèques d’Espagne*. Les sources inédites de l’histoire du Maroc, 452. Paris: E. Laroux, 1905.

Mármol, Luis del. *Descripción general de África*. 2 vols. Málaga, 1599.

Martínez de Leyva, Miguel. *Remedios preservatives y curativos, para en tiempo de la peste y otras curiosas experiencias: Dividido en dos cuerpos*. Madrid: Imprenta Real, 1597. https://play.google.com/books/reader?id=LDZkAAAAcAAJ&hl=en&pg=GBS.PA150-IA1.

Martínez, Miguel. *Front Lines: Soldiers’ Writing in the Early Modern Hispanic World*. Chicago: University of Chicago Press, 2016.

Massinger, Philip. *Believe as You List*. Edited by T. Crafton Croker. London: The Percy Society, 1849.

Massumi, Brian. “The Autonomy of Affect.” *Cultural Critique* 31 (1995): 83–109.

———. “The Future Birth of the Affective Fact: The Political Ontology of Threat.” In *The Affect Theory Reader*, edited by Melissa Gregg and Gregory J. Seigworth, 52–70. Durham, NC: Duke University Press, 2010.

Matsakis, Louise. “Body Cameras Haven’t Stopped Police Brutality. Here’s Why.” *Wired*, June 17, 2020. https://www.wired.com/story/body-cameras-stopped-police-brutality-george-floyd/.

Mbembe, Achille. “Necropolitics.” *Public Culture* 15, no. 1 (2003): 11–40.

——. *Necropolitics*. Durham, NC: Duke University Press, 2019.

McMurdo, Edward. *The History of Portugal from the Reign of D. João II to the Reign of D. João V.* London, 1889.

Mediano, Fernando Rodríguez. "Justice, Crime and Punishment in 10th/16th-Century Morocco." In *Public Violence in Islamic Societies: Power, Discipline, and the Construction of the Public Sphere, 7th–19th Centuries CE*, edited by Christian Lange and Maribel Fierro, 179–200. Edinburgh: Edinburgh University Press, 2009.

——. "The Post-Almohad Dynasties in al-Andalus and the Maghrib (Seventh–Ninth/Thirteenth–Fifteenth Centuries)." In *The Western Islamic World, Eleventh to Eighteenth Centuries*, edited by Maribel Fierro, 106–43. Cambridge: Cambridge University Press, 2010.

Meisami, Julie Scott. "History as Literature." *Iranian Studies* 33, no. 1/2 (2000): 15–30.

Mendes Pinto, Fernão. *The Travels of Mendes Pinto*. Edited by Rebecca D. Catz. Chicago: University of Chicago Press, 1989.

Mendonça, Jeronimo de. *Jornada de África*. 1607. Porto: Imprensa Recreativa do Instituto Escholar de S. Domingos, 1878.

——. *Jornada de África*. Bibliotheca de Clássicos Portugueses. Edited by Mello de Azevedo. Vol. 1 & 2, Lisbon: Livraria Clássica Editora, 1904.

Menocal, María Rosa. *The Arabic Role in Medieval Literary History: A Forgotten Heritage*. Philadelphia: University of Pennsylvania Press, 1987.

——. *Ornament of the World: How Muslims, Jews, and Christians Created a Culture of Tolerance in Medieval Spain*. New York: Little, Brown and Company, 2002.

——. *Shards of Love: Exile and the Origins of the Lyric*. Durham, NC: Duke University Press, 1992.

Mercer, Patricia. "Palace and Jihād in the Early ʿAlawī State in Morocco." *The Journal of African History* 18, no. 4 (1977): 531–54.

Meyerson, Mark. *The Muslims of Valencia in the Age of Fernando and Isabel: Between Coexistence and Crusade*. Berkeley: University of California Press, 1991.

Mignolo, Walter D. "Cartas, crónicas y relaciones del descubrimiento y la conquista." In *Historia de la literatura hispanoamericana: Época colonial*, edited by Luis Iñigo Madrigal, 57–116. Madrid: Cátedra, 1982.

"Miguel Leitão de Andrade." In *Diccionario Bibliográfico Português*, edited by Innocencio Francisco da Silva, 240–41. Lisbon: Imprensa Nacional, 1862.

More, Anna. *Baroque Sovereignty: Carlos de Sigüenza y Góngora and the Creole Archive of Colonial Mexico*. Philadelphia: University of Pennsylvania Press, 2013.

Morton, Nicholas. *The Field of Blood: The Battle for Aleppo and the Remaking of the Medieval Middle East*. New York: Basic Books, 2018.

Moura, Cristobal de. "Copia de carta original de D. Cristóbal de Mora al rey, fecha en Lisboa á 2 de setiembre de 1578." In *Colección de documentos inéditos para la historia de España*, edited by Pedro José Pidal y Carniado, 141–47. Madrid: Calera, 1862.

Mulvey, Laura. *Death 24x a Second: Stillness and the Moving Image*. London: Reaktion Books, 2006.
Munson, Henry, Jr. *Religion and Power in Morocco*. New Haven, CT: Yale University Press, 1993.
Murray, Noëleen, and Louise Green. "Notes for a Guide to the Ossuary." *African Studies* 68, no. 3 (2009): 370–86.
Nalle, Sara T. "A Saint for All Seasons: The Cult of St. Julián." In *Culture and Control in Counter-Reformation Spain*, edited by Anne J. Cruz and Mary Elizabeth Perry, 25–50. Minneapolis: University of Minnesota Press, 1992.
Newitt, Malyn. *A History of Portuguese Overseas Expansion, 1400–1668*. London: Routledge, 2005.
Newstok, Scott. *Quoting Death in Early Modern England: The Poetics of Epitaphs beyond the Tomb*. New York: Palgrave Macmillan, 2009.
Nirenberg, David. *Communities of Violence: Persecution of Minorities in the Middle Ages*. Princeton, NJ: Princeton University Press, 1996.
Noble-Olson, Michael. "Reviving the Elephant; or, Cinema Plays Dead." *Cultural Critique* 97 (2017): 84–104.
Nudelman, Franny. *John Brown's Body: Slavery, Violence, and the Culture of War*. Chapel Hill: University of North Carolina Press, 2004.
Olds, Katrina B. "The Ambiguities of the Holy: Authenticating Relics in Sixteenth-Century Spain." *Renaissance Quarterly* 65 (2012): 135–84.
Olyan, Saul W. "The Instrumental Dimensions of Ritual Violence against Corpses in Biblical Texts." In *Ritual Violence in the Hebrew Bible: New Perspectives*, edited by Saul W. Olyan, 125–36. Oxford: Oxford University Press, 2015.
Orso, Steven N. *Art and Death at the Spanish Court: The Royal Exequies for Philip IV*. Columbia: University of Missouri Press, 1989.
Osswald, Maria Cristina. "O martírio de Inácio de Azevedo e dos seus trinta e nove companheiros (1570) na hagiografia da Companhia de Jesus entre os séculos XVI e XIX." *Cultura: Revista de História e Teoria das Ideias* 27 (2010): 163–86. https://journals.openedition.org/cultura/354.
Padrón, Ricardo. *The Spacious Word: Cartography, Literature, and Empire in Early Modern Spain*. Chicago: University of Chicago Press, 2004.
Pagden, Anthony. *European Encounters with the New World: From Renaissance to Romanticism*. New Haven: Yale University Press, 1992.
———. "Ius et Factum: Text and Experience in the Writings of Bartolomé de Las Casas." *Representations* 33 (1991): 147–62.
Park, Katharine. "The Criminal and the Saintly Body: Autopsy and Dissection in Renaissance Italy." *Renaissance Quarterly* 47 (1991): 1–33.
Pastor, Reyna. "Claudio Sánchez-Albornoz y sus claves de la historia medieval de España." *Revista de historia Jerónimo Zurita* 73 (1998): 117–32.
Pearson, Michael N. "First Contacts between Indian and European Medical Systems." In *Warm Climates and Western Medicine: The Emergence of Tropical Medicine, 1500–1900*, edited by David Arnold, 20–41. Amsterdam: Rodopi, 1996.

Peele, George. *The Battell of Alcazar, fought in Barbarie betweene Sebastian King of Portugall, and Abdelmalec King of Marocco. With the death of Captaine Stukeley.* London, 1594.

Peirce, Charles S. “What Is a Sign?” In *The Essential Peirce*, edited by Peirce Edition Project, 4–10. Bloomington: Indiana University Press, 1998.

Pérez Fadrique, Juan Eulogio. *Moda práctica de embalsamar cuerpos defuntos para preservarlos incorruptos y eternizarlos en lo posible.* Seville: Thomé Miranda, 1666. https://play.google.com/books/reader?id=LDZkAAAAcAAJ&hl=en&pg=GBS.PA150-IA1.

Peterson, Kaara L. “Elizabeth I's Virginity and the Body of Evidence: Jonson's Notorious Crux.” *Renaissance Quarterly* 68 (2015): 840–71.

Philip II of Spain. Philip II to Christoval de Mora [*sic*], 5 October, 1578. Archivo General de Simancas.

——. Philip II to Christoval de Mora [*sic*], 20 October, 1578. Archivo General de Simancas.

Pianel, Georges. “Les préliminaires de la conquête du Soudan par Moulaye Ahmed el-Mansôur, d'après trois documents inédits.” *Hespéris* 40 (1953): 185–99.

Pines, Noam. “Deixis.” In *The Princeton Encyclopedia of Poetry & Poetics*, 4th ed., edited by Roland Greene, 344. Princeton, NJ: Princeton University Press, 2012.

Posel, Deborah, and Pamela Gupta. “The Life of the Corpse: Framing Reflections and Questions.” *African Studies* 68, no. 3 (2009): 299–309.

Pupo-Walker, Enrique. *La vocación literaria del pensamiento histórico en América: Desarollo de la prosa de ficción—siglos XVI, XVII, XVIII y XIX.* Madrid: Gredos, 1982.

Queiroz Velloso, José Maria de. *D. Sebastião.* Lisbon: Empresa nacional de publicidade, 1935.

Ray, Jonathan. “Iberian Jewry between West and East: Jewish Settlement in the Sixteenth-Century Mediterranean.” *Mediterranean Studies* 18 (2009): 44–65.

——. *The Sephardic Frontier: The Reconquista and the Jewish Community in Medieval Iberia.* Ithaca, NY: Cornell University Press, 2006.

Riches, David. “The Phenomenon of Violence.” In *The Anthropology of Violence*, edited by David Riches, 1–27. Oxford and New York: Blackwell, 1986.

Ricouer, Paul. *Oneself as Another.* Translated by Kathleen Blamey. Chicago: University of Chicago Press, 1992.

——. *Time and Narrative, Volume 1.* Translated by Kathleen McLaughlin and David Pellauer. Chicago: University of Chicago Press, 1984.

Rodríguez-Salgado, M. *The Changing Face of Empire: Charles V, Philip II, and Habsburg Authority, 1551–1559.* Cambridge: Cambridge University Press, 1988.

Roosen, William. “Early Modern Diplomatic Ceremonial: A Systems Approach.” *Journal of Modern History* 52 (1980): 452–76.

Ross, Kathleen. “Historians of the Conquest and Colonization of the New World: 1550–1620.” In *The Cambridge History of Latin American Literature*, edited by Roberto González Echevarría and Enrique Pupo-Walker, 101–42. Cambridge: Cambridge University Press, 1996.

Rouhi, Leyla. "Miguel de Cervantes, Early Modern Spain, and the Challenges to the Meaning of Islam." *Middle East Journal of Culture and Communication* 4 (2011): 7–22.

Rucquoi, Adeline. "De los reyes que no son taumaturgos: Los fundamentos de la realeza en España." *Relaciones: Estudios de Historia y Sociedad* 13, no. 51 (1992): 55–100.

Ruggles, D. Fairchild. "Mothers of a Hybrid Dynasty: Race, Genealogy, and Acculturation in al-Andalus." *Journal of Medieval and Early Modern Studies* 34, no. 1 (2004): 65–94.

Ruiz, Teofilo F. "Unsacred Monarchy: The Kings of Castile in the Late Middle Ages." In *Rites of Power: Symbolism, Ritual and Politics since the Late Middle Ages*, edited by Sean Wilentz, 109–44. Philadelphia: University of Pennsylvania Press, 1985.

Saldanha, António de. *Crónica de Almançor Sultão de Marrocos (1578–1603)*. Edited by António Dias Farinha. Translated by León Bourdon. Lisbon: Instituto de Investigação Científica Tropical, 1997.

San Román de Rivadeneyra, Antonio de. *Jornada y muerte del rey Don Sebastián de Portugal*. Valladolid, 1603.

Sánchez-Albornoz. *España: Un enigma histórico*. Barcelona: Editora y Distribuidora Hispanoamericana, 1954.

Sawday, Jonathan. *The Body Emblazoned: Dissection and the Human Body in Renaissance Culture*. New York: Routledge, 1995.

——. "The Fate of Marsyas: Dissecting the Renaissance Body." In *Renaissance Bodies: The Human Figure in English Culture c. 1540–1660*, edited by Lucy Gent and Nigel Llewellyn, 111–35. London: Reaktion Books, 1990.

Scarry, Elaine. *The Body in Pain: The Making and Unmaking of the World*. New York: Oxford University Press, 1985.

Schmitz, Timothy J. "The Spanish Hieronymites and the Reformed Texts of the Council of Trent." *The Sixteenth Century Journal* 37 (2006): 375–99.

Schneider, Rebecca. "Judith Butler Is My Hands." In *Bodily Citations: Religion and Judith Butler*, edited by Ellen Armour and Susan St. Ville, 225–51. New York: Columbia University Press, 2006.

——. *Performing Remains: Art and War in Times of Theatrical Reenactment*. London: Routledge, 2011.

Schwartz, Margaret. *Dead Matter: The Meaning of Iconic Corpse*. Minneapolis: University of Minnesota Press, 2015.

Seigworth, Gregory J., and Melissa Gregg. "An Inventory of Shimmers." In *The Affect Theory Reader*, edited by Melissa Gregg and Gregory J. Seigworth, 1–25. Durham, NC: Duke University Press, 2010.

Sell, Jonathan P. A. *Rhetoric and Wonder in English Travel Writing, 1560–1613*. Burlington, VT: Ashgate, 2006.

Sentilles, Sarah. "When We See Photographs of Some Dead Bodies and Not Others." *New York Times Magazine*, August 14, 2018. https://www.nytimes.com/2018/08/14/magazine/media-bodies-censorship.html.

Sérgio, António. *O Desejado: Depoimentos de contemporaneos de D. Sebastião sôbre êste mesmo rei e sua jornada de África*. Lisbon: Livrarias Aillaud e Bertrand, 1924.
Silva, Juan de. "Correspondencia de D. Juan de Silva con Felipe II, relativo, en su mayor parte, á la expedición de D. Sebastian a África." In *Colección de documentos inéditos para la historia de España*, edited by Marquis of Pidal, Marquis of Miraflores and Miguel Salvá, vol. 39, 465–574; vol. 40 5–131. Madrid, 1861.
———. Juan de Silva to Philip II, 6 March 1576. Archivo General de Simancas.
———. Juan de Silva to Philip II, 5 June, 1578. Archivo General de Simancas.
Silverblatt, Irene. "Imperial Dilemmas, the Politics of Kinship, and Inca Reconstructions of History." *Comparative Studies in Society and History* 30, no. 1 (1988): 83–102.
Silverstein, Michael. "Hierarchy of Features and Ergativity." In *Grammatical Categories in Australian Languages*, edited by Richard Dixon, 112–71. Canberra: Australian Institute of Aboriginal Studies, 1976.
Siraisi, Nancy. *Medicine and the Italian Universities, 1250–1600*. Leiden: Brill, 2001.
Skidmore, Chris. *Death and the Virgin: Elizabeth, Dudley, and the Mysterious Fate of Amy Robsart*. London: Phoenix, 2011.
Smith, Richard. *Aḥmad al-Manṣūr: Islamic Visionary*. New York: Pearson Education, 2006.
Sobchack, Vivian. "Inscribing Ethical Space: Ten Propositions on Death, Representation, and Documentary." *Quarterly Review of Film Studies* 9, no. 4 (1984): 283–300.
Soifer, Maya. "Beyond *Convivencia*: Critical Reflections on the Historiography of Interfaith Relations in Christian Spain." *Journal of Medieval Iberian Studies* 1, no. 1 (2009): 19–35.
Spragins, Elizabeth L. "Cuerpos, cuernos, and espadas ceñidas: Sedimenting Gender through Violence in La monja alférez." *ConSecuencias* 1, no. 1 (2019). https://ejournals.bc.edu/index.php/consecuencias/article/view/11769.
———. "Embodied Authority: The Virgin, Audience, and the Body of the Devotee in Marian Miracles." *La corónica* 45, no. 2 (2017): 9–36.
Steedman, Carolyn. "Something She Called a Fever: Michelet, Derrida, and Dust." *American Historical Review* 106, no. 4 (2001): 1159–80.
Stein, Rachel. "Re-composing the Global Iberian Monarchy through the Lisbon Press of Pedro Craesbeeck (1597–1632)." PhD dissertation, Columbia University, 2017.
Stewart, Susan. *Poetry and the Fate of the Senses*. Chicago: University of Chicago Press, 2002.
Subrahmanyam, Sanjay. "Connected Histories: Notes toward a Reconfiguration of Modern Eurasia." *Modern Asian Studies* 31, no. 3 (1997): 735–62.
"Sur la dynastie saadienne." Translated by E. Fagnan. In *Extraits inédits relatifs au Maghreb (Géographie et histoire)*, 360–457. Algiers: Jules Carbonel, 1924.
Szpiech, Ryan. "The Convivencia Wars: Decoding Historiography's Polemic with Philology." In *A Sea of Languages: Rethinking the Arabic Role in Medieval*

Literary History, edited by Suzanne Conklin Akbari and Karla Mallette, 135–61. Toronto: University of Toronto Press, 2013.
Tārīkh al-dawla al-sa'diyya. Edited by George S. Colin. Rabat, 1921.
Tārīkh al-dawla al-sa'diyya al-Takmadārtiyya. Edited by 'Abd al-Raḥīm Benḥādda. Marrakesh: Maṭba'a Tīnmal, 1994.
"The Battle of Alcazar." Calendar of State Papers Foreign, Elizabeth, 1558–1589. The National Archives.
Tortorici, Zeb. "Reading the (Dead) Body: Histories of Suicide in New Spain." In *Death and Dying in Colonial Spanish America*, edited by Martina Will de Chaparro and Miruna Achim, 53–77. Tucson: University of Arizona Press, 2011.
Touati, Houari. *Islam and Travel in the Middle Ages*. Chicago: University of Chicago Press, 2010.
Tritton, A. S. "Djanāza." In *Encyclopedia of Islam, Second Edition*, edited by P. Bearman, Thomas Bianquis, Clifford E. Bosworth, E. van Donzel, and W. P. Heinrichs. Leiden: Brill Online, 2012–. http://dx.doi.org/10.1163/1573-3912_islam_SIM_1985.
Valladares, Rafael. *La conquista de Lisboa: Violencia militar y comunidad política en Portugal, 1578–1583*. Madrid: Marcial Pons, 2008.
Valverde de Hamusco, Juan. *Historia de la composición del cuerpo humano*. Rome: Antonio Salamanca and Antonio Lafrerii, 1556. https://dl.wdl.org/10631/service/10631.pdf.
Varela, Javier. *La muerte del rey: El ceremonial funerary de la monarquía española (1500–1885)*. Madrid: Turner, 1990.
Vázquez, Miguel Ángel. *Desde la penumbra de la fosa: La concepción de la muerte en la literatura morisca*. Madrid: Editorial Trotta, 2007.
Venegas, Alexo. "Agonía del tránsito de la muerte: Con avisos y consuelos que cerca della son provechosos (1536)." In *Escritores místicos españoles*, edited by Miguel Mir. Nueva Biblioteca de Autores Españoles, 129–33. Madrid, 1911.
Verdery, Katherine. *The Political Lives of Dead Bodies: Reburial and Postsocialist Change*. New York: Columbia University Press, 1999.
Vieira Guimarâes, José. *A Ordem de Christo*. Lisbon, 1901.
Vogel, Amos. "Grim Death." *Film Comment* 16, no. 2 (1980): 78.
Voigt, Lisa. *Writing Captivity in the Early Modern Atlantic: Circulations of Knowledge and Authority in the Iberian and English Imperial Worlds*. Chapel Hill: University of North Carolina Press, 2009.
Vollendorf, Lisa. "Reading the Body Imperiled: Violence against Women in María de Zayas." *Hispania* 78, no. 2 (1995): 272–82.
Wacks, David A. *Double Diaspora in Sephardic Literature: Jewish Cultural Production before and after 1492*. Bloomington: Indiana University Press, 2015.
———. *Framing Iberia: Maqāmāt and Frametale Narratives in Medieval Spain*. Leiden: Brill, 2007.
———. *Medieval Iberian Crusade Fiction and the Mediterranean World*. Toronto: University of Toronto Press, 2019.

Wallace, Stephen. "Figure and Ground: The Interrelationships of Linguistic Categories." In *Tense-Aspect: Between Semantics and Pragmatics*, edited by P. J. Hopper, 201–26. Philadelphia: John Benjamins, 1982.

Wazzaz al-Fasi, al-Hassan ibn Muhammad al-. *The History and Description of Africa of Leo Africanus*. Vol. 2. Edited by Robert Brown. Translated by John Pory. London: The Hakluyt Society, 1896.

Weissberger, Barbara F. *Isabel Rules: Constructing Queenship, Wielding Power*. Minneapolis: University of Minnesota Press, 2003.

Wey Gómez, Nicolás. *The Tropics of Empire: Why Columbus Sailed South to the Indies*. Cambridge, MA: MIT Press, 2008.

White, Joshua. *Piracy and the Law in the Ottoman Mediterranean*. Stanford, CA: Stanford University Press, 2017.

Willis, John R. "The Western Sudan from the Moroccan Invasion (1591) to the Death of al-Mukhtasar al-Kunti (1811)." In *History of West Africa*, edited by J. F. Ade Ajayi and Michael Crowder, 441–84. London: Longman, 1971.

Wittman, Laura. *The Tomb of the Unknown Soldier, Modern Mourning, and the Reinvention of the Mystical Body*. Toronto: Toronto University Press, 2011.

Wright, W. *Arabic Grammar*, vol. 1. Edited by W. Robertson Smith and M. J. de Goege. Mineola, NY: Dover Publications, 2005.

Yahya, Dahiru. *Morocco in the Sixteenth Century: Problems and Patterns in African Foreign Policy*. Atlantic Highlands, NJ: Humanities Press, 1981.

Young, Craig, and Duncan Light. "Corpses, Dead Body Politics and Agency in Human Geography: Following the Corpse of Dr. Petru Groza." *Transactions of the Institute of British Geographers* 38, no. 1 (2012): 135–48.

Yuan, Jada. "Burials on Harts Island, Where New York's Unclaimed Dead Lie in Mass Graves, Have Risen Fivefold." *Washington Post*, April 16, 2020. https://www.washingtonpost.com/national/hart-island-mass-graves-coronavirus-new-york/2020/04/16/a0c413ee-7f5f-11ea-a3ee-13e1ae0a3571_story.html.

Zayas, María de. *Desengaños amorosos*. 7th ed. Edited by Alicia Yllera. Madrid: Cátedra, 2009.

Zmora, Hillay. *Monarchy, Aristocracy, and the State in Europe, 1300–1800*. New York: Routledge, 2000.

Index

1492: historical significance of, 13, 153n58

'Abd al-Raḥmān, 86
'Abd al-Malik, Abū Marwān, 1–2, 5–9, 20–21, 46, 48; cover up of death of, 111; death of, 61, 63, 111, 149n27; illness of, 61–62; al-Manṣūr on, 66–68; name of, 146n1; Valencia on, 61–63, 67–68
'Abd al-Mu'min, 5
Abū al-'Abbas, Aḥmad, 5
Achim, Miruna, 175n48
active necroviolence, 116–17
Adorno, Roleno, 159n12
affect: affective power of corpses, 83–84; necroviolence and, 117–18
agency: of corpses, 72–73, 95–96; defining, 172n7; of Leitão de Andrade, 177n70; of nonhuman objects, 79–80, 176n58
Ahmed, Sara, 193n79
Akbari, Suzanne Conklin, 153n52; on temporality and spatiality, 158n90
alternative facts, 138
anaphora, 155n70
Andalusi literature, 153n54
the Andes, 135
Andrade, Diogo de, 70, 75; background of, 171n1
animacy, 176n57
Arbery, Ahmaud, 138
al-Aṣghār, Muḥammad Shaykh, 112
Asilah, 61
assemblages: corpses as, 95–96; defining, 92; diplomatic, 96–100; Schwartz on, 96; of service, 91–96; Silva in, 96; of vital matter, 109
Astren, Fred, 176n51
Atocha bombings, 151n39
authority, 30–31
Azevedo, Ignacio de, 171n1
Aznar, José María, 151n39

Balbale, Abigail Krasner, 150n34
Baptista, João, 42, 43, 71
Barca, Calderón de la, 18
Battle of Alcácer. *See* Battle of al-Qaṣr al-Kabīr
Battle of Lepanto, 2
Battle of al-Qaṣr al-Kabīr, 2–8, 14, 22–23; Conestaggio account of, 28–30; conflicting accounts of, 28–30; corpses from, 2–3; deaths in, 8–9; impact of, in Spain and Morocco, 9–10; in *Jornada de África*, 27–29; martyrdom at, 158n5; Mendonça, J. de, on, 28–31, 42–43, 156n85; narration of, 136; Portuguese in, 28; as proxy war, 147n6; Rivadeneyra on, 29–30; royal death at, 136–37; social and political consequences of, 18; woodcut of, 42
Battle of Tell Danith, 189n39
Battle of the Three Kings, 2. *See* Battle of al-Qaṣr al-Kabīr
Battle of Wādī al-Makhāzin, 2, 4

Bazin, André, 20; on death, 50, 155n73; on obscenity, 46–47
Benḥādda, ʿAbd al-Raḥīm, 113–14
Bennett, Jane, 73, 79–80
Bertelli, Sergio, 51; on the body of the king, 161n36, 177n72, 177n73
Biblioteca Nacional in Madrid, 113
Bibliothèque Nationale du Royaume du Maroc, 114
Bidāyat al-mujtahid (Ibn Rushd), 126
bin Laden, Osama: corpse of, 137–38
biopower, 115–16; necroviolence and, 117
Black Lives Matter movement, 138
the body: anatomical discoveries, 31; Bertelli on, of the king, 161n36, 177n72, 177n73; of the king, 94–95, 102–3; narrative authority and, 30; Renaissance understanding of, 31; Silva on, of the king, 102–3; the state and metaphors of, 51
Borja, Juan de, 94; Silva and, 180n19
Bossong, Georg, 172n8, 176n57
Braudel, Fernand, 150n34, 152n44, 152n50
Brown, Elizabeth A. R., 78; on corpse desecration, 161n36
Brown, Peter, 176n48
Brown, Vincent, 176n48
Buesterien, John, 138–39
burial, 21–22, 120; mass, 138
Bush, George W., 189n42

Camões, Luis de, 173n18
Capela dos Ossos, 135
captatio benevolentiae, 55
The Captive Sea (Hershenzon), 152n51
captivity networks, 152n51, 158n93
Caravaggio, 135
Carracedo, Almudena, 188n35
cartas relatorias, 154n60, 159n12
Castile, 152n48
Castilian exceptionalism, 11
Castro, Américo, 10–11; attack on, 150n37; on Iberian Peninsula, 150n36
Catherine (Queen), 90, 97; death of, 99–100; Silva and, 98–99
Catlos, Brian, 189n39
Cervantes, Miguel de, 163n42
Ceuta, 4, 103–4
Charles V (Emperor), 5, 6; reorganization of court of, 180n21
Christianity, 11, 83, 152n43
chrononormativity, 168n36
Chronique anonyme de la dynastie Saʿdienne (Colin), 113–14
cinema. *See* film
Cirurgião, António, 75
Colin, Georges S., 113–14
Columbus, Christopher, 31, 153n58
composite histories, 154n62
Conestaggio, Girólamo de, 27, 160n21, 163n43; on Battle of al-Qaṣr al-Kabīr, 28–30; Mendonça, J. de, on account of, 28–31, 37–38, 43–44, 54–55
Consejo de Estado, 178n3, 182n48
Convento de Nossa Senhora da Luz, 74
convergers, 164n56
convivencia: defining, 10; reframing of, 11; rivalries undergirding, 151n38; Szpiech on, 151n38
Cooper, Ursula, 166n16
Cornell, Vincent J., 185n9, 191n65
coronavirus pandemic, 138
corpse care, 72, 80; Laquer on, 188n32; necroviolence and, 116; in *Tārīkh al-dawla al-saʿdiyya al-takmadārtiyya*, 119
corpse desecration, 115; blame for, 116; Brown, E., on, 161n36. *See also* necroviolence
corpses: affective power of, 83–84; agency of, 72–73, 95–96; as assemblages, 95–96; from Battle of al-Qaṣr al-Kabīr, 2–3; of bin Laden, 137–38; defining, 95–96, 118; deictics and, 36–37; efficacy of, 84–88; Eire on, 95; as empty signifiers, 41–42; as guarantee of mimetic reality, 16; identification of, 71–72; identification of royal, 119–20; as indexes, 15–18, 35, 40–41, 49, 80–81; itinerant, 105–9; Leitão de Andrade on, 73–74, 83–84; locating, 40–41, 70–71; Mendonça, J. de, on, 25, 26, 33; in *Miscellânea*, 74; of al-Mutawakkil II, 110–11, 118–19; narrative and, 17, 20–21; narrative authority and, 2–3; narrative danger of, 128–29; as objects, 80–81, 132; ontology of, 72, 73; as referential object, 3–4, 16, 73, 80–81; representation of, 15–16, 27–28; role of, in necroepistemology, 26; Schwartz on, 27, 95–96; of Sebastian I, 105–9; Sobchak on, 175n44; societal boundaries mapped via, 175n48; as subjects, 80–81, 88, 111–12; as temporal sign, 49; as vibrant matter,

81–82; witnessing of, 33. *See also* grammar of the corpsej\
The Corrupting Sea (Horden & Purcell), 152n50
Cory, Stephen, 185n9, 185n10
Corzo, Andrea Gasparo, 90, 103, 178n2; La Véronne on, 146n6, 147n9; Philip and, 108–9; Silva on, 103–4, 105–6, 108–9, 183n57, 183n61, 183n64
Council of Trent, 78, 174n35
Counter-Reformation, 135
Coutinho, Gonçalo: Valencia on, 60
Covarrubias, Sebastián de, 92–93, 97, 102
Craesbeeck, Pedro, 26, 158n3, 160n23
credibility, 30–31
Cuz, Bernardo da, 148n14

dead matter, 73
death: of 'Abd al-Malik, 61, 63, 111, 149n27; in Battle of al-Qaṣr al-Kabīr, 8–9; Bazin and Vogel on, 155n73; Bazin on, 50; of Catherine, 99–100; documentation of, 66; film and, 155n73; Laquer on, 172n5; Leitão de Andrade on, 84; of al-Manṣūr, 61; media studies on, 165n3; physical signs of, 49–50; representation of, 50–52, 155n73, 165n3; of Sebastian I, 57–58; semiotics of, 16; Sobchak on, 33, 66; temporality of, 49–50, 87–88. *See also* royal death
"Death Every Afternoon" (Bazin), 46
De humani corporis fabrica (Vesalius), 31
deictics, 106; corpses and, 36–37; Fludernik on, 155n70; narrative and, 36; relationality of, 35; spatial, 34; Stewart on, 36
De León, Jason, 111, 115, 184n2; on necroviolence, 188n34
Deleuze, Gilles, 80
Dell'unione (Conestaggio), 29, 75
Devereux, Andrew, 150n34
Dias Farinha, 6, 148n18
Díaz del Castillo, Bernal, 31
Diffie, Bailey W., 160n21
digital turn, 155n73
Dinshaw, Carolyn, 166n16, 168n36
diplomatic assemblages: Silva in, 96–100
disgust, 117
dispositif, 92
Doane, Mary Ann: on film, 166n15
Do Autor Mighel Leitão d'Andrada, etat 73, 72
documentary film, 167n25
Dubrow, Heather, 15, 156n77; on convergers, 164n56

Eire, Carlos, 79; on corpses, 95; on Philip II, 181n28
Elizabeth of Valois, 178n4
embalming: temporality of, 51–52
embodiment: Mendonça, J. de, on, 56
endangered evasion: of Mendonça, J. de, 53–59; of Valencia, 65
endangered gaze, 47
endangered vision: Sobchak on, 56
Erauso, Catalina de, 145n7
España (Sánchez-Albornoz), 150n37
European imperialism, 13
evasion, 47
eyewitness testimony, 26–27; film and photography as analogous to, 54; Frisch on, 159n8; of Mendonça, J. de, 54–57; Pagden on, 159n12; of Valencia, 65–66

Fagnan, Edmond, 113
faits notoires, 54
Fanjul, Serafín, 151n41
Fierro, Maribel, 190n50
film: death and, 155n73; Doane on, 166n15; documentary, 167n25; eyewitness testimony as analogous to, 54; Sobchak on gaze of filmmaker, 167n25
Finkel, Caroline, 147n6
al-Fishtālī, 113, 114
Fitz-Fulk, Robert, 189n39
flesh archive, 169n51
flesh memory, 160n19
Floyd, George, 138
Fludernik, Monika, 155n70
Folger, Robert A., 92, 154n60; on colonial writing, 161n27
Fontein, Joost, 82
The Forgotten Frontier (Hess), 150n34
Foucault, Michel, 92, 115–16
Freeman, Elizabeth, 47, 168n36
Frisch, Andrea, 54, 76; on eyewitness testimony, 159n8
Front Lines (Martínez), 174n22
Frow, John, 177n64

Gama, Vasco da, 31
García-Arenal, Mercedes, 60, 114, 150n34, 169n55; on al-Manṣūr, 149n25

gaze: endangered, 47; interventional, 47
gender, performance of, 145n7
al-Ghālib, ʿAbd Allah, 4–5, 147n9
Gómez-Rivas, Camilo, 150n34
González Echevarría, Roberto, 161n30
grammar of the corpse, 15–16, 18–23
Granada, 152n48
Greer, Margaret, 153n55
Guattari, Felix, 80
Gunning, Tom, 154n67
Gupta, Pamela, 82; on necropolitics, 116

Habsburg Empire, 11, 95; decline of, 151n42
Halevi, Leor, 190n49
Hamet, Muley. *See* al-Manṣūr bi-amr Allah
Hamilton, Michelle, 153n54
Hanks, William, 35, 155n70, 164n51; on indexicality, 165n76
Harries, John, 82
Hebrew literature, 153n54
Helgerson, Richard A., 164n64
Hendrickson, Jocelyn, 191n64
Henri, Castries de, 59–60
Hersh, Seymour, 137–38
Hershenzon, Daniel, 152n43, 152n51, 153n53
Hess, Andrew C., 150n34, 156n82
Horden, Peregrine, 152n50
Houdas, Octave, 114
Hunwick, John O., 114, 187n18
Hussein, Saddam, 189n42
Hutcheson, Gregory, 153n54

Iberian Peninsula, 18; Castro on, 150n36; cultural intermingling in, 11–13; harmonious existence of, 150n36; interfaith relationships in, 10–12; Muslim "invasion" of, 151n39
Ibn Al-Qāḍī, Aḥmad ibn Muḥammad, 113
Ibn Barṭāl, 192n67
Ibn Rushd, 120–21, 126
Ibn ʿAskar, Abū ʿAbdullah, 121
al-Ifrānī, 6–7, 19, 114, 187n18, 191n56
impotence: of Silva, 101–5
Inca cultural politics, 145n7
indexes, 34; corpses as, 15–18, 35, 40–41, 49; defining, 93–94; Hanks on, 165n76; photographic image indexicality, 155n73; Schwartz on, 35–36, 93–94; in semiotics, 15; Silva as indexical presence, 93–94
interventional gaze, 47
interventional ventriloquism, 59–68
Islam, 11, 152n43
Islamic eschatology, 127–29; Vázquez on, 145n2

Jakobson, Roman, 163n48
Jespersen, Otto, 163n48
Jesuits, 160n21
Jewish migration, 170n58
João I (King of Portugal), 4
João III (King of Portugal), 5, 172n13
Jornada de África (Mendonça), 20–21, 25, 32, 35, 38, 43, 48, 53, 74, 75; Battle of al-Qaṣr al-Kabīr in, 27–29; financing of, 160n23; reediting of, 160n20
Jornada y muerte del rey D. Sebastián de Portugal (Rivadeneyra), 29–30
Judaism, 11; mourning rituals in, 176n51

Kamen, Henry, 6
Kantorowicz, Ernst, 51, 165n5, 179n14
Kay, Sarah, 193n80
khilāf, 126
Kinoshita, Sharon, 152n52
Knights Templar, 172n13
Korsmeyer, Carolyn, 193n78
Krmpotich, Cara, 82

Lange, Christian, 127–28
Laquer, Thomas, 34, 40–41, 75–76; on corpse care, 188n32; on death, 172n5
Latour, Bruno, 171n4; actants defined by, 175n43; on subjectivity, 72–73
La Véronne, Chantal: on Corzo, 146n6, 147n9
Leitão de Andrade, Miguel, 19, 21, 32, 42, 69, 101; agency of, 177n70; background of, 74–75; on body of king, 94–95; on corpses, 73–74, 83–84; on death, 84; on Mendonça, J. de, 160n20; narrative passivity of, 82–84; on royal death, 85–86; as subject and object, 83–84, 87; wounds of, 77–78, 111
Leitão do Rosario, Nicolão, 70
"Lettre d'un médecin juif a son frère," 59–60
Levin, Michael J., 180n20
Lévi-Provençal, Evariste, 113, 186n12, 186n13
linguistic polysystem, 153n53; of Mediterranean, 12–13
Lisbon, 7; plague in, 147n8

Loukkos River, 7–8
Lybarger, Loren D., 175n47

Machado, Diogo Barbosa, 5; on Mendonça, J. de, 25–26
MacKay, Ruth, 6, 97; on Philip, 147n12
Madrid, 151n42
Maghreb, 4, 7
Makhāzin River, 7–8
Maliki law, 126
Malkowski, Jennifer, 155n73
Manāhil al-ṣafā fī-akhbār al-shurafā, 113
Mann, Charles C., 153n58
Manoel, Fadrique, 41–42
Manso, Antonio, 149n29
al-Manṣūr bi-amr Allah, 1, 8, 10, 46, 64–65, 111, 122; on ʿAbd al-Malik, 66–68; death of, 61; García-Arenal on, 149n25; al-Mutawakkil and, 124–25, 130–31; new regime of, 118–19; Songhay Empire conquered by, 150n33
Manuel, João, 5
Martínez, Miguel, 30–31, 76, 174n22; on narrative authority, 157n88
Martínez de Levya, Miguel, 162n40
al-Maslūkh. *See* al-Mutawakkil II, Abū ʿAbdallah Muḥammad
mass burials, 138
Massinger, Philip, 18
Massumi, Brian, 189n42
Mazagão, 60
Mbembe, Achille, 115–16, 116
Mediano, Fernando Rodríguez, 127, 192n68
media studies, 155n73; on death, 165n3
Mediterranean: cultural intermingling in, 11–13; linguistic polysystem of, 12–13
Mediterranean studies, 10, 11–14; classic, 152n50; impact of, 153n52
Meisami, Julie Scott, 185n8
memory, flesh, 160n19
Mendonça, Jerónimo de, 19–21, 48, 64, 75; background of, 25–26; on Battle of al-Qaṣr al-Kabīr, 28–31, 42–43, 156n85; on bravery of Portuguese, 58–59; on Conestaggio account, 28–31, 37–38, 43–44, 54–55; on corpses, 25, 26, 33; corroboration of story of, 28; dead named by, 32–33, 39–41; on embodiment, 56; endangered evasion of, 53–59; eyewitness testimony of, 54–57; financing of, 160n23; Leitão de Andrade on, 160n20; Machado on, 25–26; reliability of, 58; on Sebastian I, 53–54, 57–58; in *terço dos aventureiros*, 25–26; witnessing of, 33; as writer, 55
Mendonça, Nuno Furtado de, 41
Menezes, Henrique de, 32
Menezes, Manoel de, 32
Menezes, Simão de, 32, 36
Menocal, María Rosa, 150n36
Mexico City, 151n42
Mignolo, Walter D., 154n60, 159n12
mimetic reality: corpse as guarantee of, 16
Miscellânea do Sitio de Nossa Senhora da Luz do Pedrogão Grande (Leitão de Andrade), 19, 42, 69, 71, 83, 84–85; characters in, 172n20; corpses in, 74; information about, 75; printing of, 172n11
Moluco, Muley, 46
monarchy: temporality of, 51–52
Montaña de Monserrate, 78
Moors, 11–12
More, Anna, 151n42
Moriscos, 11
Morton, Nicholas, 187n24
Moura, Cristobal, 149n28, 181n29, 182n49
al-Muntaqā al-maqṣūr ʿalā maʾathir al-khilāfat Abī al-ʿAbbās al-Manṣūr, 113
Murad III, 89
al-Mutawakkil II, Abū ʿAbdallah Muḥammad, 1–2, 5–9, 128; corpse of, 110–11, 118–19; flaying of, 110–11, 123–30; al-Manṣūr and, 124–25, 130–31; necroviolence towards, 111–12; recovery of body of, 118–20, 123

Nalle, Sara T., 176n48
narrative: of Battle of al-Qaṣr al-Kabīr, 136; corpses and, 17, 20–21; deictics and, 36; Martínez on authority of, 157n88; temporal specificity of, 51–52
narrative authority: the body and, 30; corpses and, 2–3
narratology, 17
an-Nāṣirī, Aḥmad ibn Khālid, 156n82
necrocapitalism, 138–39
necroepistemology: defining, 2–3; reactive, 22; role of corpse in, 26
necronominalism, 34, 37–44, 164n74
necropolitics, 138–39; defining, 115–16; Posel and Gupta on, 116

necroviolence: active, 116–17; affect theory on, 117–18; biopower and, 117; corporeal texts generated by, 111–12; corpse care and, 116; defining, 111, 115–16, 184n2; De León on, 188n34; grammatical logic of, 129–30; living targeted by, 115; mediation of, 116; toward al-Mutawakkil II, 111–12; passive, 116; prohibition of, 126; semiotics of, 117; sources of, 115–16
Newitt, Malyn, 148n16
Noble-Olson, Matthew, 166n15
nonhuman objects, 79–80; agency of, 79–80, 176n58
Nuzhat al-ḥādī bi akhbār mulūk al-qarn al-ḥādī, 19, 114, 121

object of threat, 111–12, 117–120, 128–32
obscenity: Bazin on, 46–47; of royal death, 48–53
Oliveira, Amaral de, 156n82
Oran fatwa, 192n66
Order of Christ, 172n13
origo, 34
Osswald, Maria Cristina, 171n1
Ottoman Empire, 11, 18, 146n6, 147n12; transition in, 148n13

Padrón, Ricardo, 184n69
Pagden, Anthony, 159n8; on eyewitness testimonial, 159n12
passive necroviolence, 116
Peele, George, 18
Peregrinação (Pinto), 146n4
Pérez Fadrique, Juan Eulogio, 45, 51, 69, 78, 89
Philip II (King of Spain), 9, 19, 78–79, 89, 91, 95, 100, 106, 123, 172n13, 175n38, 178n4; burial of, 181n29; Corzo and, 108–9; Council of Trent reinforced by, 174n35; Eire on, 181n28; MacKay on, 147n12; reorganization of court of, 180n21; Silva and, 98, 108–9, 147n13, 182n48
Philip III (King of Spain), 79, 95
photography, 15–16; eyewitness testimony as analogous to, 54; indexicality of, 155n73; truth claim of, 154n67
Pinheiro, Matheus, 75
Pinto, Fernão Mendes, 146n4
plague, 162n40; in Lisbon, 147n8
plotting, 51–52
polygamy, 149n25
Posel, Deborah, 82; on necropolitics, 116
power transitions: Valencia smoothing, 64
prominence, 96
punishment, 127
Purcell, Nicholas, 152n50

al-Qaeda, 137
al-Qaṣr al-Saghīr, 4
Quran, 127–28, 192n74

Ray, Jonathan, 170n58
reanimation: royal death and, 52–53
reference, 155n70
relationality: of deictics, 35
reliability: of Mendonça, J. de, 58; of Silva, 90–91; of Valencia, 65–66
Remedios preservativos y curativos, para entiempo de la peste y otras curiosas experiencias (Martínez de Levya), 162n40
Renaissance: the body in, 31
representation: of corpses, 15–16, 27–28; of death, 50–52, 155n73, 165n3; limits of, 165n3
de Resende, Sebastian, 9
Ribeiro dos Sanctos, António, 173n18
Ricoeur, Paul, 167n23
Rivadeneyra, Antonio de San Román de, 28; on Battle of al-Qaṣr al-Kabīr, 29–30
Rivera, Isidro, 165n77
Rodríguez-Salgado, M., 182n37
Ross, Jill, 158n90
royal death, 46; at Battle of al-Qaṣr al-Kabīr, 136–37; corpse identification, 119–20; discovery of, 85; Leitão de Andrade on, 85–86; obscenity of, 48–53; reanimation and, 52–53; recovery of remains, 118–23; Silva on, 91, 107–8; temporality of, 51–52; Valencia on, 62; vibrant matter and, 90; witnessing, 47–48, 52, 122–23, 136–37
Rucquoi, Adeline, 167n29
Ruiz, Teofilo F., 167n29

sabiʿa, 120
Sá e Menezes, Francisco de, 25
Saldanha, António de, 157n85
Sánchez-Albornoz, Claudio, 150n37
Sawday, Jonathan, 31
Saʿdī dynasty, 112, 114, 185n10, 186n12
Scarry, Elaine, 26, 38–39
Schneider, Rebecca, 160n19

Schwartz, Margaret, 16; on assemblages, 96; on corpses, 27, 95–96; indexes defined by, 35–36, 93–94
Sebastian I (Kingof Portugal), 1–2, 5–7, 8, 9, 22, 32, 49, 64, 118, 121; Africa as interest of, 148n18; corpse of, 105–9; court of, 180n21; critics of, 148n14; death of, 57–58; failure of, 43; identification of body of, 122; Mendonça, J. de, on, 53–54, 57–58; men recruited by, 74–75; recovery of body of, 122–23; Sebastianism, 150n30; Silva on, 89–90, 104–5, 148n14
Sebástica (Oliveira), 156n82
Second War of the Alpujarras, 2
semiotics, 163n48; of death, 16; indexes in, 15; of necroviolence, 117
Senhora da Luz do Pedrogão Grande, 75, 83
service: assemblages of, 91–96; defining, 92–93, 97
al-Shāfiʿī, 126
al-Shaykh al-Mahdī, Muḥammad, 113
al-Shaykh al-Maʾmūn, Muḥammad, 113
al-Shaykh al-Saʿdī, Muḥammad, 4
shifters, 34; defining, 164n48
signs, classification of, 163n48
Silva, Juan de, 18–19, 22, 32, 88; in assemblages, 96; on the body of the king, 102–3; Borja and, 180n19; captivity of, 182n48; Catherine and, 98–99; on Corzo, 103–4, 105–6, 108–9, 183n57, 183n61, 183n64; in diplomatic assemblages, 96–100; impotence of, 101–5; indexical presence of, 93–94; injury of, 90; narrative power of, 104; Philip and, 98, 108–9, 147n13, 182n48; political capital of, 97–98; professional failings of, 101–2; reliability of, 90–91; religious fanaticism of, 148n14; royal body familiarity of, 97–99; on royal death, 91, 107–8; on Sebastian I, 89–90, 104–5, 148n14; service of, 91–96; on spatiality, 106–7; on subjectivity, 109; on temporality, 107
Silveira, João da, 32
Silverblatt, Irene, 145n7
skin, as textual object, 130
Sobchak, Vivian, 81; on corpses, 175n44; on death, 33, 66; on endangered vision, 56; on gaze of filmmaker, 167n25
Songhay Empire: al-Manṣūr conquering, 150n33
Les sources inédites de l'histoire du Maroc (Castries), 59–60
spatial deictics, 34
spatiality: Akbari on, 158n90; Ross on, 158n90; Silva on, 106–7
Stacey, Jackie, 193n79
the state: bodily metaphors of, 51
Stein, Rachel, 160n23
Stewart, Susan: on deictics, 36
subjectivity: of corpses, 80–81, 88, 111–12; defining, 72–73; Latour on, 72–73; of Leitão de Andrade, 83–84, 87; Silva on, 109
suicide, 176n48
Szpiech, Ryan: on *convivencia*, 151n38

Tārīkh al-dawla al-saʿdiyya al-takmadārtiyya, 19, 112–15; corpse care in, 119
tashhīr, 127
de Távora, Christóvão, 8–9
Taylor, Breonna, 138
temporal drag, 47
temporality: Akbari on, 158n90; of death, 49–50, 87–88; of embalming, 51–52; of monarchy, 51–52; of narrative, 51–52; Ross on, 158n90; of royal death, 51–52; Silva on, 107
terço dos aventureiros: Mendonça, J. de, in, 25–26
testimony. *See* eyewitness testimony
threat, object of. *See* object of threat
Three Kings, 4–5
Tomb of the Unknown Soldier, 164n74
Tortorici, Zeb, 176n48
The Tropics of Empire (Wey Gómez), 153n58
Trump, Donald, 138
Tudor model of kingship, 51

Valencia, Joseph, 8, 19, 46, 48, 52–53, 61; on ʿAbd al-Malik, 61–63, 67–68; Coutinho, 60; endangered evasion of, 65; eyewitness testimony of, 65–66; power transitions smoothed by, 64; reliability of, 65–66; on royal death, 62; ventriloquism of, 59–60; visual vocabulary of, 65
Valladares, Rafael, 148n16
Vázquez, Miguel Ángel: on Islamic eschatology, 145n2
Vega, Garcilaso de la, 164n64
Vega, Lope de, 18

ventriloquism, 47, 52–53, 68; of Valencia, 59–60
Vesalius, Andrea, 31
vibrant matter, 73; corpse as, 81–82; royal death and, 90
Virgin of Pedrogão Grande, 21, 74
vital matter: assemblages of, 109
Vogel, Amos: on death, 155n73

Wacks, David A., 153n52, 153n53, 153n54
Wādī al-Makhāzin, 9–10, 60, 110–11, 112, 119, 123–24
water bodies, as connecting medium, 152n43
Wattasid dynasty, 4
Wey Gómez, Nicolás, 153n58
wheat scarcity, 148n18
Winius, George D., 160n21
witnessing, 28–29, 30; of corpses, 33; interventional, 52–53; of Mendonça, J. de, 33; royal death, 47–48, 52, 122–23, 136–37. *See also* eyewitness testimony
Wittman, Laura, 164n74
wounds: display of, 82–84; of Leitão de Andrade, 77–78; of Silva, 90
Writing as Poaching (Folger), 154n60

Zayas, Gabriel de, 89, 106–7, 147n13
Zidān, Mulay, 60
al-Ziyani, 186n13

Elizabeth Spragins is Assistant Professor of Spanish at the College of the Holy Cross.

www.ingramcontent.com/pod-product-compliance
Lightning Source LLC
Chambersburg PA
CBHW020406080526
44584CB00014B/1189